RETHINKING THE GOSPEL SOURCES

VOLUME 2: THE UNITY AND PLURALITY OF Q

Society of Biblical Literature

Early Christianity and Its Literature

Gail R. O'Day, General Editor

Editorial Board

Number 1

RETHINKING THE GOSPEL SOURCES
VOLUME 2: THE UNITY AND PLURALITY OF Q

RETHINKING THE GOSPEL SOURCES

VOLUME 2: THE UNITY AND PLURALITY OF Q

by

Delbert Burkett

Society of Biblical Literature
Atlanta

RETHINKING THE GOSPEL SOURCES
VOLUME 2: THE UNITY AND PLURALITY OF Q

Library of Congress Cataloging-in-Publication Data

Burkett, Delbert Royce.
Rethinking the Gospel sources. Volume 2, The unity and plurality of Q / by Delbert Burkett.
        p. cm. — (Society of Biblical Literature early Christianity and its literature ; no. 1)
    Includes bibliographical references and indexes.
    ISBN 978-1-58983-412-5 (paper binding : alk. paper)
    1. Two source hypothesis (Synoptics criticism) 2. Q hypothesis (Synoptics criticism)
I. Title. II. Title: Unity and plurality of Q.
BS2555.52.B86 2009b
    226'.066—dc22
                                                   2009017569

Contents

PREFACE

This book constitutes the second of a series on the Synoptic Problem. The first volume, *Rethinking the Gospel Sources: From Proto-Mark to Mark* (T&T Clark, 2004), offered a new theory about the sources of the material that Mark shares with Matthew and/or Luke. The present book continues the former by examining "Q," the presumed source of the non-Markan material common to Matthew and Luke. I address two disputed issues in the study of Q: Is it necessary to hypothesize such a source, and, if so, did the Q material come from a single source or more than one? In chapter 1, I address the first issue and conclude that some form of the Q hypothesis is necessary. In chapters 2–11, I address the second issue. I conclude that Q existed as a single written source unified by recurring features of style and theme. I then identify the reasons why Matthew and Luke often disagree in the wording of Q. Chapter 12 summarizes my conclusions. Several appendices then set out significant results of this study.

Where appeal to the Greek has been necessary, I have used the Greek text common to the twenty-seventh edition of Nestle-Aland and the fourth edition of the United Bible Societies text. Where appeal to the Greek has not been necessary, I have used my own fairly literal English translation.

I am grateful to several scholars who read the first draft and offered perceptive criticism: Dale Allison, David Neville, Leif Vaage, Joseph Verheyden, and William O. Walker Jr. In response to their comments, I rewrote the entire book, from chapter 2 forward. I am also grateful to John Kloppenborg, who reviewed the book for publication. In response to his perceptive critique, I rewrote most of the book a second time.

ABBREVIATIONS

AB	Anchor Bible
ABD	*The Anchor Bible Dictionary*. Edited by David Noel Freedman. 6 vols. New York: Doubleday, 1992.
AnBib	Analecta Biblica
BETL	Bibliotheca Ephemeridum Theologicarum Lovaniensium
CBQ	*Catholic Biblical Quarterly*
CRINT	Compendia Rerum Iudicarum ad Novum Testamentum
ETL	*Ephemerides Theologicae Lovanienses*
ExpT	*Expository Times*
FRLANT	Forschungen zur Religion und Literatur des Alten und Neuen Testaments
FZPT	*Freiburger Zeitschrift für Philosophie und Theologie*
ICC	International Critical Commentary
JBL	*Journal of Biblical Literature*
JSNT	*Journal for the Study of the New Testament*
JSNTSup	Journal for the Study of the New Testament Supplement Series
JTS	*Journal of Theological Studies*
NovT	*Novum Testamentum*
NovTSup	Supplements to Novum Testamentum
NTOA	Novum Testamentum et Orbis Antiquus
NTS	*New Testament Studies*
RHPR	*Revue d'histoire et de philosphie religieuses*
SBLSP	Society of Biblical Literature Seminar Papers
SBT	Studies in Biblical Theology
SemeiaSt	Semeia Studies
SNTSMS	Society for New Testament Studies Monograph Series
SNTU	*Studien zum Neuen Testament und seiner Umwelt*
TJT	*Toronto Journal of Theology*
WUNT	Wissenschaftliche Untersuchungen zum Neuen Testament
ZNW	*Zeitschrift für die neutestamentliche Wissenschaft*

Abbreviations and Symbols in Tables

In the tables and the text, I use the following abbreviations and symbols.

L	Luke's special material
M	Matthew's special material
PMkA	Proto-Mark A: a revision of Proto-Mark used by Mark and Matthew
PMkB	Proto-Mark B: a revision of Proto-Mark used by Mark and Luke
Q	A source common to Matthew and Luke
R	Redaction

—	A line indicates a place where one Evangelist or the other has probably omitted material.
→	An arrow preceding a reference in smaller font (e.g., → 4:6b) indicates a place to which one Evangelist or the other probably moved the material so indicated. While the reference appears where the material originally stood in its source, the arrow points to the place to which the Evangelist moved it.
( )	Parentheses indicate passages where material from one source has been conflated with parallel material from another source.
[ ]	Brackets, unless otherwise indicated, enclose wording that is uncertain in the Greek text.
{ }	Braces, unless otherwise indicated, enclose wording from a source different than the one under consideration.

1

THE NECESSITY OF Q

The Gospels of Matthew and Luke have a good bit of non-Markan material in common. Two primary explanations for this material have been proposed. According to the Two-Document hypothesis, Matthew and Luke drew this material from the same source, traditionally known as "Q." The primary alternative to the Q hypothesis proposes that this material originated with the Gospel of Matthew and that Luke took it from there.[1] Several theories adopt this alternative, including Farrer's theory, the Three-Source hypothesis, the Augustinian hypothesis, and the Neo-Griesbach or Two-Gospel hypothesis.[2] Proponents of Farrer's theory in particular have argued against the Q hypothesis in favor of the view that Luke used Matthew. I will therefore examine the arguments on both sides of the issue. From that examination, I conclude that the arguments for Luke's use of Matthew lack substance, while the arguments for Q are quite strong.

ARGUMENTS FOR LUKE'S USE OF MATTHEW

Proponents of the Neo-Griesbach hypothesis have provided few arguments for Luke's use of Matthew. When William R. Farmer revived Griesbach's theory,[3] he directed most of his effort toward criticizing the priority of Mark rather

---

1. Less common is the view that Matthew used Luke: Ronald V. Huggins, "Matthean Posteriority: A Preliminary Proposal," *NovT* 34 (1992): 1–22; repr. in *The Synoptic Problem and Q: Selected Studies from Novum Testamentum* (ed. David E. Orton; Leiden: Brill, 1999), 204–25; Martin Hengel, *The Four Gospels and the One Gospel of Jesus Christ: An Investigation of the Collection and Origin of the Canonical Gospels* (Harrisburg, Pa.: Trinity Press International, 2000), 169–207.

2. For a brief explanation of each of these theories, see Delbert Burkett, *Rethinking the Gospel Sources: From Proto-Mark to Mark* (New York: T&T Clark, 2004), 1–5.

3. William R. Farmer, *The Synoptic Problem: A Critical Analysis* (New York: Macmillan, 1964; repr. Dillsboro, N.C.: Western North Carolina Press, 1976).

than producing new arguments for Luke's use of Matthew.[4] Some of Farmer's successors have produced a volume demonstrating how they think Luke used Matthew,[5] but for two reasons this volume does not demonstrate that Luke did so. First, the volume presupposes the theory; it does not provide evidence for it. From the perspective of the Neo-Griesbach hypothesis, it demonstrates, given the assumption that Luke used Matthew, how Luke would have gone about doing so. But this is not the same thing as demonstrating that Luke did in fact use Matthew. The authors do point to a few details of Luke's usage that seem to support this view. However, I responded to these in my previous volume.[6] Second, since the authors suppose that Luke used not only Matthew but also certain hypothetical "non-Matthean traditions," their objection to Q as a hypothetical source loses credibility.[7]

The most comprehensive case for Luke's use of Matthew has come from proponents of Farrer's theory. Michael D. Goulder in particular has championed this view.[8] However, his work has been criticized extensively by others, so I will not discuss it further here.[9] I will instead examine more recent

---

4. Antonio Gaboury, *La structure des évangiles synoptiques* (Leiden: Brill, 1970), 27–28.

5. Allan J. McNicol, with David L. Dungan and David B. Peabody, eds., *Beyond the Q Impasse—Luke's Use of Matthew: A Demonstration by the Research Team of the International Institute for Gospel Studies* (Valley Forge, Pa.: Trinity Press International, 1996).

6. Burkett, *From Proto-Mark to Mark*, 46–47, 53, 54–55.

7. This point is made by Robert A. Derrenbacker Jr., "The Relationship of the Gospels Reconsidered," *TJT* 14 (1998): 83–88, esp. 85, 87.

8. E.g., Michael D. Goulder, *Midrash and Lection in Matthew* (London: SPCK, 1974); idem, "On Putting Q to the Test," *NTS* 24 (1978): 218–34; idem, "The Order of a Crank," in *Synoptic Studies: The Ampleworth Conferences of 1982 and 1983* (ed. C. M. Tuckett; JSNTSup 7; Sheffield: JSOT Press, 1984), 111–30; idem, *Luke: A New Paradigm* (2 vols.; JSNTSup 20; Sheffield: Sheffield Academic Press, 1989); idem, "Is Q a Juggernaut?" *JBL* 115 (1996): 667–81; idem, "Self-Contradiction in the IQP," *JBL* 118 (1999): 506–17.

9. Christopher M. Tuckett, "On the Relationship between Matthew and Luke," *NTS* 30 (1984): 130–42; idem, "The Existence of Q," in *The Gospel behind the Gospels: Current Studies in Q* (ed. Ronald A. Piper; Leiden: Brill, 1995), 31–45; rev. and repr. in idem, *Q and the History of Early Christianity: Studies on Q* (Edinburgh: T&T Clark, 1996), 1–39; David R. Catchpole, "Did Q Exist?" in idem, *The Quest for Q* (Edinburgh: T&T Clark, 1993), 1–59; Mark Goodacre, *Goulder and the Gospels: An Examination of a New Paradigm* (Sheffield: Sheffield Academic Press, 1996); John S. Kloppenborg Verbin, "Goulder and the New Paradigm: A Critical Appreciation of Michael Goulder on the Synoptic Problem," in *The Gospels according to Michael Goulder* (ed. Christopher A. Rollston; Harrisburg, Pa.: Trinity Press International, 2002), 29–60; Robert A. Derrenbacker Jr., "Greco-Roman Writing Practices and Luke's Gospel: Revisiting 'The Order of a Crank,'" in Rollston, *Gospels according to Michael Goulder*, 61–83.

arguments for this position put forward by Mark Goodacre and some of his associates.[10] Goodacre takes what he believes are the strongest aspects of Goulder's work and expands on them. In his work *The Synoptic Problem*, he presents six negative arguments that seek to refute arguments for Q, and four positive arguments for Luke's use of Matthew. His subsequent work, *The Case against Q*, expands on nine of these ten arguments. Several scholars have previously responded to some of these arguments.[11] I will begin my own response by addressing Goodacre's four positive arguments for the view that Luke used Matthew. In the subsequent section, where I consider arguments for Q, I will address the attempts of Goodacre and others to refute these arguments.

1. Goodacre first argues that the minor agreements of Matthew and Luke against Mark show that Luke depended on Matthew.[12] He gives three examples of significant minor agreements which, in his view, test the Two-Document hypothesis and find it wanting. He also criticizes several defensive tactics that proponents of the Two-Document hypothesis use to minimize the problem posed for their theory by the minor agreements.

In making these arguments, Goodacre is clearly in dialogue with proponents of the Two-Document hypothesis, and that fact is both the strength and the weakness of his presentation. On the one hand, Goodacre is correct that the minor agreements pose a serious problem for the Two-Document hypothesis. And his critics have not adequately responded to this argument. Kloppenborg consciously omits consideration of it, and Foster simply repeats the same defensive tactics that Goodacre criticizes.[13] Since Goodacre wrote, the minor agreements have become even more of a problem for the Two-Document hypothesis. Prior to my own work, the discussion of minor agreements focused almost exclusively on agreements of inclusion, that is, places where Matthew and Luke include wording that differs from Mark's. My own work showed that agreements of omission, places where Matthew and Luke both lack what is in Mark, pose an even greater problem for the Two-Document

---

10. Mark Goodacre, *The Synoptic Problem: A Way through the Maze* (The Biblical Seminar 80; Sheffield: Sheffield Academic Press, 2001), 144–56; idem, *The Case against Q: Studies in Markan Priority and the Synoptic Problem* (Harrisburg, Pa.: Trinity Press International, 2002); Mark Goodacre and Nicholas Perrin, eds., *Questioning Q: A Multidimensional Critique* (Downers Grove, Ill.: InterVarsity Press, 2004).

11. F. Gerald Downing, "Dissolving the Synoptic Problem through Film?" *JSNT* 84 (2001): 117–19; Paul Foster, "Is It Possible to Dispense with Q?" *NovT* 45 (2003): 313–37; John S. Kloppenborg, "On Dispensing with Q? Goodacre on the Relation of Luke to Matthew," *NTS* 49 (2003): 210–36; Christopher Tuckett, review of *The Case against Q: Studies in Markan Priority and the Synoptic Problem* by Mark Goodacre, *NovT* 46 (2004): 401–3.

12. Goodacre, *Synoptic Problem*, 144–48; *Case against Q*, 152–69.

13. Kloppenborg, "On Dispensing with Q," 226–27; Foster, "Is It Possible," 324–26.

hypothesis. These "omissions" represent a level of Markan redaction that is completely unknown to either Matthew or Luke, a clear indication that neither Matthew nor Luke used Mark as a source.[14]

On the other hand, Goodacre draws an erroneous conclusion from the minor agreements. He claims that they show that Luke used Matthew. He bases this claim on the assertion that "if Luke sometimes agrees with Matthew against Mark in important ways, then Matthew and Luke were not written independently of one another."[15] This assertion, however, is erroneous. Agreements between Matthew and Luke can be explained without assuming that one depended on the other. In fact, several theories besides the Two-Document hypothesis explain the minor agreements of Matthew and Luke while still maintaining that Matthew and Luke worked independently. These include the theory of a primitive Gospel used by all three Synoptics, as well as theories of a Proto-Mark or Deutero-Mark. In my own theory, most of the minor agreements arose when Matthew and Luke both preserved the reading of Proto-Mark, while Mark revised it. Since in this theory all the Synoptics are independent of the others, Luke did not use Matthew, so the need for Q remains.

Goodacre's argument thus fails because he assumes that if the Two-Document hypothesis cannot account for the minor agreements while his own theory can, then his own theory must be true. He fails to consider that other theories can also account for the minor agreements. Goodacre's argument does contain one element of truth: Luke's minor agreements with Matthew, as traditionally conceived, pose less of a problem for Farrer's theory, in which Luke knew Matthew, than for the Two-Document hypothesis, in which he did not. Even that claim, however, must now be abandoned in light of the evidence that I presented in my previous volume.[16] The agreements of omission that I consider there are inconsistent with any theory of Markan priority and thus pose just as much of a problem for Farrer's theory as for the Two-Document hypothesis.

In his book *Goulder and the Gospels*, Goodacre identified six striking minor agreements featuring language that he judges to be positively Matthean and at the same time un-Lukan.[17] Robert H. Gundry compiled a more comprehensive list of these, arguing from the perspective of the Three-Source

---

14. Burkett, *From Proto-Mark to Mark*, 7–42.

15. Goodacre, *Synoptic Problem*, 145.

16. Burkett, *From Proto-Mark to Mark*, 7–42.

17. Goodacre, *Goulder and the Gospels*, ch. 3. These six examples were reviewed by Frans Neirynck, "Goulder and the Minor Agreements," *ETL* 73 (1997): 84–93. Goodacre includes one of these in *Synoptic Problem* (146–47) and *Case against Q* (154–55).

hypothesis.[18] Gundry discusses twenty-four such agreements, finding that they contain non-Lukan or anti-Lukan features, which indicate that Luke did not compose them. They do, however, exemplify characteristically Matthean interests and diction, an indication that Matthew did compose them. Gundry therefore concludes that Luke drew them from Matthew.[19]

The flaw with this argument is that, for the most part, it identifies Matthean and Lukan redaction by assuming the priority of Mark. Gundry assumes throughout that Matthew and Luke copied Mark and explains differences from Mark as the result of redaction by Matthew and/or Luke. For example, where Luke 8:10 and Matthew 13:11 agree on the reading δέδοται γνῶναι τὰ μυστήρια against Mark 4:11, τὸ μυστήριον δέδοται, Gundry assumes that Mark preserves the more original reading, that Matthew revised this, and that Luke followed Matthew's revision.[20] If, however, we take seriously the problems with Markan priority that I have mentioned above, such differences from Mark must be explained otherwise.[21] In this instance, Matthew and Luke agree because they both preserve the more original reading, while Mark has revised it. If so, Gundry bases his identification of Matthean and Lukan redaction on a false premise.

Thus the argument from minor agreements, as presented by either Goodacre or Gundry, does not necessitate the view that Luke used Matthew. While the minor agreements do require some explanation other than Markan priority, they do not require the explanation that Luke used Matthew. And if Luke did not use Matthew, then we still need Q.

2. Goodacre's second argument focuses on "passages in which Mark is not the middle term," i.e., passages described as "Mark-Q overlaps" in the Two-Document hypothesis.[22] As an example, he cites John's prediction of the

---

18. Proponents of this theory accept the Two-Document hypothesis in general but find it inadequate to account for the minor agreements of Matthew and Luke against Mark in the triple tradition. To account for these agreements, they suppose that Luke knew Matthew as well as Q.

19. Robert H. Gundry, "Matthean Foreign Bodies in Agreements of Luke with Matthew against Mark: Evidence That Luke Used Matthew," in *The Four Gospels 1992* (ed. F. van Segbroeck et al.; 3 vols.; BETL 100; Leuven: Leuven University Press, 1992), 2:1466–95. Neirynck and Gundry spar over one of Gundry's examples: Frans Neirynck, "Luke 10:25–28: A Foreign Body in Luke?" in *Crossing the Boundaries: Essays in Biblical Interpretation in Honour of Michael D. Goulder* (ed. Stanley E. Porter et al.; Biblical Interpretation Series 8; Leiden: Brill, 1994), 149–65; Robert H. Gundry, "A Rejoinder on Matthean Foreign Bodies in Luke 10, 25–28," *ETL* 71 (1995): 139–50.

20. Gundry, "Matthean Foreign Bodies," 2:1470–71.

21. Burkett, *From Proto-Mark to Mark*, 7–42.

22. Goodacre, *Synoptic Problem*, 148–51; *Case against Q*, 163–65.

greater one to come (Matt 3:11–12; Mark 1:7–8; Luke 3:16–17). He argues that such a passage poses a problem for the Q hypothesis because the overlap between Mark and Q must have included some verbatim agreement, which is odd if Mark and Q were independent. By contrast Farrer's theory is "much more straightforward" in explaining this passage as a place where Matthew elaborated on Mark and was followed by Luke. Support for this explanation comes from the fact that Matthew's presumed elaboration features characteristic themes of Matthew, such as judgment, separation, and hell-fire. Passages of this type contradict the assertion that Luke never features Matthew's modifications of Mark in the triple tradition.[23] They also establish a continuum that makes good sense in Farrer's theory: they stand in the middle on a scale of Matthew's influence on Luke, between triple tradition passages that feature minor agreements, and double tradition passages where Luke depends solely on Matthew.

Goodacre might be correct if the passage he cites were the only one that required explanation. We should start with the "more straightforward" theory and use it until it proves inadequate. The problem is that Farrer's theory soon proves inadequate once we move on to other passages of a similar kind. Let us take for example the pericope on the unforgivable sin (Matt 12:31–37; Mark 3:28–29; Luke 12:10), shown in table 1.1.

TABLE 1.1. UNFORGIVABLE SIN

Matthew 12:31–37	Mark 3:28–29	Luke 12:10
31 For this reason I say to you, every sin and blasphemy will be forgiven to men,	28 Amen I say to you that all the sins and the blasphemies will be forgiven to the sons of men,	
	however much they blaspheme,	
but the blasphemy of the Spirit will not be forgiven.	29 but whoever blasphemes against the Holy Spirit has no forgiveness	

---

23. This positive argument for Luke's use of Matthew overlaps with Goodacre's attempt to refute one of the arguments for Q, namely the argument that Luke does not include Matthew's additions to Mark (Goodacre, *Synoptic Problem*, 128–31; *Case against Q*, 49–54). Goodacre's attempted refutation, but not his positive formulation of the argument, is addressed by Kloppenborg ("On Dispensing with Q," 219–22) and Foster ("Is It Possible," 326–28).

32 And whoever speaks a word against the Son of Man, it will be forgiven to him;		10 And everyone who will speak a word against the Son of Man, it will be forgiven to him;
but whoever speaks against the Holy Spirit, it will not be forgiven to him,		but to the one who blasphemes against the Holy Spirit, it will not be forgiven.
neither in this age nor in the one to come.	forever, but is guilty of an eternal sin.	

According to Farrer's theory, Mark came first, Matthew elaborated on Mark, while Luke followed Matthew. The problem is that here Luke does not follow Matthew but only Matthew's elaboration. Luke strangely omits everything in Matthew that would have come from Mark (Matt 12:31, 32c) and includes only the material that Matthew would have added to Mark (Matt 12:32ab). It is as though Luke were following not Matthew, but Matthew's additions. And that recognition leads directly to the Q hypothesis: Luke was following not Matthew, but the source from which Matthew made these additions. And we call that source (or those sources) Q.

Another example is similar. F. Gerald Downing (see below) makes the same point with respect to the Beelzebul debate.[24] Luke follows not Matthew, but only Matthew's elaboration. Again, it is more likely that Luke was following not Matthew, but the source from which Matthew added the extra material.

Thus while the theory that Luke used Matthew might explain a few of the Mark-Q overlaps, it soon runs out of steam, and we must move on to the next most "straightforward" theory, namely that Luke used the same source as Matthew. This theory can explain those passages that the first theory cannot, as well as those that it can.

Goodacre thinks it odd that Q should overlap with Mark even to the extent of verbatim agreement in some cases. I suggest that it is odd only if one has a preconceived idea about what should be the case. As Christopher M. Tuckett observes, "the theory that some parts of the gospel tradition were

---

24. F. Gerald Downing, "Towards the Rehabilitation of Q," *NTS* 11 (1964/65): 169–81; repr. in *The Two-Source Hypothesis: A Critical Appraisal* (ed. Arthur J. Bellinzoni Jr., Joseph B. Tyson, and William O. Walker Jr.; Macon, Ga.: Mercer University Press, 1985), 269–85, esp. 277.

preserved in more than one strand is not inherently unlikely."[25] If so, then one might expect some agreement in wording in the overlaps.

3. Goodacre's third argument is that the material ascribed to Q contains not only sayings material but also a narrative sequence in its first third. It therefore does not resemble a sayings source such as the Gospel of Thomas, so the discovery of Thomas does not make the existence of Q more plausible. Such a narrative sequence, however, would make sense on the view that it was generated by Luke's use of non-Markan material in Matthew. He finds this view confirmed by the presence of Matthean redaction in Luke's version of the sequence: for example, in Luke 7:1 (parallel to Matt 7:28–29; 8:5), Luke has a formula similar to that which Matthew uses at the end of each of his five discourses. Furthermore, the narrative sequence in Luke presupposes elements in Matthew that were not taken over by Luke, thus betraying its origin in Matthew.[26]

Two points must be addressed here. First, the presence of narrative in Q does affect the question of its genre and its relation to Thomas. Q and Thomas exhibit both similarities and differences, and Goodacre's argument serves as a warning against focusing only on the similarities in assessing the genre of Q. However, other scholars have made the same point without denying the existence of Q.[27] Foster, while recognizing the differences between Thomas and Q, still finds that the discovery of Thomas makes the existence of Q more plausible:

> what *Thomas* and the synoptic gospels do is mark endpoints on a continuum of Christian writings about Jesus, and to find that the genre of Q sits comfortably between these two extremes gives plausibility to inferring that the genre of reconstructed Q is well within the realms of possibility.[28]

To this we can add that the question of Q's existence does not ultimately depend on the question of its relation to Thomas. Q existed as a theory before Thomas came on the scene, and even if Thomas had never existed, some form of the Q theory would continue to be the most plausible explanation for the double tradition. Questions concerning the genre of Q do not render

---

25. Christopher M. Tuckett, "Synoptic Problem," *ABD* 6:269.

26. Goodacre, *Synoptic Problem*, 151–54; *Case against Q*, 170–85.

27. E.g., Werner H. Kelber, "The Verbal Art in Q and *Thomas*: A Question of Epistemology," in *Oral Performance, Popular Tradition, and the Hidden Transcript in Q* (ed. Richard A. Horsley; SemeiaSt 60; Atlanta: Society of Biblical Literature, 2006), 25–42.

28. Foster, "Is It Possible," 323.

the hypothesis itself untenable or show that Luke's use of Matthew provides a better theory.

The second point is addressed by Kloppenborg, who provides a detailed refutation of Goodacre's view that Luke drew from Matthew the narrative sequence that is generally ascribed to Q.[29] To this we can add a response to Goodacre's claim that Luke 7:1 provides an instance of Matthean redaction in Luke's version of the narrative sequence. Luke 7:1 does have a formula similar to Matthew's, but it provides no greater support for Farrer's theory than for the Q hypothesis, as I have shown elsewhere.[30] The Q hypothesis attributes the formula to Q and must explain why Matthew added several more instances of it; Farrer's theory attributes the formula to Matthew and must explain why Luke included only one instance of it and omitted the other four instances. Neither explanation has a clear advantage over the other in this particular case.

4. Goodacre's fourth and final argument is based on "editorial fatigue," a term coined by Goulder.[31] According to this view, certain inconsistencies in narration are best explained as the result of inconsistent editing: an editor makes changes at the beginning of his source but fails to sustain the changes throughout the account. The editor becomes "fatigued" and lapses into "docile reproduction" of the source. Goodacre finds examples in the double tradition in Luke but not Matthew. With respect to these, he makes the argument that Luke became fatigued not with Q, but with Matthew, because

> if the Two Source Theory is correct, one will expect to see not only Luke but also Matthew showing signs of fatigue in double tradition material.... On the Q theory it does strain plausibility that Luke should often show fatigue in double tradition material and that Matthew should never do so, especially given Matthew's clearly observable tendency to become fatigued in his editing of Mark.[32]

To fully address this argument requires that we examine the examples that Goodacre cites from Q. I have therefore postponed a full consideration of this argument to appendix A, following my examination of the Q material in the present study. Here I will simply summarize the conclusions that I reach in appendix A.

---

29. Kloppenborg, "On Dispensing with Q," 231–36.

30. Burkett, *From Proto-Mark to Mark*, 54–55.

31. Goodacre, *Synoptic Problem*, 71–76, 154–56. A fuller discussion appeared earlier in idem, "Fatigue in the Synoptics," *NTS* 44 (1998): 45–58.

32. Goodacre, "Fatigue in the Synoptics," 57–58.

This argument manifests several problems. The first is Goodacre's assumption that we should expect Matthew to show editorial fatigue when editing Q since he shows such fatigue when editing Mark. We do not know enough about the circumstances of Matthew's editing to make such an assumption. Perhaps Matthew was tired when he edited Mark (or Proto-Mark) but well rested when he edited Q and therefore less prone to fatigue. Perhaps he simply paid more attention to Q than to the Markan source. The second is Goodacre's assumption that we should expect Matthew to show editorial fatigue when editing Q because Luke does. We have no reason to think that Matthew's style of editing Q would necessarily be the same as Luke's. Matthew may simply have been more careful than Luke in editing Q. Third, Foster argues that Matthew does show editorial fatigue at least once in the double tradition. Matthew tends to replace the phrase "the kingdom of God" with "the kingdom of the heavens," but in Matthew 12:28/Luke 11:20 he lapses back into using the phrase "the kingdom of God" from his source.[33] Fourth, not all of the six inconsistencies in Luke cited by Goodacre arose from editorial fatigue. Four of them probably arose because Luke conflated two somewhat inconsistent sources, neither of which was Matthew. And in the remaining instances, we can just as easily suppose that Luke used Q as that he used Matthew. Since Luke apparently created only a few such inconsistencies in the Q material, we should not take it as significant if Matthew created one or even none. Goodacre's argument therefore does not pose a problem for the Q hypothesis or make it more likely that Luke used Matthew than that he used Q.

ARGUMENTS FOR Q

I have not found Goodacre's arguments for Luke's use of Matthew persuasive. We must now consider arguments against Luke's use of Matthew. As these have been formulated by proponents of the Q hypothesis, they are at the same time arguments for the existence of Q. I will begin with eight arguments that in my opinion make the strongest case for Q. While some of these have been challenged by Goodacre and others, in my judgment they have not been overthrown.

1. Streeter formulated the classic argument against Luke's use of Matthew:

> subsequent to the Temptation story, there is not a single case in which Matthew and Luke agree in inserting the same saying at the same point in the Marcan outline. If then Luke derived this material from Matthew, he

---

33. Foster, "Is It Possible," 330–32.

must have gone through both Matthew and Mark so as to discriminate with meticulous precision between Marcan and non-Marcan material; he must then have proceeded with the utmost care to tear every little piece of non-Marcan material he desired to use from the context of Mark in which it appeared in Matthew—in spite of the fact that contexts in Matthew are always exceedingly appropriate—in order to re-insert it into a different context of Mark having no special appropriateness. A theory which would make an author capable of such a proceeding would only be tenable if, on other grounds, we had reason to believe he was a crank. [34]

Streeter's argument actually combines two distinct aspects, one primary and one secondary. The primary aspect compares how Matthew and Luke position the non-Markan material with respect to Mark: they never insert the same material at the same point in the Markan outline. The secondary aspect compares Luke's placement of the non-Markan material unfavorably with that of Matthew: Matthew places this material in more appropriate contexts than Luke does.

Table 1.2 illustrates the primary aspect, that is, the main point of the argument. While material in the Markan outline is in standard font, selected instances of Q material are shown in bold italics.

TABLE 1.2. SELECTED Q MATERIAL IN MARK'S OUTLINE

	Matthew	Mark	Luke
Region of Jordan			*3:3a*
Isaiah 40:3	3:3	1:2a, 3	3:4
Region of Jordan	*3:5b*		
Greater one	3:11	1:7–8	3:16
Wheat and chaff	*3:12*		*3:17*
Jesus' baptism	3:16–17	1:9–11	3:21–22
Jesus tested	4:1	1:12–13a	4:1b–2a
Three temptations	*4:2–11a*		*4:2b–13*
To Galilee	4:12b	1:14b	4:14a
Jesus teaches	5:2	1:21b	4:31b
Sermon on mount	*5:3–7:28a*		

---

34. Burnett Hillman Streeter, *The Four Gospels: A Study of Origins* (rev. ed.; London: Macmillan, 1930), 183; cf. G. M. Styler, "The Priority of Mark," in C. F. D. Moule, *The Birth of the New Testament* (3rd ed.; San Francisco: Harper & Row, 1982), 285–316, esp. 302; Tuckett, "Synoptic Problem," 268.

People astonished	7:28b–29	1:22	4:32
Centurion's boy	*8:5–13*		
At Peter's house	8:14–15	1:29–31	4:38–39
Etc.			
Old and new	9:16–17	2:21–22	5:36–38
Jesus and John	*11:2–19*		
Plucking grain	12:1–4, 8	2:23–26, 28	6:1–5
Withered hand	12:9–14	3:1–6	6:6–11
Ministry to crowd	12:15–16	3:7–12	6:17–19
Jesus chooses 12		3:13–19	
Jesus beside himself		3:20–21	
Sermon on plain			*6:20–7:1a*
Centurion's boy			*7:1b–10*
Jesus and John			*7:18–35*
Beelzebul debate	12:24–29	3:22–27	
Unforgivable sin	12:31–32	3:28–30	
Sign of Jonah	*12:38–42*		
Jesus' true family	12:46–50	3:31–35	8:19–21
Parable of sower	13:1–9	4:1–9	
Reason for parables	13:10–13	4:10–12	
Sower interpreted	13:18–23	4:13–20	
Short sayings		4:21–25	
Growing seed		4:26–29	
Mustard seed	13:31–32	4:30–32	
Parable of leaven	13:33		
Use of parables	13:34	4:33–34	
Views of Jesus	14:1–2	6:14–16	9:7–9
Etc.			
On greatness	18:1–5	9:33–37	9:46–48
Unknown exorcist		9:38–40	9:49–50
Cup of water		9:41	
Offender's fate	18:6	9:42	
Offender's fate	*18:7*		
Cut off member	18:8–9	9:43–48	
Lost sheep	18:10–14		
Correct a brother	*18:15*		
Forgive 7 times	*18:21–22*		

Sign of Jonah			*11:16, 29–30*
Mustard seed			13:18–19
Parable of leaven			13:20–21
Spoiled salt		9:49–50	14:34–35
Jesus goes to Judea	19:1–2	10:1	
Teaching on divorce	19:3–8	10:2–9	
Ruling on divorce	19:9	10:11–12	16:18
Offender's fate			*17:1–2*
Correct a brother			*17:3*
Forgive 7 times			*17:4*
Jesus and children	19:13–14	10:13–14	18:15–16
Etc.			

After the temptation narrative, Matthew and Luke never agree in placing the same Q material at the same point in the Markan outline. For example, Matthew places the "Sermon on the Mount" between Mark 1:21 and 1:22,[35] while Luke places his corresponding "Sermon on the Plain" later between Mark 3:21 and 3:22. Matthew has the material "Jesus and John" between Mark 2:22 and 2:23, while Luke has it later between Mark 3:21 and 3:22. Likewise, Matthew and Luke disagree in their placement of all the rest of the Q material. The only exceptions are at the beginning, where Q overlapped with Mark. Both Mark and Q included "Greater one," followed by "Wheat and chaff" in Q; and both included "Jesus tested," followed by "Three temptations" in Q. Since in both cases, the Markan parallel determines the position of the Q material, it is to be expected that Matthew and Luke would agree here in their placement of the Q material. Apart from these exceptions, Matthew and Luke always disagree in where they place the Q material with respect to the Markan outline.

This disagreement poses a major difficulty for the view that Luke used Matthew, particularly in the theories of Augustine and Farrer, in which Luke used both Matthew and Mark. If Luke used Matthew, we would expect to

---

35. On this point, see Hajo Uden Meijboom, *A History and Critique of the Origin of the Marcan Hypothesis 1835–1866: A Contemporary Report Rediscovered* (trans. and ed. John J. Kiwiet; New Gospel Studies 8; Macon, Ga.: Mercer University Press, 1993), 152, 154; Frans Neirynck, "The Sermon on the Mount in the Gospel Synopsis," *ETL* 52 (1976): 350–57; repr. in *Evangelica: Gospel Studies—Études d'évangile: Collected Essays* (ed. F. van Segbroeck; BETL 60; Leuven: Leuven University Press, 1982), 729–36; idem, "Matthew 4:23–5:2 and the Matthean Composition of 4:23–11:1," in *The Interrelations of the Gospels* (ed. David L. Dungan; BETL 95; Leuven: Leuven University Press, 1990), 23–46, esp. 23–25, 46.

find the Markan and Q material combined in much the same order in Luke as in Matthew, since Luke would have inherited from Matthew the order in which Matthew combined these two types of material. For Luke to use Matthew in these theories, he would have to do so in a peculiar way, by going through Matthew, leaving the Markan material where it was, but taking the Q material out of its place in Matthew and transferring it elsewhere in his own Gospel. In so doing, Luke would have effectively concealed the fact that he knew Matthew, since he would have removed all trace of Matthew's order from his own Gospel, leaving only Mark's order and, to a lesser degree, the order of Q. But if Luke lacks any trace of Matthew's order in his own Gospel, we have no reason to think that he knew Matthew at all. If he knows the order of the Markan source and the order of Q, but not the order of Matthew, it is probable that he knew the Markan source and Q separately, not as they were combined in Matthew.

What would constitute evidence for the view that Luke used Matthew? It would help the theory if the Markan and non-Markan material were combined in the same order in Luke as in Matthew. One could then infer that this combination arose in Matthew and was copied by Luke. Since that is not the case, the theories of Augustine and Farrer start from a deficit, a lack of evidence that Luke used Matthew. Proponents of these theories must therefore make up the deficit by explaining why this particular evidence for their theory does not exist. And they attempt to do so essentially by claiming that Luke destroyed the evidence. At every point where Luke allegedly used Matthew, he hid the fact by separating the non-Markan material from the Markan and moving it elsewhere. And at every point where Luke did this, proponents of these theories have to speculate as to why. To put the matter generously, this alleged editorial procedure of Luke does not commend itself as the most obvious explanation for the lack of evidence that Luke used Matthew.

The first aspect of Streeter's argument poses a different problem for the Neo-Griesbach or Two-Gospel hypothesis, since in this theory Luke knew only Matthew—Mark had not yet come along. Thus Luke knew no Markan or non-Markan material, but only Matthean material, some of which he kept in the same order as Matthew and some of which he rearranged. Later, Mark came along and omitted this rearranged material (i.e. Q) precisely because Matthew and Luke disagree regarding its placement. The problem for this theory, then, is the lack of evidence that Mark ever knew this material that he supposedly omitted.

While the different placement of non-Markan material in Matthew and Luke thus poses a problem for the assumption that Luke used Matthew, it is precisely what we would expect to find if Matthew and Luke independently combined the non-Markan material with the Markan source. Working independently, Matthew and Luke would rarely if ever place the same non-Markan material in the same place with respect to the Markan outline. Thus it appears most likely that Matthew and Luke each used some form of the Markan source and one or more sources containing non-Markan material. And this non-Markan material that they shared we call Q.

The secondary aspect of Streeter's argument compares the organization of Matthew with the organization of Luke. He finds that Matthew places the Q material at points in Mark's outline that are "always exceedingly appropriate," but that Luke places them at points "having no special appropriateness." It is therefore unlikely that Luke used Matthew, since it is not likely that Luke would have turned Matthew's appropriate organization into something less appropriate. In Streeter's work, this aspect of the argument played a subsidiary role in support of the main point. In the subsequent debate, however, it has taken on a life of its own. Reginald H. Fuller, for example, stated it thus:

> Matthew has tidily collected the Q material into great blocks. Luke, we must then suppose, has broken up this tidy arrangement and scattered the Q material without rhyme or reason all over his gospel—a case of unscrambling the egg with a vengeance![36]

A few opponents of the Q hypothesis have tried to counter Streeter's argument. E. P. Sanders, for example, addressed the main point, in trying to show that Luke does sometimes have the non-Markan material at the same place in the Markan outline as Matthew.[37] He cites two passages as "Points where Matthew and Luke agree, to some extent at least, in placing the same material at the same place in the Markan outline, where such agreement cannot be attributed to the influence of Q."[38] Sanders cites as the first such passage the parable of the leaven (Matt 13:33/Luke 13:20–21). However, it is not the case that Matthew and Luke place this parable "at the same place in the Markan outline." It is true that both Matthew and Luke place it after the parable of the mustard seed, but as table 1.2 shows, Matthew places these between Mark 4:29 and 4:33, while Luke places them between Mark 9:48 and 9:49. Thus Matthew and Luke agree in having the two parables together, but they do not agree on having them at the same place in the Markan outline as Sanders claims.

---

36. Reginald H. Fuller, *The New Testament in Current Study* (New York: Charles Scribner's Sons, 1962), 74.

37. E. P. Sanders, "The Argument from Order and the Relationship between Matthew and Luke," *NTS* 15 (1968–69): 249–61; repr. in Bellinzoni, *Two-Source Hypothesis*, 409–25. In citing page numbers I refer to the reprint.

38. Sanders, "Argument from Order," 424.

The second passage of this type listed by Sanders is Matthew 18:10–22/ Luke 17:3–4, where following a saying on offenses that all three Synoptics have (Mark 9:42; Matt 18:6–7; Luke 17:1–2), both Matthew and Luke have sayings on correcting a brother (Matt 18:15/Luke 17:3) and forgiving seven times (Matt 18:21–22/Luke 17:4). However, once again it is not true that Matthew and Luke have their parallel material "at the same place in the Markan out-line." As table 1.2 shows, Matthew has two versions of the saying "Offender's fate," one parallel to Mark 9:42 (Matt 18:6) and one immediately after (Matt 18:7). Matthew has the other two elements of this material, "Correct a brother" (18:15) and "Forgive seven times" (18:21–22), between Mark 9:48 and 9:49. Luke has all three elements together, between Mark 10:12 and 10:13.

Thus neither passage adduced by Sanders provides the type of agreement that he attributes to them. It remains true that Matthew and Luke do not put the non-Markan material at the same place relative to the Markan outline. This fact suggests that Matthew and Luke independently added the non-Markan material (Q) to material that they shared with Mark.

Goodacre has replied to both aspects of Streeter's argument, which he refers to as an argument concerning "Luke's order."[39] His first point is that Streeter mischaracterizes the evidence by misrepresenting an important fact.

> As he well knew, most of the pieces of Luke's double tradition do not appear in a "different context of Mark," whether appropriate or otherwise, because hardly any of Luke's double tradition occurs in a Markan context at all. That is, whereas Matthew often features Q in Markan contexts, Luke rarely does, for most of Luke's Q material occurs in 6:20–8:3 and 9:51–18:14, and there is famously little use of Mark in these sections.[40]

Goodacre appears to have misinterpreted Streeter's meaning. When Streeter speaks of Luke moving non-Markan material to "a different context of Mark," the context of Streeter's statement makes clear that he means to a different "point in the Marcan outline." And all of the Q material can be related to some point in the Markan outline. It is true, as Goodacre notes, that Luke has put together several items of Q material in Luke 6:20–8:3. Yet this entire section occurs at a particular point in the Markan outline, specifically between Mark 3:21 and 3:22 (see table 1.2). Understood properly, Streeter's statement does not mischaracterize the evidence.[41]

---

39. Goodacre, *Synoptic Problem*, 123–28; *Case against Q*, 59–61, 81–132.

40. Goodacre, *Case against Q*, 84–85; cf. *Synoptic Problem*, 124.

41. Foster points out that this particular critique of Goodacre "does not seem to answer Streeter's fundamental charge" ("Is It Possible," 317). While this is true, Goodacre does address the fundamental charge subsequently.

Goodacre's second point is that the argument from Luke's order depends on "a dubious value judgment."[42] In making this point, Goodacre is addressing the secondary aspect of Streeter's argument, in which Streeter claims that Matthew places the Q material at points in Mark's outline that are "always exceedingly appropriate," while Luke places them at points "having no special appropriateness." As we saw above, other scholars have reiterated this view. Following Sanders,[43] Goodacre objects that comments such as these are based on a purely subjective value judgment that regards Luke's order and arrangement as inferior to Matthew's. Such a negative judgment of Luke, he says, is difficult to maintain since literary critics are able to make good sense of Luke's order and literary design. Jeffrey Peterson and Mark Matson have made similar arguments.[44]

These scholars make a valid point, which should serve as a corrective to unsupported claims that Matthew's organization is superior to Luke's or that Luke's order lacks any rhyme or reason. However, two considerations blunt the edge of this point somewhat. First, most Q scholars today would probably agree with Goodacre that Luke's order shows evidence of literary design. Christopher Tuckett, for example, asserts that "no one today would deny that Luke's ordering can be seen to have some rhyme and reason to it."[45] Second, while Goodacre's point is well taken against the subsidiary aspect of Streeter's argument, it does not touch the main point. As Tuckett points out, "The argument[46] is not that Luke's order per se is incoherent; it is that Luke's *changes to Matthew's order* may be difficult to conceive."[47]

Goodacre's third point does address the main point of Streeter's argument. He claims that "it is easy to see why Luke might have wanted to alter [Matthew's order]," since "Luke would not have found Matthew's restructuring of

---

42. Goodacre, *Synoptic Problem*, 124–25, 126–27; *Case against Q*, 85–86.

43. E. P. Sanders and Margaret Davies, *Studying the Synoptic Gospels* (Philadelphia: Trinity Press International, 1989), 114.

44. Jeffrey Peterson, "Order in the Double Tradition and the Existence of Q," in Goodacre and Perrin, *Questioning Q*, 28–42; Mark A. Matson, "Luke's Rewriting of the Sermon on the Mount," in Goodacre and Perrin, *Questioning Q*, 43–70.

45. Tuckett, review of *Case against Q*, 402. Tuckett may go too far, however, when he states that "No one has ever doubted that Luke's order may make (Lukan) sense" (402). Stein, for example, refers to Luke's arrangement of the material as "artistically inferior" to that of Matthew: Robert H. Stein, *Studying the Synoptic Gospels: Origin and Interpretation* (2nd ed.; Grand Rapids: Baker, 2001), 104.

46. I would correct this to "the *primary* argument."

47. Tuckett, review of *Case against Q*, 402. Foster makes the same point ("Is It Possible," 318–19).

Mark congenial."[48] Goodacre mentions two primary ways in which Luke found Matthew's presentation uncongenial. First, Luke objected to Matthew's order.[49] In Luke 1:3, where Luke states that he will set out the story "in order," Luke shows that he is critical of his predecessors' work, specifically its order.[50] Goodacre supposes that Luke had known Mark for some time before he discovered Matthew. He therefore kept Mark's order for the most part, but thought that he could do a better job than Matthew of integrating Matthew's non-Markan material into Mark.[51] Since most of this material consisted of sayings, he felt greater liberty in rearranging it than he did with rearranging Mark's narrative. Second, Luke objected to Matthew's long discourses. In *The Synoptic Problem*, Goodacre follows Goulder in arguing that Luke "has a certain reticence over lengthy discourses" like those in Matthew, and so would have been concerned to shorten them.[52] Both Kloppenborg[53] and Tuckett[54] take issue with this claim, and Goodacre himself in *The Case against Q* refines it: Luke "does not dislike lengthy discourses *per se*" but objects to them when they impede the flow of the narrative, as Matthew's Sermon on the Mount does.[55]

To illustrate and make plausible the view that Luke reordered Matthew, Goodacre focuses on Luke's supposed reordering of Matthew's Sermon on the Mount.[56] According to Goodacre, this discourse does impede the flow of the narrative, so Luke would want to shorten it. He would also want to eliminate Matthean emphases that he found uncongenial, such as Matthew's emphasis on the Law. Since the last half of the Sermon consists of "a series of loosely related sayings,"[57] Luke redistributed these to appropriate contexts. Goodacre argues that narrative criticism makes good sense out of Luke's reordering of the Sermon on the Mount.[58] Furthermore the way that modern Jesus films

---

48. Goodacre, *Synoptic Problem*, 125.

49. Ibid., 127–28; *Case against Q*, 86–91, 103–104.

50. Foster finds little support for this view in the text of Luke ("Is It Possible," 319–21).

51. Kloppenborg allows the plausibility of this view ("On Dispensing with Q," 227); Foster doubts it ("Is It Possible," 318).

52. Goodacre, *Synoptic Problem*, 125–26, esp. 125.

53. John S. Kloppenborg Verbin, *Excavating Q: The History and Setting of the Sayings Gospel* (Minneapolis: Fortress, 2000), 16–17; Kloppenborg, "On Dispensing with Q," 229–30.

54. Tuckett, "Existence of Q," 41; *Q and the History of Early Christianity*, 26–27.

55. Goodacre, *Case against Q*, 91–96, 97, esp. 95.

56. Goodacre, *Case against Q*, 96–132; cf. Matson, "Luke's Rewriting of the Sermon on the Mount."

57. Kloppenborg takes issue with this assertion ("On Dispensing with Q," 227–29).

58. Goodacre, *Case against Q*, 105–120.

have treated the Sermon resembles the way Luke would have used Matthew.[59]

The length and detail of Goodacre's argument tend to obscure its most important point. Goodacre has attempted to imagine a plausible scenario in which Luke might have treated Matthew in the way required by Farrer's theory. That is, he has tried to make plausible the view that Luke took almost every piece of non-Markan material out of its place in Matthew and moved it to a different place in Mark's outline. Essential to this endeavor are Goodacre's suppositions that Luke had a preference for Mark because he knew it before he discovered Matthew, that he did not like the way Matthew added material to Mark, and that he thought he could do a better job.

Is this scenario possible? Yes. Is it plausible? Opinions may differ. Is it probable? No. To make a theory probable, one must do more than simply imagine that it might have happened. One must provide some sort of evidence to suggest that it actually did happen. And whether plausible or not, Goodacre's scenario does not provide evidence to suggest that Luke used Matthew. We have no evidence that Luke ever knew this material in the combination that it has in the Gospel of Matthew. Those scholars who claim that he did must argue that Luke destroyed all such evidence by completely rearranging this material.

Thus the main point of Streeter's argument for Q remains unanswered, and this argument makes it probable that Luke did not use Matthew. The essential and indisputable point is that Luke's combination of Markan and non-Markan material differs from Matthew's. Luke shares with Matthew the order of the Markan source and, to a lesser degree, the order of the non-Markan material; but Luke does not share with Matthew the order in which Matthew has combined these two types of material. On the one hand, if Luke used Matthew, we would expect to find some evidence that he knew Matthew's order. The fact that Luke lacks any trace of Matthew's order in his own Gospel makes it probable that he did not use Matthew. On the other hand, since there is evidence that Luke knew the order of the Markan source and the order of Q separately, it is probable that he knew the Markan source and Q separately, not as they were combined in Matthew. Thus the more probable explanation is that the Markan material and the Q material came from different sources that Matthew and Luke independently combined.

---

59. Ibid., 121–32. This chapter appeared previously as "The Synoptic Jesus and the Celluloid Christ: Solving the Synoptic Problem through Film," *JSNT* 80 (2000): 31–44. Downing criticizes Goodacre for using anachronistic comparisons ("Dissolving the Synoptic Problem"). Goodacre responds in Mark Goodacre, "On Choosing and Using Appropriate Analogies: A Response to F. Gerald Downing," *JSNT* 26 (2003): 237–40.

2. As Streeter's second argument for Q, he affirms that

> Sometimes it is Matthew, sometimes it is Luke, who gives a saying in what
> is clearly the more original form. This is explicable if both are drawing from
> the same source, each making slight modifications of his own; it is not so if
> either is dependent on the other.[60]

If Luke drew the double tradition exclusively from Matthew, Matthew would
always have the more primitive version of it, while Luke's version would always
be secondary. Goulder, representing Farrer's theory, argues that such is the
case: "I have given reasons for thinking that at all points the Lucan form is secondary, carrying over Matthaean expressions and theology, and adapting them
with Lucan expressions and theology."[61] Proponents of the Q hypothesis, on
the other hand, claim that it is sometimes Matthew and sometimes Luke that
appears to have the more primitive version of the double tradition.[62] Tuckett,
for example, cites several instances where Luke seems to have the more primitive version: some of the Beatitudes (Matt 5:3, 6/Luke 6:20–21), the doom
oracle (Matt 23:34/Luke 11:49), the Lord's Prayer (Matt 6:9–13/Luke 11:2–4),
and the saying concerning the sign of Jonah (Matt 12:40/Luke 11:30).[63]

Goodacre discusses this argument under the heading "alternating
primitivity."[64] He first attempts to minimize the degree to which Luke can
be viewed as having the more primitive reading. He argues that when "Matthaean language" appears in Matthew's version of a Q saying but not in Luke's,
Q theorists assume that Matthew added it and that Luke preserves the more
original version.[65] However, such logic works only if one has already assumed
the Q hypothesis. If one instead assumes that Luke used Matthew, one expects
to see Luke eliminating Matthean language in the process of rewording the
Matthean original.[66] To illustrate this point, Goodacre shows how Matthew's
version of the blessing on the hungry (Matt 5:6) can be viewed as more original than Luke's version (Luke 6:21) if one accepts the view that Luke used

---

60. Streeter, *Four Gospels*, 183.

61. Goulder, *Midrash and Lection in Matthew*, 452. Cf. A. M. Farrer, "On Dispensing
with Q," in *Studies in the Gospels: Essays in Memory of R. H. Lightfoot* (ed. D. E. Nineham;
Oxford: Blackwell, 1955), 55–88; repr. in Bellinzoni, *Two-Source Hypothesis*, 321–56, esp.
332.

62. E.g., Styler, "Priority of Mark," 302; Catchpole, "Did Q Exist," 1–59.

63. Tuckett, "Synoptic Problem," 268.

64. Goodacre, *Synoptic Problem*, 133–40; *Case against Q*, 61–66, 133–51.

65. Kloppenborg objects that Goodacre misstates the usual procedures for reconstructing Q ("On Dispensing with Q," 223–24).

66. Goodacre, *Synoptic Problem*, 134.

Matthew. He makes a similar demonstration for the blessing on the poor (Matt 5:1b–3/Luke 6:20).

Goodacre is correct that a scholar's presuppositions about sources affect that scholar's judgment as to whether Matthew or Luke has the more primitive version of a saying. His argument therefore illustrates the need to distinguish between two different enterprises, both of which involve evaluations of primitivity. One enterprise is conducted by scholars who presuppose the Q hypothesis and wish to reconstruct the original wording of Q. In this enterprise, scholars legitimately take the Q hypothesis as a starting point and make evaluations of primitivity from that perspective. The other enterprise is conducted by scholars who are making an argument for a particular source theory, such as the Q hypothesis or the view that Luke used Matthew. In this enterprise, scholars must be careful that their argument does not presuppose the theory for which they are arguing. Goodacre seems to confuse these two enterprises, since his argument is directed against those who assume the Q hypothesis.

The relevant issue here, however, is Streeter's argument, which affirms that, without presupposing one theory or the other, we can find double tradition passages in which Luke has a more primitive version than Matthew. For example, Luke probably preserves the more original form of the sign of Jonah (Luke 11:30/Matt 12:40). It is easy to understand why Matthew would have added a reference to Jesus' resurrection, but less easy to understand why Luke would have removed it had he known it. Likewise, in the Beelzebul debate, Luke's "finger of God" is probably more original than Matthew's "Spirit of God" (Matt 12:28/Luke 11:20). It is unlikely that Luke, who elsewhere adds references to the Spirit (Luke 10:21; 11:13), would have substituted a different expression if he had found "Spirit of God" in his source. So too in the pericope on faithful and unfaithful slaves, Luke's "unbelievers" is probably more original than Matthew's "hypocrites" (Matt 24:51/Luke 12:46). While Luke shows no aversion to the term "hypocrites" (Luke 6:42; 12:56; 13:15), Matthew shows a positive affinity for it, using it fourteen times. It is more likely therefore that Matthew introduced the term than that Luke dispensed with it. If in these and other instances[67] Luke preserves a more original form of the Q material than Matthew, then Luke did not get it from Matthew. We should not imagine therefore that Luke used Matthew, but that both Matthew and Luke used Q independently.

In Goodacre's second main response to this argument, he acknowledges that Luke may occasionally have a more primitive version of a saying than

---

67. Other instances are proposed by Kloppenborg, "On Dispensing with Q," 224–25.

Matthew in the double tradition. He attributes this, however, not to Luke's knowledge of Q but to Luke's knowledge of oral tradition. He gives two examples of such sayings: the words of institution of the Eucharist, and the Lord's Prayer.[68] According to Goodacre, "The number of such passages is probably not large."[69]

Ultimately, then, Goodacre fails to refute Streeter's second argument for Q. He has to acknowledge that Luke sometimes has the more original version in the double tradition. His appeal to oral tradition to account for these does not help his case, since this explanation may work for liturgical tradition like the two examples that Goodacre gives, but is less likely to explain Luke's priority in nonliturgical passages such as those mentioned above.[70] Furthermore if he can appeal to hypothetical oral traditions known to Luke independently of Matthew, then he has no basis for objecting to a hypothetical written source such as Q.[71] He has thus eliminated the main appeal of Farrer's theory, which Farrer and Goulder framed precisely to avoid any need for hypothetical sources.[72]

3. A third argument for Q, similar to the second, affirms that sometimes Matthew, sometimes Luke, preserves a more original form of the triple tradition. Goodacre does not respond to this argument, perhaps because it speaks especially against the Griesbach and the Augustinian hypotheses. Since in these theories Matthew was the first Gospel, Matthew should always have the more original form of the tradition, whether double or triple. Yet it sometimes seems that Matthew's version of the triple tradition is secondary to that of Luke. For example, Peter's confession in Matthew, which identifies Jesus as "the Christ, the son of the living God" (Matt 16:16), is probably less original than the versions of Mark and Luke, which identify him only as "the Christ" (Mark 8:29) or "the Christ of God" (Luke 9:20). It is easy to see why Matthew would have added an identification of Jesus as the son of God, but not easy to see why Mark and Luke would have omitted it, had they known it from Matthew.

This type of argument does not in every instance affect Farrer's theory, specifically in those instances in which Mark preserves the earliest form of the tradition. Since Farrer's theory assumes that Mark was the first Gospel, its

---

68. Goodacre, *Synoptic Problem*, 138–39; *Case against Q*, 63–66.

69. Goodacre, *Case against Q*, 66.

70. Kloppenborg, "On Dispensing with Q," 224; Tuckett, review of *Case against Q*, 403.

71. As Tuckett points out, "if appeal is made too often to parallel traditions (oral or otherwise) available to Luke independently of Matthew, some form of 'Q' starts creeping in by the back door again!" (review of *Case against Q*, 403).

72. Foster, "Is It Possible," 321–22.

proponents can argue that both Matthew and Luke received the triple tradition from Mark and that either could sometimes preserve the more original
form of it. However, if Luke has a more original form of the tradition than
either Matthew or Mark, such instances speak against every form of the
theory that Luke used Matthew. Since Matthew provided the triple tradition
in the Griesbach hypothesis, and Mark did in Farrer's theory, the Gospel of
Luke should never have the earliest form of the triple tradition in any of these
theories. Yet there is good reason to think that it does. One example occurs at
the end of the story about plucking grain on the Sabbath (table 1.3).

TABLE 1.3. PLUCKING GRAIN

Matthew 12:5–8	Mark 2:27–28	Luke 6:5
5 Or have you not read in the Law that on the Sabbaths the priests in the Temple defile the Sabbath and are guilt-less? 6 But I say to you that something greater than the Temple is here. 7 But if you had known what 'I desire mercy and not sacrifice' means, you would not have con-demned the guiltless.		
	27 And he said to them,	5 And he said to them,
	"The Sabbath was made for humans and not humans for the Sabbath.	
8 For the son of man is Lord of the Sabbath."	28 So the son of man is lord even of the Sab-bath."	"The son of man is lord of the Sabbath."

Here both Matthew and Mark make secondary interpolations into the
story, while Luke preserves the more original version without these interpolations. Matthew 12:5–7 is one of two places where Matthew interpolates
the same scriptural quotation: "I desire mercy and not sacrifice." In the first
instance (Matt 9:13a), its secondary character is shown by the fact that it
interrupts the two parts of a comparison in which the sick represent sinners
and the well represent the righteous. In both instances, Mark and Luke lack
the interpolation. Since the theme of the interpolation would be acceptable

to both Mark and Luke, both writing for Gentile Christian audiences with no attachment to the Jewish sacrificial system, it is difficult to believe that either, much less both, would omit this theme twice had they known it. The agreement of Mark and Luke against Matthew shows clearly in this case that Matthew's interpolation is secondary. Likewise Mark interpolated the statement "The Sabbath was made for humans and not humans for the Sabbath" in Mark 2:27. As I have shown elsewhere, proponents of Markan priority have had difficulty explaining why Matthew and Luke, supposedly following Mark, do not include this saying.[73] Luke, in particular, would have welcomed it for its expression of the same theme as the parable of the good Samaritan (Luke 10:29–37): that human need outweighs the requirements of the law. More likely therefore, Mark added this saying for the same reason that Matthew added Matthew 12:5–7. The story of plucking grain provided a justification for the church's Sabbath conduct. Since the church tended to want more arguments for its position, not fewer, Matthew and Mark each added another justification to the original argument. Luke, who includes neither interpolation, thus preserves a more original form of the story's ending than either Matthew or Mark.

Another example occurs in the Synoptic accounts of the Last Supper. Luke includes an account of the Passover meal and the Passover cup (Luke 22:15–18) followed by the bread and cup of the Lord's Supper (Luke 22:19–20). Matthew and Mark have an account in which these two meal traditions have been combined into one (Matt 26:26–29/Mark 14:22–25). This conflated version, however, left out the account of the Passover meal that Luke includes in 22:15–16.[74] Thus Luke again appears to preserve the most original form of the tradition. Such instances in which Luke preserves a more original form of the tradition than either Matthew or Mark are not consistent with any theory in which Luke used Matthew.

4. A fourth argument for Q is the fact that either Matthew or Luke sometimes includes an overlap between the Markan source and Q, i.e. two versions of the same material in the same Gospel. In some cases, the Gospel preserves the two versions separately, thus creating doublets; in other cases it combines the two versions into a single conflated version.[75] For instance, Matthew includes two versions of the pericope in which Jesus' opponents seek a sign from him, one shared with Mark (Matt 16:1, 4/Mark 8:11–13) and one shared

---

73. Burkett, *From Proto-Mark to Mark*, 232–33.

74. Ibid., 217–20.

75. Joseph A. Fitzmyer, "The Priority of Mark and the 'Q' Source in Luke," in idem, *To Advance the Gospel: New Testament Studies* (New York: Crossroad, 1981), 16–23; Styler, "Priority of Mark," 303–304; Tuckett, "Existence of Q," 27.

with Luke (Matt 12:38–40/Luke 11:16, 29–30). Such a doublet suggests that Matthew found this pericope in two different sources: one shared with Mark (the Markan source) and one shared with Luke (Q).

We saw above that Goodacre's second argument for Luke's use of Matthew focuses on "passages in which Mark is not the middle term," i.e. passages described as "Mark-Q overlaps" in the Two-Document hypothesis. However, in examining that argument, we saw that Farrer's theory has difficulty explaining these overlaps, such as the saying on the unforgivable sin. In such cases, it appears that Luke followed not Matthew, but what Matthew added to the Markan source from another source, i.e. Q. Therefore the overlaps that Goodacre makes his second argument for Luke's use of Matthew are better regarded as part of our fourth argument for Q.

Another example of such an overlap is the Beelzebul debate (Mark 3:22–27 parr). Here Matthew stands as the "middle term," agreeing in part with Mark and in part with Luke, while Mark and Luke have few agreements against Matthew. F. Gerald Downing has made a detailed analysis of this pericope, finding that Luke includes none of the material in which Matthew reproduces Mark verbatim but almost all of the material from Matthew that has no parallel in Mark. He concludes that "Luke in fact seems to be using Matthew's extra material without Matthew's obviously Markan additions. *But Matthew's extra material without the Markan additions is not Matthew's gospel; it is Matthew's other source(s).*"[76] Here too it appears that Luke followed not Matthew, but what Matthew added from Q to the Markan source.

While the Q hypothesis provides a reasonable explanation for such overlaps, other theories do not. Christopher Tuckett describes the strange editorial procedure required of Luke by the Farrer hypothesis in such passages:

> Mark must have written first, Matthew then adding to Mark. Luke, who usually follows Mark and ignores Matthew when they run parallel, must have decided here to remove very carefully all the Markan material from Matthew, retaining only the parts peculiar to Matthew.

Tuckett goes on to describe the strange editorial procedure required of Mark by the Neo-Griesbach hypothesis in these same passages:

> Matthew must have written first; Luke, writing second, must have reproduced only some parts of Matthew. Then Mark, writing third, must have

---

76. Downing, "Towards the Rehabilitation of Q," in Bellinzoni, *Two-Source Hypothesis*, 277.

taken an aversion to anything which Luke had taken from Matthew and so reproduced only those parts of Matthew which Luke had omitted.[77]

The Q hypothesis relieves both Mark and Luke of such peculiarities: the Markan source preserved one version of these pericopes, Luke another (Q), while Matthew conflated the two. Thus the inability of other theories to account for these passages provides a positive argument for the existence of Q.

5. A fifth argument for Q represents a broader application of the fourth. It looks beyond the overlaps to include the wider phenomenon of the minor agreements rejected by any evangelist writing third. F. Gerald Downing presented this argument subsequent to the appearance of Goodacre's work.[78] He bases it on "the disagreements of each evangelist with the minor close agreements of the other two." The Neo-Griesbach hypothesis has Mark writing third, while Farrer's theory has Luke writing third.[79] Downing shows that in each theory, the supposed third author, in copying from the two earlier Gospels, very frequently refuses to copy his sources where they agree verbatim or very closely, even while precisely copying one or the other in the same context. While other ancient authors preferred to use material where their sources agreed, these authors would have gone to considerable effort to avoid copying such agreements. While the strange editorial procedure required of the author by these theories makes them implausible, such strange behavior is not required by a theory that incorporates Q.[80]

6. A sixth argument for Q points out that the material common to Matthew and Luke does not begin until after the infancy narratives and ceases prior to the resurrection narratives. This suggests that what Luke shared with Matthew was not the Gospel of Matthew itself but only certain parts of Matthew between the infancy narratives and the resurrection narratives, i.e., Q.[81]

Against this argument, Goodacre finds evidence that Luke did know Matthew's birth narrative. Such knowledge appears in the fact that they agree on matters otherwise not found in the New Testament, such as Jesus' birth in

---

77. Tuckett, "Synoptic Problem," 269.

78. F. Gerald Downing, "Disagreements of Each Evangelist with the Minor Close Agreements of the Other Two," *ETL* 80 (2004): 445–69.

79. Downing does not discuss the theory of Matthean posteriority, which has Matthew writing third.

80. From his study, Downing draws the conclusion that "positing Mk and Q as the sources used independently by Mt and by Lk remains the only credible solution to the synoptic problem" ("Disagreements," 469). Here he overstates the case, since my own theory positing Proto-Mark and Q also avoids the problems that he points out.

81. Styler, "Priority of Mark," 302–303.

Bethlehem, the name of Jesus' father as Joseph, and the virginal conception. Furthermore they even have the same wording in the sentence "She/you will give birth to a son and you shall call him Jesus" (Matt 1:21; Luke 1:31).[82]

Goodacre's argument founders for two reasons. First, most of the elements common to Matthew and Luke in the birth narratives do not involve any agreement in wording. Therefore these show only that Matthew and Luke knew some of the same traditions, not that one depended on the other. Second, the one sentence where the two Gospels agree in wording is a quotation of Isaiah 7:14. From this passage both evangelists include the sentence "She/you will give birth to a son and you shall call him. . . ," (Matt 1:21; Luke 1:31), and Luke also includes the phrase "you will become pregnant" (Luke 1:31). It is doubtful that Luke drew his version of Isaiah 7:14 from Matthew, since Matthew does not include all of Isaiah 7:14 that Luke quotes. Thus if one Gospel depended on the other, it was more likely Matthew drawing from Luke, not the reverse. However, the resemblance between Matthew and Luke here most likely results not from dependence of one on the other but from their common use of Isaiah 7:14. The one striking agreement is the substitution of the name "Jesus" for "Immanuel" in both Matthew's and Luke's quotation of Isaiah 7:14. However, one such agreement in the entirety of the birth narratives does not suffice to establish dependence of one narrative on the other. In this case, Matthew and Luke probably relied on a common tradition of interpreting Isaiah 7:14 as a prediction about Jesus.

7. A seventh argument for Q is the evidence that the Gospel of Matthew includes a layer of redaction that was unknown to either Mark or Luke. I set out much of this evidence in the previous volume in this series subsequent to Goodacre's work.[83] Not only passages, but also less noticeable features of Matthew's style such as recurring words, phrases, grammatical constructions, themes, and redactional techniques characteristic of Matthew are absent from both Mark and Luke. For instance, Matthew includes numerous quotations of Scripture that are introduced by a special formula, such as "This took place to fulfill what was spoken by the prophet" (Matt 1:22–23; 2:15; 2:17–18; 2:23; 4:13–16; 8:17; 12:15–21; 13:35; 21:4–5; 26:56; 27:9–10; cf. 2:5–6). Neither Mark nor Luke includes any of these, despite the fact that both evangelists agreed that Jesus fulfilled scripture. Similarly, Matthew uses the verb προσκυνέω with Jesus as object ten times (Matt 2:2; 2:8; 2:11; 8:2; 9:18; 14:33; 15:25; 20:20; 28:9; 28:17). Neither Mark nor Luke includes any of these, despite the fact that both use the same verb with Jesus as object else-

---

82. Goodacre, *Synoptic Problem*, 132; *Case against Q*, 56–57.
83. Burkett, *From Proto-Mark to Mark*, 43–59.

where (Mark 5:6; Luke 24:52; cf. Mark 15:19). Likewise, Matthew uses the verb μεταβαίνω six times, none of which are included by either Mark or Luke. These instances, and many others that I have cited elsewhere, are best explained as Matthean redaction that was unknown to either Mark or Luke.

Since these features occur repeatedly in Matthew, what requires explanation is not the absence from Mark and Luke of individual words or sentences in Matthew, but the absence of entire themes and recurring features of Matthew's style. And since these pervasive features of Matthew's style are generally benign, that is, neither grammatically nor ideologically objectionable, it is difficult to explain why either Mark or Luke would have omitted them had they known them. If Luke knew Matthew, then he either intentionally omitted these features of Matthew's style or he eliminated them unintentionally in the process of making other revisions. Since these features are generally benign, it is difficult to explain why he would omit them intentionally, especially since he uses some of them in contexts other than parallels to Matthew. Since they are numerous, individually and collectively, it is also difficult to explain how he could have unintentionally omitted them all in the process of making other revisions. Most likely, therefore, Luke did not include these stylistic features of Matthew because he did not use Matthew's Gospel. Instead, Matthew and Luke shared a non-Markan source or set of sources that each redacted independently. And we call such a source or sources "Q."

8. An eighth argument for Q takes into consideration form criticism and, as far as I know, appears here for the first time. In the stage of oral tradition, stories and sayings probably circulated independently or as part of short collections or discourses.[84] Luke's organization better reflects this early stage than Matthew's. While Luke has the Q material in short groups of sayings, such as the section "On prayer" (Luke 11:1–13) or the section "On light" (Luke 11:33–36), Matthew has combined this material into five much lengthier discourses, such as the Sermon on the Mount. Luke's organization thus appears to stand closer to the origin of the tradition than Matthew's and for that reason must be judged more primitive. But if Luke exhibits a more original form of organization than Matthew, then Luke did not use Matthew. Instead, both used Q.

---

84. This view is accepted even by more recent advocates of oral tradition: e.g., James D. G. Dunn, *Jesus Remembered* (vol. 1 of *Christianity in the Making*; Grand Rapids: Eerdmans, 2003), 245–48.

Unused Arguments for Q

I have now discussed eight arguments that appear to me to be the strongest arguments against Luke's use of Matthew and for Q. A number of other arguments for Q remain that I have not used. Here I briefly consider five of these, not only for the sake of completeness, but because Goodacre responds to some of these in his critique of Q.

1. Goodacre responds to one of the most common arguments for the existence of Q: the fact that Luke does not show any knowledge of Matthew's additions to Mark in the triple tradition. He finds this argument given by Kümmel, Tuckett, Fitzmyer, Kloppenborg, Allison, and Stein.[85] This argument is a nonstarter against the Neo-Griesbach hypothesis since, as it is usually formulated, it presupposes Markan priority. Even in a more neutral formulation, such as that of Kloppenborg,[86] the argument presupposes Luke's knowledge of Mark. In the Neo-Griesbach hypothesis, which puts Matthew first and Mark third, there are no Matthean additions to Mark, and Luke does not know Mark. The material under consideration would result from Luke abridging Matthew, and Mark then following Luke's abridgment. So the problem does not exist in that theory.

With respect to Farrer's theory, which does presuppose Markan priority, the argument is somewhat inaccurate. As Goodacre points out, in that theory, Luke does include some of Matthew's additions to Mark, such as those in the John the Baptist complex, the temptation narrative, and those passages labeled "Mark/Q overlaps" by proponents of Q. With respect to the Matthean additions to Mark that Luke omits, the question is whether it is reasonable to think that Luke would have omitted them in favor of Mark alone. Goodacre, at least, thinks that it is. Several proponents of Q have argued that it is not.[87] While I think that the proponents of Q make the better case, I have chosen not to use this argument because of its weaknesses.

---

85. Goodacre, *Synoptic Problem*, 128–31; *Case against Q*, 49–54, which expands and revises Goodacre, "A Monopoly on Marcan Priority? Fallacies at the Heart of Q," in *Society of Biblical Literature 2000 Seminar Papers* (Atlanta: Society of Biblical Literature, 2000), 538–622, esp. 592–99.

86. "Or, to put it more neutrally, in Lukan material for which there are Matthean and Markan parallels, Luke rarely reflects what is distinctive of Matthew when it is compared with Mark" (Kloppenborg Verbin, *Excavating Q*, 41).

87. Kloppenborg, "On Dispensing with Q," 219–22; Foster, "Is It Possible," 326–28; Tuckett, review of *Case against Q*, 401–2.

2. Goodacre also responds to the argument that Luke lacks the "M" material and therefore did not know Matthew.[88] This argument does not particularly discomfit either the Neo-Griesbach hypothesis or Farrer's theory. Both have explanations for the material unique to Matthew. The former sees it as Matthean material that both Luke and Mark omitted; in the latter, it is Matthean material that Luke omitted. Goodacre thinks that Luke omitted it because it was not congenial to his own perspective, and Kloppenborg criticizes this view.[89] I have omitted the whole argument.

3. Goodacre points out an argument for Q that has emerged more recently than most other such arguments. This is the idea that Q is distinctive, that it "distinguishes itself from the other material in the Synoptics … because it is held to have a special theology, vocabulary, history, structure, and style."[90] Goulder disputes this view, claiming that the theology of Matthew and the theology of Q are indistinguishable. Goodacre also finds much overlap between the style of Q and the style of M. He does find that the double tradition material has a distinctive profile, but he explains this by Farrer's theory: Luke chose the "Luke-pleasing" elements in Matthew's non-Markan material (Q), but omitted the "Luke-displeasing" material (M). Kloppenborg defends the coherence of Q against Goodacre's critique.[91]

It will be one of the primary tasks of the present volume to show that Q does in fact exhibit a stylistic and thematic unity. However, I do not use this unity as an argument for the existence of Q. Instead I establish the existence of Q on other grounds (the eight arguments above) and then proceed to identify the stylistic and thematic unity of Q. If the results of this study are persuasive, they may serve to confirm our initial conclusion that Q existed.

4. Goodacre responds to one further argument for Q, namely, that "the success of redaction-criticism" argues in favor of the two-source hypothesis.[92] Goodacre criticizes this argument, among other reasons, for circularity. Kloppenborg agrees that this argument is hardly a compelling one.[93]

---

88. Goodacre cites Fitzmyer and Stein as proponents of this argument (Goodacre, *Synoptic Problem*, 131–33; *Case against Q*, 54–59).

89. Kloppenborg, "On Dispensing with Q," 222–23.

90. Goodacre, *Synoptic Problem*, 140–42; *Case against Q*, 66–75, esp. 66–67.

91. Kloppenborg, "On Dispensing with Q," 225–26.

92. Goodacre, *Synoptic Problem*, 142–44; *Case against Q*, 75–77.

93. Kloppenborg, "On Dispensing with Q," 226.

5. I include here one final argument that Goodacre does not mention: an argument from ancient scribal practices. Downing[94] and Derrenbacker[95] in particular have developed the view that plausible solutions to the Synoptic problem must take into account the normal practices of ancient scribes and the physical limitations that they faced as they produced manuscripts. Both scholars find that the Two-Document hypothesis is less problematic than alternative theories when viewed from the perspective of ancient scribal practices. These scholars have made an important contribution by highlighting what is known of scribal practice. I do not use their argument, however, for two reasons. First they imagine a scenario in which a single scribe alone produced a Gospel. However, as Christopher Tuckett points out, the author of a Gospel may have dictated to a scribe, in which case the physical limitations of a single scribe might be less relevant.[96] Jeffrey Peterson makes a similar point, with respect to the question of whether it was technically possible for the evangelists, specifically Luke, to relocate material from their sources:

> this concern is addressed easily enough if we credit Luke's likely patron Theophilus with the resources and inclination to supply the Evangelist with a scribe (cf. Romans 16.22) and a quantity of *tabellae* for taking notes and composing drafts in wax before committing the finished product to papyrus.[97]

Second, our knowledge of ancient scribal practice is sketchy and probably reflects what scribes did normally with normal projects. We do not know what ingenuity they may have exercised when confronted with an unusual task or when they wished to accomplish a task in an unusual manner.

---

94. F. Gerald Downing, "Redaction Criticism: Josephus' *Antiquities* and the Synoptic Gospels," *JSNT* 8 (1980): 46–65; 9 (1980): 29–48; idem, "Compositional Conventions and the Synoptic Problem," *JBL* 107 (1985): 69–85; idem, "A Paradigm Perplex: Luke, Matthew and Mark," *NTS* 38 (1992): 15–36; idem, "Word Processing in the Ancient World: The Social Production and Performance of Q," *JSNT* 64 (1996): 29–48; idem, *Doing Things with Words in the First Christian Century* (JSNTSup 20; Sheffield: Sheffield Academic Press, 2000).

95. Robert A. Derrenbacker Jr. "Greco-Roman Writing Practices"; idem, *Ancient Compositional Practices and the Synoptic Problem* (BETL 186; Leuven: Peeters, 2005).

96. Christopher Tuckett, review of *Ancient Compositional Practices and the Synoptic Gospels* by R. A. Derrenbacker, *JTS* 58 (2007): 187–90, esp. 189. Tuckett attributes this insight to his colleague, Dr. Andrew Gregory.

97. Peterson, "Order in the Double Tradition," 37.

CONCLUSION

Mark Goodacre's work marks a step forward for the view that Luke used Matthew, because he has formulated in a systematic manner the arguments for that position. Despite his best efforts, however, these arguments fall short of their purpose. The evidence is simply lacking to indicate that Luke used Matthew. To the contrary, at least eight arguments suggest that Luke did not use Matthew but that both used a common source or sources. Goodacre and others have attempted to refute some of these arguments but without success. Goodacre has envisioned "a world without Q,"[98] a dream apparently shared by other opponents of the Q hypothesis. Such a vision is destined to remain nothing more than a dream so long as the evidence strongly supports the Q hypothesis and fails to support the view that Luke used Matthew. In the rest of this volume, I presuppose the Q theory as the best way to account for the non-Markan material common to Matthew and Luke.

---

98. Goodacre, *Case against Q*, 187; idem, "A World Without Q," in Goodacre and Perrin, *Questioning Q*, 174–79.

2

Q: Unity or Plurality?

Once we accept the need for Q, we must next ask whether the Q material came from one source or more than one. Does it exhibit unity or plurality? Here I will survey previous scholarship on this issue in order to determine the state of the question.

Scholarship Advocating the Unity of Q

Much scholarship on Q presupposes that it was a single text. Members of the International Q Project, for example, take this position. Their reconstruction of Q presupposes "that there was a written Greek text of Q which functioned as an archetype, copies of which were available to the Matthean and Lukan communities and used by their Evangelists."[1] Their critical edition of Q seeks to reconstruct the original wording of this single Greek text. Many other scholars have also thought of Q as a single text. Far fewer, however, have actually provided arguments to support this view. From those who have, two basic arguments have emerged, one based on the order of Q and one on its literary unity.

Argument from Order

Most commonly, scholars have used the order of Q as an argument for its unity. Since Matthew and Luke have much of the Q material in the same order, one could infer that they drew it from a single text.

---

1. James M. Robinson, Paul Hoffmann, and John S. Kloppenborg, eds., *The Critical Edition of Q: Synopsis Including the Gospels of Matthew and Luke, Mark and Thomas with English, German, and French Translations of Q and Thomas* (Hermeneia; Minneapolis: Fortress; Leuven: Peeters, 2000), lxvii; idem, *The Sayings Gospel Q in Greek and English with Parallels from the Gospels of Mark and Thomas* (Leuven: Peeters, 2001), 65.

Streeter used this common order of Q parallels in conjunction with their common wording to argue that Q was a document rather than oral tradition. While recognizing that proverbial sayings might reach both Evangelists through oral tradition, he affirmed that where "a number of consecutive sayings occur in two Gospels with approximately the same wording," the source was more likely a document.[2] He found considerable agreement between Matthew and Luke in the order in which they arranged material from Q. Differences in order, he thought, resulted primarily from the editorial activity of Matthew. While Luke better preserved the order of Q, Matthew reordered material by incorporating it into his major discourses.[3]

Vincent Taylor examined the order of Q in two articles.[4] He presupposed the "working hypothesis" that Q was a single document.[5] He then sought to explain, given this theory, why much of the material common to Matthew and Luke does not follow the same order in both Gospels. He broke the material into six distinct segments, one for each of Matthew's five major discourses and one for material outside of these discourses. He sought to show that in each segment Matthew and Luke have much of the Q material in the same order and that exceptions could be explained as the result of redaction by Matthew or Luke. He took these results as confirmation that Matthew and Luke knew the same document Q with the same material in the same original order. In fact, his study shows no such thing. At the end of his study he seems to have forgotten that he presupposed his conclusion as a working hypothesis from the beginning. Furthermore, his identification of six interwoven segments of Q material does little to support the unity of Q. It could just as easily be taken to show that Matthew and Luke knew six distinct collections of Q material that they combined independently.[6] Instead, since Taylor presupposes that Q was a single document, he must assume that "Matthew scanned Q several times, removing material appropriate to each of the five sermons" and keeping the order of sayings within each sermon approximately the same as in

---

2. Streeter, *Four Gospels*, 185.

3. Ibid., 271, 273–75.

4. Vincent Taylor, "The Order of Q," *JTS* NS 4 (1953): 27–31; repr. in idem, *New Testament Essays* (London: Epworth, 1970), 90–94; idem, "The Original Order of Q," in *New Testament Essays: Studies in Memory of Thomas Walter Manson, 1893–1958* (ed. A. J. B. Higgins; Manchester: Manchester University Press, 1959), 246–69; repr. in Taylor, *New Testament Essays*, 95–118; repr. in Bellinzoni, *Two-Source Hypothesis*, 295–317.

5. Taylor, "Original Order," in Bellinzoni, *Two-Source Hypothesis*, 297.

6. This point is most easily seen from the chart in the earlier of Taylor's two articles (*JTS*, 1953, 29–30).

Luke.[7] In criticizing Taylor, Kloppenborg points out that "Given a sufficient number of scannings, *any two lists* of common elements can be reconciled in order." The more scans necessary to reconcile the lists, the less convincing the solution, and Kloppenborg suggests that it would take fifteen scans to fully reconcile the material in Taylor's table.[8] Taylor's argument from order for the unity of Q thus has little to recommend it.

Other scholars have also employed the argument from order. Werner Georg Kümmel showed that 13 of 23 sections of Q have the same order in Matthew as in Luke. He concluded that "Such agreement can be no accident and proves a common, written source."[9] John Kloppenborg Verbin points out that Matthew and Luke agree in placing 27 of 67 pericopes in the same sequence. From this common order he infers that the two Evangelists used a single document for the Q material.[10]

The common order of Q in Matthew and Luke indicates that at least some of this material came to the Evangelists in the form of a document with a fixed order. By itself, however, this common order falls short of proving that all of the Q material came from the same source. If we use Kloppenborg Verbin's figures, the argument would apply only to the 27 pericopes in the same order in Matthew and Luke. The lack of a common order for the other 40 pericopes could indicate that they came from a different source than the 27 or from oral tradition. And even if all 67 pericopes originally had the same order in a written source, there may have been more than one version of this source, versions that differed more in wording than in content or order. Thus to assess the unity or plurality of Q, we must consider not only order, but other factors as well.

ARGUMENT FROM LITERARY UNITY

The literary unity of Q material provides a second argument for a single Q source. According to Arland D. Jacobson, Adolf Harnack was the first to argue for such unity.[11] Harnack pointed out certain linguistic and formal characteristics of Q, such as its vocabulary, grammar, and style, but had to

---

7. John S. Kloppenborg, *The Formation of Q: Trajectories in Ancient Wisdom Collections* (Philadelphia: Fortress, 1987), 68–69.

8. Ibid., 69.

9. Werner Georg Kümmel, *Introduction to the New Testament* (rev. ed.; Nashville: Abingdon, 1975), 65–66.

10. Kloppenborg Verbin, *Excavating Q*, 67–72.

11. Arland D. Jacobson, *The First Gospel: An Introduction to Q* (Sonoma, Calif.: Polebridge, 1992), 23–25.

confess that these features fell short of a convincing proof that Q came from a single document.[12]

Jacobson himself tried to improve on Harnack's effort. He offered three types of evidence for the literary unity of Q, recognizing that without such evidence one could not maintain that Q was a single document.[13] He first compared forms in Mark and Q. He pointed to forms that are common in Q but rare in Mark (such as macarisms, woes, the eschatological correlative, prophetic threats, paired figurative sayings) and to forms common in Mark but rare in Q (conflict stories; miracle stories; parables, similitudes, comparisons; apocalyptic predictions; chreiai). He concluded not only that Mark and Q represent independent traditions, but also that Q shows a considerable measure of literary unity in terms of form and general content. Second he compared traditions shared by Mark and Q, finding certain distinctive recurrent themes in Q (i.e. the impenitence of Israel, judgment, and the consequences of rejecting God's messengers). Third, he pointed to the deuteronomistic tradition, involving rejection of Israel's prophets, as the theological basis for the literary unity of Q.

Kloppenborg Verbin cited Jacobson's arguments with approval and gave further examples of thematic connections between different Q pericopes. Without claiming that Q was homogeneous, he saw signs of unity that extend over large sections of Q and that make it preferable, he says, to assume that Q was a single document.[14]

In making these arguments, Jacobson and Kloppenborg Verbin must walk a fine line, because while they argue that Q is a literary unity, at the same time they argue that it is *not* a literary unity. Both think that Q developed in stages, in which disparate layers of material were successively added. Kloppenborg Verbin argues that Q began with a "formative stratum" of material (Q1) united by paraenetic, hortatory, and instructional concerns. To this was subsequently added a "main redaction" (Q2), a stratum of material united by the motifs of judgment, polemic against "this generation," a deuteronomistic understanding of history, and allusions to the story of Lot. At a third stage,

---

12. Adolf Harnack, *The Sayings of Jesus: The Second Source of St. Matthew and St. Luke* (trans. J. R. Wilkinson; New York: Putnam's Sons, 1908), 146–72.

13. Jacobson, *First Gospel*, 61–76; idem, "The Literary Unity of Q," *JBL* 101 (1982): 365–89; repr. in part in *The Shape of Q: Signal Essays on the Sayings Gospel* (ed. John S. Kloppenborg; Minneapolis: Fortress, 1994), 98–115; idem, "The Literary Unity of Q: Lc 10,2–16 and Parallels as a Test Case," in *Logia: Les paroles de Jésus—The Sayings of Jesus. Mémorial Joseph Coppens* (ed. Joël Delobel; BETL 59; Leuven: Leuven University Press, 1982), 419–23.

14. Kloppenborg Verbin, *Excavating Q*, 66–67.

the temptation narrative was added.[15] Jacobson too argues that Q developed in stages. He identifies a deuteronomistic layer of material, which he uses as a basis for comparison, and finds both pre-deuteronomistic and post-deuteronomistic strata as well.[16]

For both scholars, it is precisely the lack of literary unity in Q that permits them to identify these distinctive layers of material. Jacobson makes this fact explicit in describing his procedure for analyzing Q:

> Attention is directed particularly to themes that emerge in the material and to *evidence of literary disunity* [emphasis mine]. Literary disunity is detected using the typical criteria: "hard connections" such as grammatical shifts; breaks in the train of thought; shifts in audience; shifts in tradition or theology; and so on.[17]

The view that Q consists of disparate strands of material that can be distinguished thematically and grammatically seems, at least on the surface, to negate the argument that Q is a literary unity and therefore must have been a single document. As Dunn asks, "How can one both argue for the coherence and unity of Q (as proof of its existence), and at the same time argue that internal tensions indicate disunity, without the one argument throwing the other into question?"[18] To be fair to Jacobson and Kloppenborg Verbin, however, we must recognize that both unity and disunity can occur within the same document. For example, the Gospel of Mark includes a variety of disparate traditions, yet it has been redacted into a single story within a single document. The difference between Mark and Q, of course, is that while we know that Mark is a single document despite its inconsistencies, we do not know the same for Q. It is legitimate to ask, therefore, whether the literary disunity within Q arose as a single document underwent successive stages of redaction or as the Evangelists combined multiple Q sources or versions.

Despite this caveat, we can agree that Jacobson and Kloppenborg Verbin have made a valuable contribution to the study of Q in calling attention to indications of literary unity within the Q material. Their work has particular value in demonstrating the distinctive features of Q as compared to the Markan material. It confirms that the Markan material and Q came from different sources.

---

15. Ibid., 143–53.
16. Jacobson, *First Gospel*, 251–55.
17. Ibid., 45.
18. Dunn, *Jesus Remembered*, 156.

For two reasons, however, the arguments given to date for the unity of Q fail to demonstrate that all of the Q material came from a single source. First, no one has coordinated the argument from order with the argument from literary unity. According to Kloppenborg Verbin, 27 of 67 Q pericopes have the same order in Matthew as in Luke. Furthermore within these 67 pericopes are recurrent features of style and theme. But these two uncoordinated facts leave open a number of questions. Do these unifying features of style and theme occur in the 40 pericopes that do not have a common order as well as in the 27 that do? If not, we have no reason to think that both groups came from the same source. And if such features do occur in both groups, then how many of the 40 pericopes are connected to the 27 by common features of style and theme? Without answers to these questions, we have no basis for asserting the unity of Q.

Second, even if all of the Q material came from a written source unified by recurring features of style and theme, this source could still have existed in more than one version. For instance, if the Q material existed in two different written versions, then both texts might have much the same material in much the same order with the same themes and literary forms. The two versions might differ less in content and order than in wording.

To illustrate this point, we can compare Matthew's version of the saying "Tombs of the prophets" with Luke's version (table 2.1).

TABLE 2.1. TOMBS OF THE PROPHETS

Matthew 23:29–32	Luke 11:47–48
29 Woe to you,	47 Woe to you,
scribes and Pharisees, hypocrites,	
because you build the tombs of the prophets	because you build the memorials of the prophets
and adorn the memorials of the righteous.	
30 And you say, "If we had been in the days of our fathers, we would not have been participants with them in the blood of the prophets."	while your fathers killed them.
31 Therefore you testify against yourselves that you are sons of those who killed the prophets.	48 So then you are witnesses and agree with the deeds of your fathers,
32 And you complete the measure of your fathers.	because they killed them, while you build.

Here both Matthew and Luke refer to the rejection of the prophets, one of the main themes of the deuteronomistic tradition that Jacobson sees as the theological basis for the literary unity of Q. Both express this theme in the form of a woe, one of the distinctive forms of Q to which Jacobson points. Yet the difference in wording between Matthew and Luke raises the question, did Matthew and Luke use the same version of Q or two different versions? If Matthew and Luke took this saying from the same written version of Q, then one or both must have revised the saying to such a degree that hardly any wording remains in common. While we can at least imagine this possibility, we can just as easily imagine that Matthew and Luke knew two different versions of the woe. The point here is not to argue for one alternative or the other, but to show that the unity of Q with respect to order and style is compatible with the view that more than one version of Q existed. We must take into account, therefore, not only the unity of Q with respect to order and style, but also its plurality with respect to wording.

SCHOLARSHIP ADVOCATING THE PLURALITY OF Q

We turn therefore to scholars who have argued for the plurality of Q. Most who have done so base their case on variations in the degree of verbal agreement between Matthew and Luke in Q parallels. Streeter described this phenomenon:

> The fact we have to explain is the occurrence in Matthew and Luke of two sets of parallelism, one set in which the verbal resemblances are so close as to favour, if not actually compel, the conclusion that they were derived from a common *written* source, and another set in which the divergences are so great that they cannot be explained in that way. And this distinction is not affected by the existence of border-line cases which would be susceptible of either explanation.[19]

Scholars who think of Q as a single document explain these differences in wording as the result of redaction by one Evangelist or the other. Streeter, however, found this explanation inadequate. Those parallels with close verbal agreement must have come from the same written source; but those with little verbal agreement must have come from two different documents or from variant oral traditions.[20] This alternative posed by Streeter, either different documents or variant oral traditions, divides advocates of the plurality of Q

---

19. Streeter, *Four Gospels*, 237.
20. Ibid.

into two groups: those who give a literary (i.e. documentary) explanation for the variation and those who appeal to oral tradition.

LITERARY HYPOTHESES

Wilhelm Bussmann argued that the Q material came from more than one document. He found this hypothesis necessary to explain different degrees of verbal agreement in the Q material, a phenomenon previously noticed by his predecessors Paul Ewald and Adolf Harnack.[21] To explain this phenomenon, he theorized that Q consisted of two distinct collections: collection I in Greek and collection II in Aramaic. While Matthew and Luke used the same Greek source for collection I, they used different Greek translations of the Aramaic collection II. Bussmann supported this conclusion by pointing out other differences between the two collections: they use different words for the same things; they use the same words with different meanings; each has distinctive stylistic features that the other lacks; each has *hapax legomena*; and they differ in content as well as style. Bussmann also pointed out that sayings in one collection had doublets in the other and that the connection between sayings within each collection was good.[22]

Bussmann took into account several significant features of the Q material, including differences in content and style, and doublets in the material. His attention to *hapax legomena* is less significant, since nothing can be inferred about sources from a single occurrence of a word. The lasting value of his work is the attention that he calls to the different degrees of verbal agreement between Matthew and Luke. Bussmann argues, probably correctly, that this extreme variation cannot be explained exclusively by assuming that each Evangelist revised the same source differently. In some instances, it is likely that Matthew and Luke differ in wording because they had different versions of the same material, as Bussmann supposed.

However, even if we accept this premise, Bussmann's theory still faces two significant criticisms. First, in both of his collections he mixes high-agreement pericopes with low-agreement pericopes, contrary to his original premise.[23] The pericopes in collection I, whose parallels should have almost identical wording, include several whose parallels differ significantly in wording, such as the temptation narrative (Matt 4:1–11a/Luke 4:1b–13) and the story of the centurion's boy (Matt 8:5–13/Luke 7:1b–10). Likewise the peri-

---

21. Wilhelm Bussmann, *Synoptische Studien* (3 vols. in 2; Halle [Saale]: Buchhandlung des Waisenhauses, 1925–31), 2:118–20.

22. Ibid., 2:112–56.

23. Kloppenborg Verbin makes this criticism of Bussmann (*Excavating Q*, 61).

copes in collection II, whose parallels should have quite different wording, include several whose parallels have significant agreements in wording, such as the Lord's prayer (Matt 6:9–13/Luke 11:1–4) and the pericope "Ask, seek, knock" (Matt 7:7–11/Luke 11:9–13). Second, Bussmann does not account for the data in the most economical manner. He posits three distinct documents: one used by both Evangelists, a second used only by Matthew, and a third (a variant version of the second) used only by Luke. However, we could account for the same data by positing only two documents: one used by both Evangelists for the material where they agree, and a second used by one or the other for the material where they differ.

After Bussmann, C. K. Barrett also argued for the plurality of Q.[24] Defining Q as the non-Markan material common to Matthew and Luke, Barrett suggested that Q "is derived not from one common source, but from a number of non-Markan sources."[25] To establish this position, Barrett made two main points. First, he sought to show that the wording of Q, along with the social setting implied thereby, provides no basis for thinking of Q as a single document. He argued that those parts of Q where Matthew and Luke agree closely in wording can be ascribed to a single common Greek source but that the remainder could not be explained without recourse to some parallel version. In the latter type of passage, he thought it more likely that Matthew and Luke used similar but not identical traditions, and less likely that they both used the same source which Matthew conflated with a parallel version from M.

Second, Barrett rejected the argument from order, seeking to show that the order of the Q material provides no basis for thinking of Q as a single document.[26] He pointed to the differences in order between Matthew's Sermon on the Mount and the corresponding material in Luke, finding that no common order can be traced. To the explanation that Matthew rearranged the material, he replied,

> If it be urged that Matthew's editorial methods provide an adequate explanation of the phenomena, it must be answered that the explanation itself is a confession that the evidence *as it stands* affords no grounds for belief in a single common source as the origin of the Q material. Besides, the editing which we are asked to accept is, sometimes at least, of a surprising nature.[27]

---

24. C. K. Barrett, "Q: A Re-examination," *ExpT* 54 (1942–43): 320–23; repr. in Bellinzoni, *Two-Source Hypothesis*, 259–68. I cite page numbers from the reprint.

25. Ibid., 261.

26. Ibid., 265–68.

27. Ibid., 266.

Barrett next examined Luke 10:13–11:32, a section cited by Streeter as an example of agreement in order, and found Streeter's argument unconvincing when attention is given to detail. Finally, he examined the overall outline of Q. He found no common order in the latter part of the outline, and the common order at the beginning he attributed to the influence of Mark's order on both Matthew and Luke.

Barrett's argument from the wording of Q still calls for consideration. However, his objections to the argument from order ultimately fail to convince. It is inadequate simply to point to the differences in order between Matthew and Luke without explaining the many points of agreement in order. And Barrett's view that Matthew and Luke simply followed Mark's order fails to explain why they have a common order for Q material that has no parallel in Mark.

C. J. A. Hickling modified Bussmann's view, proposing three sources for the Q material: one source which each Evangelist reproduced with a high degree of exactness, a second that one or both modified slightly, and discrete items from oral tradition or written sources other than the first two.[28] However, in his brief article of less than five pages he did not adequately develop this idea.

Other scholars have theorized that Q developed along two different trajectories into two different recensions or written versions, one used by Matthew (Q^{Mt} or Q^{Matt}) and one used by Luke (Q^{Lk} or Q^{Luke}).[29] Ulrich Luz[30] and Hans Dieter Betz[31] used this distinction to account for some of the differences between Matthew's Sermon on the Mount and Luke's Sermon on the Plain, differences that they think cannot be accounted for by the redaction

---

28. C. J. A. Hickling, "The Plurality of 'Q,'" in Delobel, *Logia*, 425–29.

29. Streeter rejects this view: *Four Gospels*, 235–38. For more detail, see Frans Neirynck, "Q^{Mt} and Q^{Lk} and the Reconstruction of Q," *ETL* 66 (1990): 385–90; Kloppenborg Verbin, *Excavating Q*, 104–111.

30. Ulrich Luz, "Sermon on the Mount/Plain: Reconstruction of Q^{Mt} and Q^{Lk}," in *Society of Biblical Literature 1983 Seminar Papers* (SBLSP 22; Chico, Calif.: Scholars Press), 473–79; idem, *Matthew 1–7* (trans. W. Linss; Continental Commentaries; Minneapolis: Augsburg, 1989), 46; idem, *Matthew 1–7: A Commentary* (trans. James E. Crouch; Hermeneia; Minneapolis: Fortress, 2007), 19.

31. Hans Dieter Betz, *The Sermon on the Mount: A Commentary on the Sermon on the Mount* (Hermeneia; Minneapolis: Fortress, 1995), 8, 42–44. For a critique of Betz's view, see Dale C. Allison Jr., *The Jesus Tradition in Q* (Harrisburg, Pa.: Trinity Press International, 1997), 67–77.

of one Evangelist or the other. Migaku Sato[32] and Daniel Kosch[33] accepted this distinction and worked it out in more detail. This theory takes seriously the wide divergence in wording between Matthew and Luke in some of the Q material, explaining it by appeal to two different versions of Q. However, if these versions differed so widely in some Q material, then why in other Q material do Matthew and Luke have almost identical wording? The theory fails to provide an adequate answer to this question; it simply pushes the problem back to an earlier stage of the tradition.

According to Thomas Bergemann, the double tradition, i.e., what other scholars generally call Q, came from more than one source.[34] Bergemann points to a central problem in the usual reconstruction of Q: scholars attribute to the same source both passages in which Matthew and Luke have almost complete verbatim agreement and passages in which they have almost no verbatim agreement. Bergemann argues that only those passages with high verbal agreement should be called "Q." As for the rest, scholars have usually explained the low verbal agreement in one of two ways. Some have theorized that Matthew and Luke used different recensions of Q (see above). Bergemann rejects this explanation because it just pushes the problem back a step: it does not explain why these recensions would agree almost completely in some passages but disagree almost completely in others. Other scholars have theorized that the differences in wording between Matthew and Luke resulted from one or both Evangelists redacting Q. This is the theory that Bergemann puts to the test. He develops a word statistical method and applies this to what is usually called the Q sermon (Luke 6:20b–49 par), most of which exhibits a low degree of verbal agreement. He finds that the differences in wording between Matthew and Luke in this material cannot be attributed to observable redactional tendencies of the Evangelists. If that is the case, it makes less plausible the assumption that Matthew and Luke found Q in essentially the same form and produced by their own redaction the differences in

---

32. Migaku Sato, *Q und Prophetie: Studien zur Gattungs- und Traditionsgeschichte der Quelle Q* (WUNT 2/29; Tübingen: Mohr Siebeck, 1988), 18–28, 47–62.

33. Daniel Kosch, *Die eschatologische Tora des Menschensohnes: Untersuchungen zur Rezeption der Stellung Jesu zur Tora in Q* (NTOA 12; Fribourg: Universitätsverlag; Göttingen: Vandenhoeck & Ruprecht, 1989); idem, "Q: Rekonstruktion und Interpretation: Eine methodenkritische Hinführung mit einem Exkurs zur Q-Vorlage des Lk," *FZPT* 36 (1989): 409–25.

34. Thomas Bergemann, *Q auf dem Prüfstand: Die Zuordnung des Mt/Lk-Stoffes zu Q am Beispiel der Bergpredigt* (FRLANT 158; Göttingen: Vandenhoeck & Ruprecht, 1993). A summary and critique of Bergemann's work is given by Adelbert Denaux, "Criteria for Identifying Q-Passages: A Critical Review of a Recent Work by T. Bergemann," *NovT* 37 (1995): 105–29; Kloppenborg Verbin also gives a critique in *Excavating Q*, 62–65.

wording. Bergemann therefore proposes an alternative theory: most of this material came not from Q, but from a separate source that Bergemann calls a "*Grundrede*." This Grundrede began as an Aramaic document, of which two different Greek translations were made. These translations underwent modification in the process of transmission before reaching the Evangelists, who did not use the same translation.

Technically Bergemann does not argue that Q consisted of more than one document, since he distinguishes between Q and the "Grundrede." However, his position amounts to much the same thing, since he posits more than one written source for the material that others ordinarily designate as Q. Bergemann's work rightly emphasizes the need to explain why the degree of verbal agreement between Matthew and Luke varies so widely in the double tradition material. It also has its weaknesses, however. Bergemann's method for determining Matthean and Lukan redaction presupposes Markan priority. That presupposition may have seemed reasonable in 1993, but it has become more problematic since my publication of new evidence against that theory.[35] Bergemann also focuses on verbal agreement to the exclusion of other criteria for determining the content of Q, such as shared sequence. Consequently he does not explain how Matthew and Luke could have independently inserted the Grundrede (Q sermon) into the same point in the sequence of Q.[36]

Maurice Casey, like Barrett, conceives of Q as a plurality of sources.[37] Casey criticizes previous scholarship on Q for assuming both that Q was a single document and that it was written in Greek. He proposes "a chaotic model of Q," in which various elements of Q circulated on wax tablets or as oral tradition. Much of Q was translated from Aramaic and represents authentic sayings of Jesus. Casey chooses three Q passages "which show some signs of having been translated literally from an Aramaic source,"[38] and he reconstructs the presumed Aramaic sources of these passages. (1) For the woes against Pharisees (Matt 23:23–36/Luke 11:39–51), Matthew and Luke used two different translations of an Aramaic original. (2) For the section on Jesus and John (Matt 11:2–19/Luke 7:18–35), the Evangelists used the same Greek translation of an Aramaic original. (3) For the Beelzebul debate, which also occurs in Mark (Mark 3:20–30; Matt 12:22–32; Luke 11:14–23; 12:10), Mark used one translation of an Aramaic original, while Matthew and Luke used another. Thus in some passages Matthew and Luke agree closely in wording

---

35. Burkett, *From Proto-Mark to Mark*, 7–42.

36. Denaux, "Criteria," 116–17.

37. Maurice Casey, *An Aramaic Approach to Q: Sources for the Gospels of Matthew and Luke* (SNTSMS 122; Cambridge: Cambridge University Press, 2002).

38. Ibid., 60.

because they are using the same Greek translation, while in other passages they do not agree closely in wording because they are using different translations of an Aramaic original.

Casey correctly recognizes the need to explain the wide range of variation in verbal agreement between Matthew and Luke in Q. And his attempt to find that explanation in a pre-Synoptic stage of Aramaic is certainly legitimate. Reviewers, however, have called attention to several problems in his work. In focusing on the plurality of Q, he has ignored evidence for its unity, such as the common order of some Q pericopes, its distinctive features, and its theological coherence.[39] By postulating that the Evangelists engaged in "vigorous editing" in the woes on Pharisees, he has made the theory that they used different translations somewhat unnecessary.[40] He assumes too readily that if he can translate a Greek passage into Aramaic, then it must have existed in Aramaic.[41] And he assumes too readily that the words of Q represent the words of Jesus.[42]

ORAL HYPOTHESES

Other advocates of the plurality of Q appeal to oral tradition to explain the variations in verbal agreement between Matthew and Luke in Q parallels.

From other disciplines, studies of oral tradition and oral performance have renewed interest among New Testament scholars in the importance of orality for understanding Q.[43] For example, Richard A. Horsley and Jonathan A. Draper conceive of Q as an "oral-derived text," i.e., an oral communication performed before a group and subsequently written down.[44] Q thus originated in oral performance, and even after it was written down it continued to be recited and performed orally. Horsley and Draper believe that they can identify characteristics of oral communication in the reconstructed text of

---

39. C. M. Tuckett, review of *An Aramaic Approach to Q: Sources for the Gospels of Matthew and Luke* by Maurice Casey, in *JTS* NS 54 (2003): 683–87, esp. 684.

40. Ibid., 686; Paul Foster, review of *An Aramaic Approach to Q: Sources for the Gospels of Matthew and Luke* by Maurice Casey, in *NovT* 46 (2004): 289–91, esp. 291.

41. Foster, review of *An Aramaic Approach*, 291.

42. Tuckett, review of *An Aramaic Approach*, 686–87.

43. For reviews of the scholarship, see Richard A. Horsley, "Recent Studies of Oral-Derived Literature and Q," in Richard A. Horsley and Jonathan A. Draper, *Whoever Hears You Hears Me: Prophets, Performance, and Tradition in Q* (Harrisburg, Pa.: Trinity Press International, 1999), 150–74; Dunn, *Jesus Remembered*, 192–210; Terence C. Mournet, *Oral Tradition and Literary Dependency: Variability and Stability in the Synoptic Tradition and Q* (WUNT 2/195; Tübingen: Mohr Siebeck, 2005), 54–99.

44. Horsley and Draper, *Whoever Hears You*; Horsley, *Oral Performance*.

Q. The basic units of Q were not individual sayings, but short speeches or discourses, in which individual sayings were embedded. These discourses reflect the perspective of a movement for the renewal of Israel, probably in Galilee, that stood in opposition to the Jerusalem leaders. The discourses were spoken in specific social settings, such as renewing a covenant, commissioning envoys to expand the movement, praying for the kingdom as a way of helping make it a social reality, pronouncing woes against the Pharisees and thus calling down divine judgment upon them, and reassuring those anxious about the necessities of life.

Horsley and Draper focus on interpreting Q within the context of oral performance, which is certainly a legitimate and illuminating approach. However, it would be equally legitimate to focus on the fate of Q once it became inscribed in writing. For Horsley and Draper, the written text Q functioned primarily to facilitate further oral performance. They recognize that Matthew and Luke incorporated Q into their Gospels, but they show little interest in this stage of the life of Q. They therefore do not address the kinds of questions that we are asking in this study: e.g., what is the relationship between Q in Matthew and Q in Luke, and how do we account for the fact that some Q parallels differ radically in wording while others agree closely?

Since Horsley and Draper envisage different oral performances of the same Q discourses, they might have used this feature of their theory to account for the differences between Q in Matthew and Q in Luke. However, Horsley at least does not take that step. At one point he states that Matthew and Luke used the same text of Q, transcribed from the same oral performance.[45] Draper, in passing, does suggest that Matthew and Luke separately inscribed Q in text, but he does not develop this idea.[46]

In contrast, James D. G. Dunn does use a theory of oral tradition to explain variations of wording in Q parallels.[47] While accepting the existence of a Q document and the general validity of the Two-Document hypothesis, Dunn doubts that all of the material common to Matthew and Luke came to them in written form. To account for the variation in wording between Matthew and Luke in some of the Q material, Dunn proposes that Matthew and Luke knew "two orally varied versions of the same tradition."[48] Dunn finds

---

45. Horsley and Draper, *Whoever Hears You*, 167.

46. Ibid., 187.

47. Dunn, *Jesus Remembered*, 173–254.

48. Ibid., 232. Dunn qualifies the Two-Document hypothesis by oral tradition to such a degree that in David Neville's judgment he thereby undermines its integrity: David Neville, "The Demise of the Two-Document Hypothesis? Dunn and Burkett on Gospel Sources," *Pacifica* 19 (Feb 2006): 78–92, esp. 79–86.

the evidence insufficient to judge between two alternative explanations: either one Evangelist or the other (or both) drew directly from oral tradition; or while both took the material from the Q document, one or the other retold it in the style of an oral storyteller.[49]

If Dunn's latter explanation were the case, his theory would not differ essentially from the view that Matthew and Luke knew a single Q document that one Evangelist or the other altered. It would simply provide an oral rather than a literary model for understanding that alteration. This explanation has implications that Dunn apparently has not considered. In much of the Q material, Matthew and Luke have almost identical wording. In utilizing these passages, both Evangelists functioned as scribes, copying more or less exactly what lay before them in the document Q. Dunn does not explain why one or the other of these Evangelists would suddenly cease to be a scribe and become a storyteller instead, retelling the Q document in his own words.

If Dunn's former alternative explanation were the case, his theory would require two or three different versions of Q, one written and one or two from oral tradition. Dunn dismisses the possibility that there may have been more than one written version of Q, claiming that such a suggestion undermines the arguments for the existence of a Q document.[50] However, we have seen above that the arguments for a unified Q source do not rule out a plurality of written Q versions. If, as Dunn believes, more than one version of Q circulated, there is no reason why they could not have been written.

A student of Dunn, Terence C. Mournet, takes much the same position as Dunn.[51] Mournet thinks the Evangelists used written sources and that the Two-Document hypothesis provides the proper framework for examining the Synoptic Problem. However, he doubts that Synoptic relations can be explained exclusively by literary dependence. The Evangelists had access not only to written sources, but also to a body of oral tradition. The theory of a common written source best explains those passages where Matthew and Luke have a high degree of verbatim agreement; but where they do not, common dependence on oral tradition may provide a better explanation. Mournet uses statistics to test those Q passages that Dunn ascribes to oral tradition and those that he ascribes to a written source. With a few exceptions, Mournet's conclusions support those of Dunn. However, Mournet recognizes that he has not provided definitive criteria for distinguishing oral from literary material in Q.

49. Dunn, *Jesus Remembered*, 232, 237.
50. Ibid., 233–34.
51. Mournet, *Oral Tradition*.

Dunn and Mournet rely on the work of Kenneth Bailey for their understanding of oral tradition.[52] Bailey drew on his experience with village life in
the Middle East to formulate a theory of "informal controlled tradition."[53]
According to this theory, villagers themselves exercise control over the tradition to ensure its accuracy. Dunn and Mournet follow Bailey in taking this
understanding as a model for the oral transmission of traditions about Jesus.
However, Bailey's work has been subjected to a damaging critique by Theodore J. Weeden Sr.[54] While it is still possible that oral tradition influenced the
Evangelists, it would be unwise to use Bailey's model as a way of understanding how that happened or defending the accuracy of that tradition.

CONCLUSION

From the preceding review of scholarship, we can sum up the state of the
question concerning the unity or plurality of Q. On the one hand, the Q material manifests a degree of unity with respect to order and features of style and
theme. No one has established, however, whether such unity pervades and
unites the entirety of the Q material or only a part of it. On the other hand, Q
manifests plurality with respect to the degree of verbal agreement in parallels,
a phenomenon suggesting that it may have existed in more than one version.
No one, however, has provided other evidence for such versions, successfully
identified their contents, or determined whether one or both Evangelists used
such versions.

In the present study, I try to delineate both the unity and the plurality of Q more clearly than previous scholarship. Chapters 3–6 focus on the
aspects of the double tradition that suggest a unity: namely, common order
of parallels in Matthew and Luke, and recurring features of style and theme.
In chapter 3, I identify a "core" of double tradition material that is unified
by order, style, and theme. In chapter 4, I show that most of the rest of the
double tradition coheres stylistically and thematically with this core. In chapter 5, I identify material unique to one Gospel that also coheres stylistically
and thematically with the core. In chapter 6, assuming that all of this material

---

52. Dunn, *Jesus Remembered*, 205–210; Mournet, *Oral Tradition*, 187–91.

53. Kenneth E. Bailey, "Informal Controlled Oral Tradition and the Synoptic Gospels," *Asia Journal of Theology* 5 (1991): 34–54; repr. in *Themelios* 20.2 (January 1995):
4–11; idem, "Middle Eastern Oral Tradition and the Synoptic Gospels," *ExpT* 106 (1995):
363–67.

54. Theodore J. Weeden Sr., "Theories of Tradition: A Critique of Kenneth Bailey,"
Forum (Westar Institute) 7.1 (2004): 45–69.

represents a unified source Q, I adopt the working hypothesis that Luke best preserves the order of Q.

Chapters 7–11 focus on that aspect of the double tradition that suggests a plurality: namely variation in verbal agreement in double tradition parallels. In chapter 7, assuming a single Q source, I identify three factors that would cause the wording of Matthew and Luke to differ in the double tradition: combining Q with Mark, with M, and with L. In chapters 8–11, I survey examples of these and other factors that caused such differences in wording. Chapter 12 summarizes my conclusions.

3
THE CORE OF Q

In chapter 2, we saw that no one has established either the unity or the plurality of Q, that is, whether it came from a single unified source or several disparate sources. In chapters 3–6, we will focus on the unity of Q, seeking to determine how much of the double tradition and related material can be attributed to a single unified source. To this point we have identified two aspects of the unity of Q: the fact that some of this material occurs in the same order in both Matthew and Luke, and the fact that it exhibits recurring features of style and theme. In the present chapter, we use both aspects of this unity in order to identify the minimal assured contents or "core" of a single unified Q source.

COMMON ORDER OF Q PARALLELS

We begin with the order of Q. If the Q material came from a written source, at least some of it should occur in the same order in both Matthew and Luke. Previous scholarship has noticed that such is in fact the case. However, different scholars have given slightly different reconstructions of this common order.[1] Table 3.1 shows the reconstructions of Streeter, Kümmel, de Solages, Allison, and Kloppenborg Verbin.[2] The table lists the relevant material in the

---

1. I leave out of consideration here Taylor's very different approach to the order of Q, which I discussed above in chapter 2 ("Order of Q"; "Original Order of Q").

2. Streeter, *Four Gospels*, 273–75; cf. idem, "On the Original Order of Q," in *Studies in the Synoptic Problem: By Members of the University of Oxford* (ed. W. Sanday; Oxford: Clarendon, 1911), 140–64; Kümmel, *Introduction to the New Testament*, 65–66; Paul Marie Bruno de Solages, *La composition des évangiles* (Leiden: Brill, 1973), 29; Dale Allison in W. D. Davies and Dale C. Allison, *A Critical and Exegetical Commentary on the Gospel according to Saint Matthew* (ICC; Edinburgh: T&T Clark, 1988), 1:117–18; Kloppenborg Verbin, *Excavating Q*, 68–71. I have standardized the names of the pericopes for ease of comparison.

order of Luke, and an asterisk indicates a pericope or section that one of these scholars includes in the common order.

TABLE 3.1. RECONSTRUCTIONS OF COMMON ORDER IN Q

	Streeter	Kümmel	de Solages	Allison	Klop-penborg
John's preaching	*	*	*	*	*
Jesus' baptism	*		*		
Jesus' temptation	*	*	*	*	*
Nazara (Q 4:16a)					*
The Q sermon	*	*	*	*	*
Centurion's boy	*	*	*	*	*
Jesus and John		*		*	*
On following	*		*		
Pray for workers	*		*		
Mission charge	*		*		
Woes on cities	*	*	*	*	*
Father and son	*	*	*	*	*
Blessed eyes				*	
Beelzebul debate	*	*	*		*
Return of spirit	?	*	?		
Seeking signs	?		?		*
On Pharisees		*		*	
Mustard seed	*		*		*
Leaven	*		*		*
Last first			*		
Deserted house		*	*	*	
Lost sheep					*
Forgive 7 times					*
Eschatology		*	*	*	*
Parable of pounds		*	*	*	*

All five scholars agree that this sequence of Q common to Matthew and Luke included "John's preaching," "Jesus' temptation," the Q sermon, "Centurion's boy," "Woes on cities," and "Father and son." All except Streeter include the sections "Eschatology" and "Parable of pounds," and these would fit in the sequence that he reconstructs as well. Accepting all of these as part of the common order, we can now examine the differences in these reconstructions to determine the most probable sequence.

1. Streeter and de Solages include the baptism of Jesus in this sequence, and it does fit, if in fact Q included an account of Jesus' baptism. Whether it did or not is a disputed issue,[3] but there are two good reasons to think that it did. First, the temptation narrative seems to presuppose the baptismal account that precedes it: that Jesus is led by the Spirit presupposes that he has received the Spirit, and that Satan tests him as the son of God presupposes that Jesus has been designated as such. Second, in the account of Jesus' baptism, Matthew and Luke include several agreements against Mark, which probably represent remnants of a common non-Markan account. I therefore include the baptism in my reconstruction of the common order.

2. Kloppenborg Verbin includes a reference to "Nazara," a term that is in fact found in the sequence common to Matthew and Luke (Matt 4:13/Luke 4:16a). But since Matthew speaks of leaving Nazareth, and Luke of arriving there, the term itself is the only common element. Since it is difficult to know what to do with a single word, I leave it out of account here.

3. Between the story of the centurion's boy and the pericope "Woes on cities," one has two alternatives for reconstructing a common order. While Kümmel, Allison, and Kloppenborg Verbin trace the common order through the section "Jesus and John," Streeter and de Solages trace it through the passages "On following," "Pray for workers," and "Mission charge." It is likely that both alternatives originally stood in the common order of parallels, but after one Evangelist transposed the two sets of passages, either alternative could be counted in the common order, but not both. Streeter thought that Matthew postponed the section on Jesus and John. Since this section presupposes that Jesus performed miracles, Matthew may have moved it to a later position in his Gospel in order to place it after some miracle stories.[4] If so, that would leave the pericopes on following and mission in their original position in the order of Q. However, this explanation presupposes that the section "Jesus and John" also originally belonged in the common order of parallels before Matthew postponed it. I will therefore include both alternatives in my reconstruction for the purpose of assessing the minimal contents or "core" of a unified Q source.

4. After the pericope "Father and son," four of the scholars trace the common order through the Beelzebul debate, while Allison traces it through the pericope "Blessed eyes." This pair of alternatives probably arose for the

---

3. For the pros and cons see Kloppenborg Verbin, *Excavating Q*, 93.
4. Streeter, *Four Gospels*, 273.

same reason as the pair discussed above: both alternatives originally stood in the common order of parallels before one of the Evangelists transposed them. Originally "Blessed eyes" probably followed "Father and son" as in Luke, while Matthew inserted it into his parable discourse in order to join it with other material on seeing and hearing (Matt 13:13–15). Since both alternatives probably stood in the original order of parallels, I include both in my reconstruction.

5. After the Beelzebul debate, the common order can be traced through either "Return of spirit" (Matt 12:43–45/Luke 11:24–26) or "Seeking signs" (Matt 12:38–42/Luke 11:29–32). Streeter mentions both, with the recognition that one Evangelist or the other transposed them. De Solages includes both as well. Kümmel puts the former in the common sequence; and Kloppenborg Verbin, the latter. This alternative probably arose because Luke moved "Return of spirit" from its original position in the common order. He placed it with the Beelzebul debate, probably because both address the theme of exorcism.[5] If so, then "Seeking signs" retains its place in the original sequence of Q. However, since "Return of spirit" originally stood in that order, I include both alternatives in my reconstruction.

6. After the section "Seeking signs," Streeter, de Solages, and Kloppenborg Verbin trace the common order of Q through the parables of mustard seed and leaven (Matt 13:31–33/Luke 13:18–21), while Kümmel and Allison trace it through the discourse against Pharisees (Matt 23:23–36/Luke 11:37–54). The latter is preferable. The parables of mustard seed and leaven probably came not from Q, but from a separate parable discourse, as I have shown elsewhere.[6]

7. With the discourse on Pharisees in the sequence, the pericope "Last first," proposed by de Solages, does not remain an option. Neither does Kloppenborg Verbin's proposed sequence, parable of the lost sheep (Matt 18:10–14/Luke 15:4–7) and the saying on forgiving seven times (Matt 18:15–22/Luke 17:3b–4). Eliminating these leaves the pericope "Deserted house" (Matt 23:37–39/Luke 13:34–35), suggested by Kümmel, de Solages, and Allison.

Table 3.2 shows our results, our reconstruction of the order of Q common to Matthew and Luke. An arrow preceding a reference in smaller font (e.g., → 11:2–19) indicates a place where one Evangelist or the other probably relocated the material so indicated.

---

5. *Contra* Manson, who thinks Matthew moved this pericope: T. W. Manson, *The Sayings of Jesus* (London: SCM Press, 1937; repr. Grand Rapids: Eerdmans, 1979), 87.

6. Burkett, *From Proto-Mark to Mark*, 172–75.

TABLE 3.2. COMMON ORDER OF Q PARALLELS

	Matthew Q	Luke Q
John's preaching	3:5b, 7–10, 11–12	3:2b–3a, 7–9, 16–17
Jesus' baptism	3:16–17	3:21–22
Jesus' temptation	4:1–11a	4:1b–13
Q sermon	5:1–7:28a	6:20–7:1a
Centurion's boy	8:5–10, 13	7:1b–10
Jesus and John	→ 11:2–19	7:18–35
On following	8:19–22	9:57–62
Pray for workers	9:37–38	10:2
Mission charge	10:9–15	10:4–12
Woes on cities	11:20–24	10:13–15
Father and son	11:25–27	10:21–22
Blessed eyes	→ 13:16–17	10:23–24
Beelzebul debate	12:22–30	11:14–15, 17–23
Seeking signs	12:38–42	11:29–32
Return of spirit	12:43–45	→ 11:24–26
On Pharisees	23:23–36	11:39–51
Deserted house	23:37–39	13:34–35
Eschatology	24:26–41	17:22–37
Parable of pounds	25:14–30	19:12–27

Table 3.2 represents one possible reconstruction of a sequence in Q that extends from John's preaching to the parable of the pounds. As we have seen, in three places alternative choices of material in the common order are possible, and I have included both alternatives in all three instances.

Did Matthew and Luke obtain this material from a written source or from oral tradition? The fact that Matthew and Luke have an extended sequence of material in the same order suggests that they received it from a written source. While we know that a written source could transmit the material in the same order to the two Evangelists, we do not know that oral tradition could do so. Though Horsley seems to think that the discourses of Q could have been performed in sequence orally,[7] Joanna Dewey, who also works with oral tradition, points out in response that

---

7. Horsley and Draper, *Whoever Hears You*, 168–69.

oral cultures do not tend to gather oral material formally into coherent
wholes.... Tellers of the Q material may well have been familiar with several
or all of the discourses, and may have performed them in various combi-
nations as appropriate on different occasions, but they are unlikely to have
thought of or performed them as one whole discourse in any sort of stable
order.[8]

For this reason, we can be fairly certain that this sequence came to Matthew
and Luke from a written source. It is conceivable that the wording of the
source might have been influenced by variants from oral tradition or other
sources, but the common order in itself most likely reflects the fixed order of
a document.

Style and Theme in the Common Order

The Q parallels in table 3.2 are unified not only by a common order but also
by recurring features of style and theme. In appendix B, I have assembled a list
of recurring features of style and theme in the Q material. I have designated
individual features with a "B" followed by a number (e.g., B.1, B.2, etc.). By
perusing the features listed in appendix B, we can determine that the following twenty-six occur in two or more passages of the Q material in table 3.2.

- B.1 Reference to John the Baptist: John's preaching; Jesus and
  John
- B.2 Implicit or explicit identification of John as a prophet: John's
  preaching; Jesus and John
- B.3 The expression "brood of vipers" (γεννήματα ἐχιδνῶν):
  John's preaching; On Pharisees
- B.4 The theme of fleeing from judgment: John's preaching; On
  Pharisees
- B.5 The theme of bearing good or bad fruit: John's preaching; Q
  sermon
- B.6 The theme of repentance (μετάνοια, μετανοέω): John's
  preaching; Woes on cities; Seeking signs
- B.7 The theme of cutting down a fruitless tree: John's preaching;
  Q sermon
- B.8 The theme of destroying something worthless by fire as an
  analogy for judgment: John's preaching; Q sermon

---

8. Joanna Dewey, "Response to Kelber, Horsley, and Draper," in Horsley, *Oral Performance*, 101–108, esp. 105–106.

- B.9 Reference to Jesus as "the one coming" (ὁ ἐρχόμενος): John's preaching; Jesus and John; Deserted house
- B.10 Reference to the Spirit: John's preaching; Jesus' baptism; Jesus' temptation; Beelzebul debate
- B.13: Identification of Jesus as God's son: Jesus' baptism; Jesus' temptation; Father and son
- B.14 The theme of the kingdom of Satan: Jesus' temptation; Beelzebul debate
- B.15 The form of a blessing (μακάριος): Q sermon; Jesus and John; Blessed eyes
- B.16 The theme of "the kingdom of God" (in Matt: "of the heavens"): Q sermon; Jesus and John
- B.17 The theme of rejected or persecuted prophets or messengers: Q sermon; Jesus and John; Seeking signs; On Pharisees; Deserted house; Eschatology
- B.18 The expression "Son of Man": Q sermon; Jesus and John; On following; Seeking signs; Eschatology
- B.19 The term "reward": three times in Q sermon
- B.20 The form of a woe (οὐαί): Q sermon; Woes on cities; On Pharisees
- B.24 The term "hypocrite(s)" (ὑποκριταί): Q sermon; On Pharisees
- B.26 The theme of hearing and doing the word: twice in Q sermon
- B.28 The expression "this generation": Jesus and John; Seeking signs; Return of spirit; On Pharisees; Eschatology
- B.29 The theme of "wisdom" (σοφία): Jesus and John; Father and son; Seeking signs; On Pharisees
- B.30 Sentence "the kingdom of God has drawn near (or come) [to you]": ἤγγικεν or ἔφθασεν [ἐφ' ὑμᾶς] ἡ βασιλεία τοῦ θεοῦ: Mission charge; Beelzebul debate
- B.32 The theme of the day of judgment: Mission charge; Woes on cities; Seeking signs
- B.33 The theme of Sodom and Lot: Mission charge, Woes on cities, Eschatology
- B.37 The eschatological correlative: Seeking signs; Return of spirit; Eschatology

These features of style and theme link together all but three of the pericopes in table 3.2: "Centurion's boy," "Pray for workers," and "Parable of pounds." Thus the material in table 3.2 is unified not only by the common order of its parallels in Matthew and Luke, but also by numerous recurring features of style and theme within the sequence. This material thus constitutes the minimal assured contents or core of a single unified Q source.

TRACTS, CLUSTERS, OR DISCOURSES

In addition to a common order in the parallels and recurring features of style and theme, the core of Q exhibits one other significant feature: the sayings are organized topically. While Q has been called a collection of sayings, many scholars have recognized that the individual sayings are usually grouped in larger complexes. Several such complexes belong to the core of Q that we have identified above. The first three pericopes, "John's preaching," "Jesus' baptism," and "Jesus' temptation," constitute a section on John the Baptist and Jesus. The Q sermon contains shorter complexes within the sermon. The section "Jesus and John" consists of the pericopes "John's question," "Jesus on John," and "Children in market." The material on following Jesus includes two, possibly three, different pericopes. A section on mission includes the pericopes "Pray for workers," "Mission charge," "Woes on cities," and perhaps "Father and son" and "Blessed eyes." The Beelzebul debate includes several pericopes. The discourse against Pharisees combines a number of different sayings, as does the discourse on eschatology.

These complexes have been variously conceived as tracts, clusters of sayings, or discourses. Wilfred L. Knox regarded some of these complexes as short tracts that had independent existence as collections of Jesus' sayings. He found evidence for such tracts especially in Luke.[9] Knox thought that these tracts circulated separately and so may have come to Matthew and Luke as separate documents. He expressed reservation concerning the existence of Q as a single document into which all these tracts had been incorporated. He thought that even if such a document existed, the tracts within it must have had an earlier independent existence. He therefore focused on identifying such tracts and only secondarily raised the question of whether these tracts had been joined into a larger whole before reaching the Evangelists.

Kloppenborg Verbin has conceived of these complexes as "topically coherent clusters" of sayings in a single document.[10] The sayings in Q were not randomly collected but grouped in these clusters. Other scholars have

---

9. Wilfred L. Knox, *St Luke and St Matthew* (vol. 2 of *The Sources of the Synoptic Gospels*; Cambridge: Cambridge University Press, 1957), 45–47.

10. Kloppenborg, *Formation of Q*, 89.

made similar identifications of shorter collections of sayings within Q.[11] In Kloppenborg Verbin's theory, the document Q went through three stages in the history of its composition. Especially in the second stage, these clusters underwent expansion as a redactor added other material to them.

Harnack described these complexes as "discourses."[12] More recently, Horsley and Draper have also argued that an oral model explains them better than a literary model: "Q is not a collection of sayings but a collection of speeches."[13] These short speeches were performed orally before a community. Individual sayings were embedded in the speeches. At some point the speeches were written down.[14] If these discourses were written down individually, then at that point the oral discourse would essentially become a written tract. Thus the theory of Horsley and Draper is compatible with that of Knox.

Whether we consider these complexes as tracts, clusters, or discourses, several belong to the core of Q that we have identified. Organization of sayings into larger complexes thus appears to be a characteristic feature of the Q source. This distinguishes Q from the Gospel of Thomas, which tends to relate individual sayings of Jesus without much attempt to connect them.

CONCLUSION

We have identified the minimal assured contents or core of a unified Q source: a series of pericopes in the double tradition that is unified by a common order in the parallels, recurring features of style and theme, and a tendency to organize sayings into larger complexes. We can conclude therefore that Q existed as a written source with a unified stylistic and thematic character. At this point, we have not demonstrated that the rest of the double tradition came from the same source as the core of Q. We will consider the extent of Q in chapters 4 and 5, using the core as a basis of comparison to determine whether other double tradition and related pericopes belong to the same source. Nor have we demonstrated that the Q source existed in only one version. Though we have identified a unified source, that source may have existed in parallel versions with different wording. We will consider the wording of Q in chapters 7–11.

---

11. Robinson in Robinson et al., *Critical Edition of Q*, lxi–lxv; idem, *Sayings Gospel Q*, 58–62.

12. Harnack, *Sayings of Jesus*, 181: Q was "a collection of discourses."

13. Horsley in Horsley and Draper, *Whoever Hears You*, 83.

14. Ibid., 7–8, 83–93; Horsley, *Oral Performance*, 2–3, 45.

4

Other Q in the Double Tradition

In chapter 3, I established the minimal assured contents or core of a unified Q source. I now ask, did the rest of the double tradition come from the same source as the core of Q? As we saw in chapter 2, some scholars doubt that all of the material in the double tradition came from a single source. Barrett, for example, pointed out that much of this material lacks agreement in wording or in order.[1] He therefore used the siglum "Q" to refer to the double tradition, without assuming that all of this material came from the same source. Other scholars assume, generally without argument, that all of the double tradition did come from the same source.

I will try to put this issue on a firmer footing by examining recurring features of style and theme in the double tradition. If the remaining double tradition material exhibits the same distinctive features of style and theme as material in the core of Q, the chances are good that it came from the same source. Such a procedure, of course, does not yield certainties, but only probabilities. The greater the number of stylistic and thematic features that a passage shares with the core or other Q material, the greater the probability that it came from Q. And the more distinctive or uncommon such shared features are, the more that probability increases. Yet in brief passages, even one or two features shared with the core may be significant, and even features that are not uncommon can show that a passage is stylistically or thematically consistent with the core.

Stylistic and Thematic Features of Q

A number of double tradition pericopes outside the core of Q are directly linked stylistically or thematically to the core. That is, they share distinctive features of style or theme with the core. The following list shows these

---

1. Barrett, "Q: A Re-examination."

pericopes and the features that they share with the core. These features are designated here as in appendix B with the letter "B" followed by a number (e.g., B.18).

- "On words" (Matt 12:33–37/Luke 6:45): the expression "brood of vipers" (B.3); theme of bearing good or bad fruit (B.5); theme of the day of judgment (B.32)
- "Lord's prayer" (Matt 6:9–13/Luke 11:1–4): reference to John the Baptist (B.1); theme of the kingdom of God (B.16); reference to John's disciples (B.25)
- "Unforgivable sin" (Matt 12:32/Luke 12:10): reference to the Spirit (B.10); the expression "Son of Man" (B.18)
- "Do not worry" (Matt 6:25–33/Luke 12:22–31): theme of gathering wheat into a granary (B.12); theme of the kingdom of God (B.16)
- "Unexpected thief" (Matt 24:43–44/Luke 12:39–40): the expression "Son of Man" (B.18); the phrase "But know this: that…" (B.31)
- "Faithful or not" (Matt 24:45–51/Luke 12:42–46): form of a blessing (B.15); the term "hypocrites" (B.24); theme of being "faithful" (B.45); the sentence "There, there will be weeping and gnashing of teeth" (B.45)
- "Few saved" (Matt 7:13a, 22–23; 8:11–12; 20:16/Luke 13:23–30): theme of the kingdom of God (B.16); the sentence "There, there will be weeping and gnashing of teeth" (B.47)
- "Great supper" (Matt 22:1–10/L Luke 14:15–24) and No garment (Matt 22:11–14): theme of the kingdom of God (B.16); theme of rejected or persecuted prophets or messengers (B.17); the sentence "There, there will be weeping and gnashing of teeth" (B.47)
- "Law until John" (Matt 11:12–13/Luke 16:16): reference to John the Baptist (B.1); theme of the kingdom of God (B.16)
- "On offenses" (Matt 18:7, 15, 21–22; 17:20b/Luke 17:1–6): theme of repentance (B.6); form of a woe (B.20)

Some of the double tradition outside the core of Q has not a direct, but an indirect link to the core. That is, this material shares features of style or theme not with the core, but with another double tradition passage that does share such features with the core.

- "Good gifts" (Matt 7:9–11/L Luke 11:11–13) linked to "Lord's prayer" and "Do not worry": reference to God as Father (B.21)

- "Good gifts" (Matt 7:9/L Luke 11:11) linked to "Do not worry": the phrase "Who (What man/woman) among you" (B.34)
- "Good gifts" (Matt 7:9/L Luke 11:11) linked to "On words": the expression "(you) being evil" (B.36)
- "On treasure" (Matt 6:19–21/Luke 12:33–34) linked to "On words": the term "treasure" (B.42)
- "On treasure" (Matt 6:19–21/Luke 12:33–34) linked to "Unexpected thief": the term "thief" (B.43); the term "break in" (B.44)
- "Man with dropsy" (Q Matt 12:10c, 11/L Luke 14:1–6) linked to "Do not worry": the phrase "Who (What man/woman) among you" (B.34)
- "Blind lead blind" (Matt 15:14b/Luke 6:39) linked to "Man with dropsy": theme of falling into a hole, βόθυνος (B.23)
- "Spoiled salt" (Matt 5:13b/Luke 14:34–35) linked to "Few saved": expression "cast out" (B.49)
- "Law to remain" (Matt 5:18/Luke 16:17) linked to "Law until John": theme of the Law

A few double tradition sayings outside the core share no features of style or theme with the core of Q or with other double tradition passages.

- "Lamp on stand" (Matt 5:15/Luke 11:33)
- "Lamp of body" (Matt 6:22–23/Luke 11:34–36)
- "Agree on way" (Matt 5:25–26/Luke 12:57–59)
- "Two masters" (Matt 6:24/Luke 16:13)
- "On divorce" (Matt 5:32/Luke 16:18a)
- "Twelve thrones" (Matt 19:28b/Luke 22:28–30)

Since all of these sayings are brief, the absence of features shared with other double tradition material may not be significant.

Apart from these few short sayings, the material considered so far shares stylistic and thematic affinities with the core of Q, either directly or indirectly. These passages are linked to the core and to each other by a web of stylistic and thematic connections. A fuller picture of these connections can be seen in appendix B, which identifies over fifty features of style and theme that unite the double tradition passages. The double tradition material thus exhibits a stylistic and thematic coherence or unity. Such unity indicates that this material came from the same milieu; and such unity is at least consistent with the view that these passages came from the same source. As a working hypothesis, therefore, I will theorize that all of this material came from the same source Q. I will refine this theory in later chapters.

ON CONFESSION

One discourse or complex of sayings in the double tradition probably did not come from Q. Table 4.1 shows this material, which I will call "On confession."

TABLE 4.1. ON CONFESSION

	Matthew	Luke
Student, teacher	10:24–25a	6:40
Beelzebul	10:25b	
Hidden shown	10:26–27	12:2–3
Whom to fear	10:28	12:4–5
On sparrows	10:29–31	12:6–7
Confess or deny	10:32–33	12:8–9
Divided house	10:34–36	12:51–53
Jesus says		14:25
Love Jesus	10:37	14:26
Take up cross	10:38	14:27
Lose life to find	10:39	17:33

While in Matthew all of this material stands together in a single discourse (Matt 10:24–39), in Luke it is split up into five different segments standing at five different places in the Gospel (Luke 6:40; 12:2–9; 12:51–53; 14:25–27; 17:33). However, these five segments occur in the same order in Luke as the corresponding material in Matthew.

Kloppenborg Verbin assumes that Luke's placement of these sayings is more original than Matthew's.[2] In his view, Matthew "scanned" Q, lifting these sayings out of their original position in that document and bringing them together. Harnack, on the other hand, thought that these sayings originally stood together as in Matthew and that Luke secondarily separated them.[3] The following considerations support this view.

1. The first saying, Luke 6:40, occurs in Luke's Q sermon but not in Matthew's. Kloppenborg Verbin thinks that it originally stood in the sermon as in Luke and that Matthew moved it out. But while we can affirm that Matthew moved material into the Q sermon, to move anything out would be contrary

---

2. Kloppenborg Verbin, *Excavating Q*, 59, 88–89.
3. Harnack, *Sayings of Jesus*, 174–75.

to his usual practice. Furthermore the saying in Luke interrupts its context, the section on judging in the Q sermon (Luke 6:37–38, 41–42). The interruptive character of the saying suggests that Luke inserted it into the sermon where it did not originally belong.

2. Luke 12:51–53 and 14:26 belong together. Both passages express a common theme, division in households, and both must be read together to get the full message: Jesus may break families apart (Luke 12:51–53), but the faithful disciple will choose Jesus over family (Luke 14:26). Here we find confirmation that Matthew preserves a unity that Luke secondarily broke apart.

3. Luke 14:27 and 17:33 originally stood together, as both Jacobson and Kloppenborg Verbin recognize.[4] Both passages encourage the same attitude: to be willing to bear one's cross or lose one's life. Furthermore the two sayings stand together in the Markan parallel (Matt 16:24–25; Mark 8:34–35; Luke 9:23–24). The evidence therefore suggests again that Luke broke up an original unity that Matthew preserved.

4. The whole of this material constitutes a single discourse on a single theme. Throughout, the putative speaker is Jesus, who exhorts his disciples not to fear, but to remain faithful to him in the midst of opposition. He reminds them that they can expect to suffer like their teacher (Matt 10:24–25a; Luke 6:40). They are to keep nothing hidden from fear, but to proclaim all that he tells them (Matt 10:26–27; Luke 12:2–3).[5] They are not to fear opponents who can kill them, but God who can cast them into Gehenna (Matt 10:28; Luke 12:4–5). They are not to fear, because God knows whatever happens to them (Matt 10:29–31; Luke 12:6–7). Jesus promises them that if they confess him before other people, he will confess them before the angels; but he warns that if they deny him before other people, he will deny them before the angels (Matt 10:32–33; Luke 12:8–9). He informs them that he came to bring division to households. In that situation, they should not put their relations with family members before him (Matt 10:34–37; Luke 12:51–53; 14:26). They should take up their cross and follow him, being willing to lose their life in order to find it (Matt 10:38–39; Luke 14:27; 17:33).

It appears therefore that Matthew did not assemble this sequence out of originally disparate pieces. Instead, it came to both Matthew and Luke as a pre-existing unit. While Matthew retained this unity, Luke did not.

There are two good reasons for doubting that this discourse came from Q. First, it does not belong to the same stylistic milieu. It has little in common stylistically or thematically with other double tradition material. Jacobson

---

4. Jacobson, *First Gospel*, 221; Kloppenborg Verbin, *Excavating Q*, 89.
5. Or, in Luke 12:2–3, they will not be able to hide anything they say.

argues that the last part of this complex (Matt 10:34–39/Luke 12:51–53; 14:26–27; 17:33), like other Q material, has been shaped by the deuteronomistic-wisdom perspective.[6] However, neither this part of the discourse nor the earlier part includes any of the distinctive stylistic or thematic features of this perspective: namely, the theme of rejected or persecuted prophets (B.17), the expression "this generation" (B.28), the eschatological correlative (B.37), the theme of wisdom (B.29), the theme of the day of judgment (B.32), or the theme of the kingdom of God (B.16).

"On confession" does share a few features of style or theme with other double tradition material, but these are generally not distinctive enough to establish that it came from the same source.

- The term οἰκοδεσπότης (housemaster) occurs in this discourse (Matt 10:25) as well as in the core of Q (Matt 24:43/Luke 12:39; Luke 13:25; 14:21) and the parable discourse unique to Matthew (Matt 13:27, 52), which, as I will argue, came from Q. However, this term also occurs in Mark (Mark 14:14/Luke 22:11), M (Matt 20:1, 11), and Matthean redaction (Matt 21:33).
- The term "Beelzebul" occurs in Matthew's version of this discourse (Matt 10:25) as well as in the core of Q (Matt 12:24, 27/Luke 11:15, 19; Luke 11:18). However, this term also occurs in Mark (Mark 3:22). Furthermore the term "Beelzebul" in Matthew 10:25 probably refers back to Matthew 9:34 (unique to Matthew) rather than forward to Matthew 12:24 (Q); and since this term does not occur in Luke's parallel, it may be Matthean redaction.
- A reference to God as "father" occurs in Matthew's version of the discourse (Matt 10:29) as well as in Q (B.21). However, such references also occur in M (Matt 5:16; 6:1, 4, 6, 8 etc.) and Mark (Mark 11:25/Matt 6:14–15). Furthermore this reference does not occur in Luke's parallel (Luke 12:6) and may therefore be Matthean redaction.
- The expression "Son of Man" occurs in Luke's version of the discourse (Luke 12:8) as well as in Q (B.18). However, this expression is not unique to Q. Furthermore the expression does not occur in Matthew's parallel (Matt 10:32) and may therefore be Lukan redaction.
- One prophetic threat occurs in this discourse (Matt 10:32–33/ Luke 12:8–9), while twelve such threats occur in Q.[7] However,

---

6. Jacobson, *First Gospel*, 76, 198–200, 220–24.
7. Ibid., 64.

the same threat occurs in Mark 8:38, and another prophetic threat occurs in Mark 12:38–40.

• One striking agreement between this discourse and Q does occur. The pericope on sparrows in this discourse draws the conclusion, "You are worth (διαφέρετε) more than many sparrows" (Matt 10:31/Luke 12:7). The Q pericope "Do not worry" makes a similar statement: "You are worth (διαφέρετε) much more than birds" (Matt 6:26/Luke 12:24). However, for the amount of material included in this discourse, a single distinctive feature of style shared with Q does not suffice to establish a common origin.

Thus while "On confession" does share some stylistic and thematic features with the rest of the double tradition, these features are for the most part either redactional or not unique to the double tradition. Their presence in this discourse, therefore, does not indicate that it came from the same source.

A second reason also makes it doubtful that "On confession" came from Q: if it did, we would have to attribute a rather peculiar procedure to Luke. He would have removed this discourse from its original position in Q and scattered it to other positions in his Gospel. Such a procedure would be contrary to his usual practice, since, as most scholars agree, Luke usually kept the Q material in its original order. Therefore if Luke found "On confession" as a unit in Q, it is likely that he would have left it as he found it. We can make sense of Luke's procedure only if he found this discourse in a different source, which he wished to integrate into a stage of his Gospel that already included Q. From the source containing "On confession," Luke took one passage at a time and integrated it into what he considered to be an appropriate place in his Gospel. In doing so, Luke kept the material of this discourse in its original order but inserted it into five different locations in the sequence of Q: the first in the Q sermon (Luke 6:40), the second after the discourse against Pharisees (Luke 12:2–9), the third after the discourse on readiness (Luke 12:51–53), the fourth after the parable of the great supper (Luke 14:25–27), and the fifth in the eschatological discourse (Luke 17:33).

These considerations indicate that "On confession" came from a different source than the material that we have identified as Q. It may have circulated independently as a short discourse or tract of prophetic exhortation. Most likely it originated as the message of a Christian prophet speaking in the name of the risen Jesus since it presupposes a situation after Jesus' death. His crucifixion has already occurred and now serves as an example for his followers (Matt 10:38/Luke 14:27). His disciples are experiencing opposition, the possibility of death, division among their families, all as a result of confessing Jesus. The situation presupposed matches that of early Christianity after the death of Jesus, not that of his disciples before his death. The risen Jesus commands, promises, and threatens in order to encourage his followers to continue to confess him despite the opposition.

Matthew and Luke have little agreement in wording throughout their respective versions of this discourse. For such an extensive amount of material, it is not reasonable to think that all of these differences arose from redaction by the Evangelists. Each Evangelist apparently knew a different version of the discourse.

CONCLUSIONS

The idea that Q was a single unified source is not a new theory. What is new in the present study is a method for testing this theory. If the double tradition material did come from the same source, we should expect it to exhibit a degree of stylistic and thematic coherence. For the most part, it does. The only major exception, apart from a few short sayings, is the discourse "On confession" (Matt 10:24–39 par). It is reasonable to think therefore that Q was a single stylistically and thematically unified source that encompassed most of the double tradition.

5

Q MATERIAL UNIQUE TO ONE GOSPEL

In determining the extent of Q, we must recognize that some Q material included by one Evangelist may have been omitted by the other. Reconstructions of Q therefore often include some material that occurs in only one Gospel.[1] For example, the International Q Project includes one passage unique to Matthew and four passages unique to Luke.[2] We must therefore consider how such passages can be identified. In the present chapter, I adopt a criterion for identifying Q material unique to Matthew or Luke, and I use that criterion to identify such material.

IDENTIFYING Q MATERIAL UNIQUE TO ONE GOSPEL

A few scholars have previously tried to establish criteria for detecting Q material unique to one Gospel. Heinz Schürmann, for example, employed a method based on "verbal reminiscences."[3] If he found a reminiscence in one Gospel of a passage unique to the other, he concluded that both Evangelists knew the passage. Kloppenborg rightly criticized this method for requiring "subtle—perhaps over-subtle—arguments,"[4] and it resulted in an excessive

---

1. For discussions, see Streeter, *Four Gospels*, 185, 289–91; Petros Vassiliadis, "The Nature and Extent of the Q Document," *NovT* 20 (1978): 49–73; Kloppenborg, *Formation of Q*, 80–87; Tuckett, *Q and the History of Early Christianity*, 92–96; Kloppenborg Verbin, *Excavating Q*, 95–101.

2. Matt 5:41; Luke 11:27–28; 12:49; 15:8–10; and 17:20–21 (Robinson et al., *Critical Edition of Q*; idem, *Sayings Gospel Q*).

3. Heinz Schürmann, "Sprachliche Reminiszenen an abgeänderte oder ausgelassene Bestandteile der Sprachsammlung im Lukas- und Matthäusevangelium," *NTS* 6 (1959/60): 193–210; repr. in idem, *Traditionsgeschichtliche Untersuchungen zu den synoptischen Evangelien* (Düsseldorf: Patmos, 1968), 111–25.

4. Kloppenborg, *Formation of Q*, 83.

number of candidates for inclusion in Q.[5] Yet it may be useful in certain cases if used judiciously.

Petros Vassiliadis proposed that a passage unique to Matthew or Luke is likely to have come from Q only if it meets some of the following conditions: (1) it is a component of a text assigned to Q on other grounds; (2) it accords with the theological ideas of Q; (3) it accords with the country-life language of Q; (4) it shows no signs of editorial activity; (5) the other Evangelist had good reason to omit it; and (6) it falls into the Q material in Luke's Travel Narrative (Luke 9:51–18:14).[6] Using these criteria, Vassiliadis found two passages unique to Matthew and seven passages unique to Luke that may have stood in Q.[7]

Kloppenborg Verbin has rightly criticized Vassiliadis's conditions 3, 4, and 6.[8] The criterion of "country-life language" is not helpful since agricultural language and metaphors are hardly unique to Q. Absence of editorial activity is no indication of Q material, since many Q pericopes show clear signs of editing by Matthew or Luke. And while much of Luke's Q material occurs in the Travel Narrative, the presence of a unique passage in this context does not mean that it came from Q.

Vassiliadis's conditions 1 and 5, while having some value, must be used with care. Condition 1, that the unique passage is a component of a text assigned to Q on other grounds, should be revised. On the one hand, the fact that a unique passage does not occur in a Q text or context does not mean that it did not come from Q. Most scholars agree that Matthew, and to a lesser extent Luke, inserted Q passages into Markan contexts. On the other hand, the fact that a unique passage is a component of a Q text or context does not guarantee that it did come from Q. The Evangelist could have composed it or added it from another source. However, if one has other reasons for thinking that a unique passage came from Q, then the fact that it forms part of a Q text or context could be used as a supporting argument.

---

5. In "Sprachliche Reminiszenen" (125), Schürmann concluded that three passages unique to Matthew and fifteen unique to Luke stood in Q: Matt 4:4b; 10:23; 21:14–16; Luke 6:24–26; 6:45; 7:1–5; 9:61–62; 10:4b; 11:2a; 11:5–8; 11:37–38; 12:1; 12:13–21; 12:35–38; 12:54–56; 12:57; 15:8–10; 16:(14)-15. In other works, he added other passages. These are listed by Frans Neirynck, "Recent Developments in the Study of Q," in Delobel, Logia, 38–39 n. 38. Kloppenborg Verbin provides a slightly revised list (Formation of Q, 83 n. 147).

6. Vassiliadis, "Nature and Extent," 67.

7. Matt 10:16b; 11:12–13 (cf. Luke 16:16); Luke 9:60b–62; 10:19–20; 11:27–28; 12:32–38; 12:54–56; 13:23–30; 21:34–36 (Ibid., 70).

8. Kloppenborg Verbin, Excavating Q, 95–96.

Vassiliadis's condition 5, that the other Evangelist had good reason to omit the passage, should also be used with care. On the one hand, in imagining why one Evangelist might have omitted a passage, we may be able to come up with a reason that is entirely plausible but completely wrong. On the other hand, an Evangelist may have omitted a passage for some reason that would not occur to anyone else. Scholarly humility should warn us that we may not always be able to accurately intuit the mental processes of the Evangelists.

Vassiliadis's most useful criterion is the second: a unique passage may come from Q if it accords with the theological ideas of Q. However, Kloppenborg Verbin suggests that coherence of style should be given priority over coherence of theological ideas.[9] By adopting this suggestion and reformulating "theological ideas" as "themes," we can formulate a more effective criterion, the criterion of style and theme. That is, if a passage unique to Matthew or Luke exhibits the same distinctive features of style and theme as Q material, the chances are good that it came from the same source. This is the same criterion that I used in chapters 3 and 4 to identify Q in the double tradition.

While this criterion would seem to offer the best method for identifying Q material unique to one Gospel, to my knowledge, no one has previously applied it in a systematic manner. In my own examination of the question, I will employ this as the main criterion. I have identified numerous recurring features of style and theme in Q, which I have listed in appendix B. In the following discussion, I use some of these recurring features to identify material unique to Matthew or Luke that may have come from Q.

To repeat the disclaimer that I made in chapter 4, such a procedure does not yield verifiable results, but only probabilities. The greater the number of stylistic and thematic features that a passage shares with Q material, the greater the probability that it came from Q. And the more distinctive or uncommon such shared features are, the more that probability increases. Yet in brief passages, even one or two features shared with Q may be significant, and even features that are not uncommon can show that a passage is stylistically or thematically consistent with Q.

Q MATERIAL UNIQUE TO MATTHEW

Several items that are unique to Matthew have significant stylistic and thematic affinities with Q. These include the pericope "On words" (Matt 12:33–37), and the parables unique to Matthew in Matthew 13 (Matt 13:24–30, 36b–52).

---

9. Ibid., 95.

ON WORDS (MATT 12:33–37/LUKE 6:45)

The pericope "On words," most of which is unique to Matthew, probably came from Q (table 5.1). While Matthew preserved the entire pericope, Luke included only two elements from it (Luke 6:45b, 45a).

TABLE 5.1. ON WORDS

	Matthew Q	Luke Q
Tree and fruit	12:33	—
Brood of vipers	12:34a	—
Fullness of heart	12:34b	→ 6:45b
Treasure of heart	12:35	→ 6:45a
Judged by words	12:36–37	—

Despite the brevity of this pericope, it shares five features of style or theme with other Q material. (1) The theme of bearing good or bad fruit (Matt 12:33) links it to two other Q pericopes where the same theme occurs (B.5). (2) The distinctive expression "brood of vipers" (Matt 12:34a) occurs in the New Testament only here and in two other Q passages (B.3). (3) The distinctive expression "(you) being evil" (Matt 12:34a) occurs in the New Testament only here and in the Q pericope "Good gifts" (B.36). (4) The term "treasure" is common to this pericope (Matt 12:35/Luke 6:45a) and the Q pericope "On treasure" (B.42). (5) The theme of the day of judgment occurs here (Matt 12:36–37) and in three other Q passages (B.32). So many features of Q in such a brief compass suggest that this pericope came from Q.

Since some of this material repeats Q material elsewhere, it might be thought that Matthew assembled 12:33–35 from other contexts in Q.[10] However, two factors weigh against this view. First, this would require of Matthew an editorial procedure that would be idiosyncratic, contrary to his normal procedure, and difficult to explain. He would have taken Matthew 12:34b–35 from the parallel to Luke 6:45 in the Q sermon. Already this raises doubt, since Matthew tended to add material to this sermon to create the Sermon on the Mount. It would be contrary to his normal procedure to take material out. Furthermore, from that same Q context, Matthew would have *repeated* the saying on tree and fruit (Matt 7:18, 16a/Luke 6:43–44a) as Matthew 12:33, in the process rewording it in a less comprehensible form than the original. Why

---

10. So, for example, Allison in Davies and Allison, *Matthew*, 2:333.

from the same context inconsistently remove one part and repeat another part? And why garble the latter in transmission? Furthermore, to formulate 12:34a, he would have gone to two other Q contexts for the expressions, "brood of vipers" (Matt 3:7b/Luke 3:7b) and "you being evil" (Matt 7:11/Luke 11:13). Taken individually, these actions seem strange. Taken together, they raise the question, to what end would Matthew do any of this?

Second, even if it were plausible to think that Matthew assembled 12:33–35, that still would not explain 12:36–37. This passage shares with other Q material the theme of the day of judgment. It suggests that Matthew used a Q text at this point, and if 12:36–37 came from this text, it is likely that the preceding material in 12:33–35 did too. Support for this view comes from the fact that 12:33–37 occurs in Matthew as a section of material between two other Q sections: the Beelzebul debate (Matt 12:22–30) and the demand for a sign (Matt 12:38–42).

If Matthew 12:33–37 came from Q, then Q included the saying on tree and fruit twice, once in the Q sermon (Matt 7:18, 16/Luke 6:43–44) and once in the pericope "On words" (Matt 12:33), in different formulations. This fact might explain Luke's procedure. To avoid the doublet, Luke omitted the pericope "On words" except for two sentences (Luke 6:45a, 45b), which he added to the pericope on tree and fruit in the Q sermon.[11]

PARABLE DISCOURSE UNIQUE TO MATTHEW

In the parable discourse that he shares with Mark, Matthew includes several parables that are unique to his Gospel. These include the parable of the weeds in the wheat (Matt 13:24–30), an explanation of this parable (Matt 13:36b–43), three shorter parables (Matt 13:44–50), and a concluding saying on new and old (Matt 13:51–52). Because this material is unique to Matthew, scholars have traditionally ascribed it to M or to Matthew himself.[12] Joachim Jeremias made the classic case for supposing that the Evangelist Matthew composed the interpretation of the parable of the weeds and the interpretation of the parable of the net.[13] I have examined his arguments in appendix E and

---

11. Bergemann (*Q auf dem Prüfstand*, 236–47) envisages a similar procedure: Matthew preserved two forms of the tradition, from Q (Matt 12:33–37) and a "Grundrede" (Matt 7:15–20), respectively, while Luke combined the two in Luke 6:43–45.

12. E.g., Francis W. Beare, *The Gospel according to Matthew: Translation, Introduction and Commentary* (Harper & Row, 1981; repr. Peabody, Mass.: Hendrickson, 1987), 303, 311; Allison in Davies and Allison, *Matthew*, 2:407, 409–10, 426–27, 434, 444.

13. Joachim Jeremias, *The Parables of Jesus* (2nd ed.; New York: Scribner's, 1972), 81–85.

found them wanting. While these pericopes do contain a modest number of Matthean characteristics, these most plausibly arose as redactional modifications to pre-existing material.

If Matthew did not compose this material, then it probably came from either M or Q. Stylistically it stands closest to Q. We find in it five, possibly six, distinctive stylistic and thematic features that are characteristic of Q.

1. The parable of the weeds (Matt 13:24–30), the explanation of this parable (Matt 13:36b–43), and the parable of the net (Matt 13:47–50) all include analogies for separating the righteous from the wicked. A similar analogy occurs in the Q saying "Wheat and chaff" (B.11). Of the three passages unique to Matthew, the parable of the weeds stands closest in wording to the Q saying. It concludes with the following analogy for separating the righteous from the wicked: "Pull up the weeds first and bind them into bundles to burn (κατακαῦσαι) them, but gather the wheat into my granary (τὸν δὲ σῖτον συναγάγετε εἰς τὴν ἀποθήκην μου)" (Matt 13:30). This dual theme of burning something worthless while gathering wheat into a granary occurs in much the same wording in the Q saying: "and he will gather his wheat into the granary (συνάξει τὸν σῖτον αὐτοῦ εἰς τὴν ἀποθήκην), but the chaff he will burn (κατακαύσει) with unquenchable fire" (Matt 3:12/Luke 3:17).

While the parable of the weeds and the Q pericope "Wheat and chaff" contain both halves of this analogy, other Q passages contain one half or the other. a) The theme of gathering wheat into a granary occurs elsewhere only in two Q pericopes and the story of the rich fool, a parable unique to Luke (B.12). b) Likewise the theme of destroying something worthless by fire as an analogy for judgment occurs elsewhere in the Synoptics only in three Q sayings (B.8).

2. The interpretation of the parable of the weeds as well as the parable of the net both include the sentence "There, there will be weeping and gnashing of teeth" (Matt 13:42; 13:50). Elsewhere this sentence is included by both Matthew and Luke from a Q passage (Matt 8:12/Luke 13:28). If we are correct in thinking that Luke did not use Matthew, then the presence of this feature of style in Luke shows that Matthew did not create it but found it in Q.

In Matthew the sentence occurs five times where it does not occur in Luke: twice in the parable material that we are considering and three other times (Matt 22:13; 24:51; 25:30). Did Matthew find this sentence once in Q and like it so much that he included it several more times? Or did Luke find it several times in Q but omit it all except once? The evidence indicates that it occurred several times in Q but that Luke had reason to omit it. First, it occurs in Matthew's version of the parable of the great supper (Matt 22:13) but not in Luke's version. I will argue in chapter 10 that Matthew's version came from Q, while Luke's came from L. Thus Luke did not include the sentence because he used a parallel from L instead of the Q parable in which the sentence occurred. Second, it occurs in Matthew's version of the pericope "Faithful or not" (Matt 24:51b), but not in Luke's version. I will argue in chapter 10 that both versions came from Q but for this sentence in Q Luke substituted a different description of eschatological judgment from L (Luke 12:47–48). Third, the sentence occurs in Matthew's version of the parable of the pounds (Matt 25:30), but not in Luke's. Again I will argue in chapter 10 that Matthew's version came from Q, while Luke's came from L. Luke did not include the sentence because he used a parallel from L instead of the Q pericope in which the sentence occurred. Thus the sentence is a typical feature of Q (B.47) even though Luke tended to omit the material in which it occurred.

3. Twice in this discourse we find the eschatological correlative, in whole or in part:

ὥσπερ ... οὕτως ἔσται (Matt 13:40, Weeds explained);
οὕτως ἔσται (apodosis only, Matt 13:49, Parable of net).

While a "prophetic correlative" occurs in the Septuagint and the literature of Qumran,[14] elsewhere in the Synoptic tradition this stylistic feature occurs only in the double tradition (table 5.2; B.37).[15]

TABLE 5.2. ESCHATOLOGICAL CORRELATIVE

	Matthew	Luke
Sign of Jonah	12:40 ὥσπερ ... οὕτως ἔσται	11:30 καθὼς ... οὕτως ἔσται
Return of spirit	12:45b οὕτως ἔσται	11:26 —
Weeds explained	13:40 ὥσπερ ... οὕτως ἔσται	
Parable of net	13:49 οὕτως ἔσται	
Like lightning	24:27 ὥσπερ ... οὕτως ἔσται	17:24 ὥσπερ ... οὕτως ἔσται
Days of Noah	24:37 ὥσπερ ... οὕτως ἔσται	17:26 καθὼς ... οὕτως ἔσται
Days of Noah	24:38–39 ὡς ... οὕτως ἔσται	17:30 κατὰ τὰ αὐτὰ ἔσται

Matthew 12:45b and 13:49 express only the conclusion of the correlative; the protasis is replaced by a paragraph describing the first term of comparison.

4. The term "treasure" (θησαυρός) in the parable "Hidden treasure" (Matt 13:44) and the conclusion "New and old" (Matt 13:52) links these sayings to

14. Kloppenborg, *Formation of Q*, 130.

15. On the eschatological correlative see Richard Alan Edwards, *The Sign of Jonah in the Theology of the Evangelists and Q* (SBT 2/18; Napierville, Ill.: Allenson, 1971), 47–58.

the Q pericopes "On words" and "On treasure," where the same term occurs (B.42). This term occurs only twice elsewhere in the Synoptics (Matt 2:11; Mark 10:21 parr).

5. The expression "cast out" (ἐκβάλλειν ἔξω) in the parable of the net (Matt 13:48) links this parable to several other Q pericopes where the same, or a similar, expression occurs (B.49; cf. B.51, B.52). Elsewhere it occurs only in Mark 12:8 parr and Luke 4:29.

6. The expression "the sons of the kingdom" (οἱ υἱοὶ τῆς βασιλείας) in the explanation of the parable of the weeds (Matt 13:38) links this explanation to the only other passage where this expression occurs, the Q pericope "Sons excluded" (B.50). However, since this expression occurs only in Matthew, it could be Matthean redaction.

How should we explain these stylistic and thematic affinities with Q in this material? Is it possible that this is not Q material but that the Evangelist Matthew's mind was so steeped in the language of Q that he added these features of Q to the material? If so, we would expect to find other non-Q passages in Matthew with a similar concentration of Q features. Yet we do not. Matthew may occasionally favor a word that also occurs in Q,[16] and he may have reused the conclusion to the Q sermon,[17] but stylistic features of Q in this same concentration do not occur elsewhere in Matthew except in Q.

It is most likely therefore that these parables came from the same stylistic milieu as Q. We can imagine three possibilities. (1) The simplest explanation is that these parables came from Q. This would explain why they have stylistic affinities with Q. It would not explain, however, why Luke does not include them, since he too knew Q. (2) As a second possibility, we can imagine that these parables came to Matthew through oral tradition from the same individual or community that created the source Q. This would explain why Luke does not include them, if he did not know this oral tradition. We wonder, however, whether oral tradition could preserve the many stylistic and thematic affinities between these parables and Q, since one of the chief characteristics of oral tradition is its variability with respect to wording. (3) The third possibility is that Matthew received these parables in a separate document, from the same individual or community responsible for Q. As a collection of parables, this discourse is precisely the type of material that we can imagine circulating as a separate document. The common origin of this parable collection and Q would explain the stylistic and thematic affinities

---

16. E.g., ὀλιγόπιστος, found in both Q (Matt 6:30/Luke 12:28) and elsewhere in Matthew (Matt 8:26; 14:31; 16:8).

17. Matt 11:1; 13:53; 19:1; 26:1; cf. Q (Matt 7:28a/Luke 7:1a).

between them; and if Luke did not know this collection, it would explain why he does not include it.

On balance, we cannot rule out either the first or the third possibility. The affinities of this material with Q indicate that it may well have formed part of that source. Why then did Luke omit it? Here my previous comment about scholarly humility applies. We may not be able to accurately intuit Luke's mental processes. Luke may have had some reason that we cannot determine for omitting these parables from Q. That reason may have been as simple as the fact that Luke knew more material than he could use. He did not so much choose these parables for omission as choose other material for inclusion. If the discourse did not stand in Q, then it may have circulated in a separate document composed by the same individual or community that was responsible for Q.

Q Material Unique to Luke

Like Matthew, Luke includes several unique passages that share stylistic and thematic affinities with Q. The following may have come from Q.

Woes on rich	Luke 6:24–26
Another follower	Luke 9:61–62
Friend at night	Luke 11:5–8
Hear and do	Luke 11:27–28
Against greed	Luke 12:15
Rich fool	Luke 12:16–21
Prophet's fate	Luke 13:31–33
Fired manager	Luke 16:1–9
Faithful in little	Luke 16:10–12

Woes on Rich (Luke 6:24–26)

The first passage that we consider contains the woes against the rich (Luke 6:24–26) that Luke includes after the Q beatitudes. Scholars are divided on whether these woes came from Q or from Luke's own hand.[18] Tuckett, for instance, judges that they probably came from Q,[19] as does Kloppenborg

---

18. Paffenroth notes a few scholars who attribute the woes to L but finds this view unconvincing: Kim Paffenroth, *The Story of Jesus according to L* (JSNTSup 147; Sheffield: Sheffield Academic Press, 1997), 39–40.

19. C. M. Tuckett, "The Beatitudes: A Source-Critical Study," *NovT* 25 (1983): 193–207, esp. 195–99; with a reply by M. D. Goulder, 207–16.

Verbin.[20] Fitzmyer, on the other hand, attributes them to Luke because they contain Lukan vocabulary.[21] This argument, however, is not conclusive since the Lukan vocabulary could have resulted as Luke redacted a Q passage.

For two reasons, we can infer that these woes probably did come from Q. First, the woes correspond to the Q beatitudes (Matt 5:11–12/Luke 6:20–23) in number, style, and theme. Like the Q beatitudes, the woes are four in number and use direct address in the second person; and each woe expresses the opposite of the corresponding beatitude. Though it is possible that Luke composed the woes to match the beatitudes, this correspondence at least creates a *prima facie* case that both forms came from the same source.

Second, "woe" is a characteristic expression in Q but not in Luke. Elsewhere in Q, the expression occurs in the pericope "Woes on cities," the discourse against Pharisees, and the pericope "Offender's fate" (B.20). Apart from these passages, the expression occurs elsewhere in Luke only in two passages in the triple tradition, where Luke has adopted it from the Markan material (Luke 21:23; 22:22). It never occurs elsewhere in a passage unique to Luke. This feature of style therefore suggests that the woes came from Q rather than from L or Luke's redaction.

Tuckett thinks that a plausible reason can be given for Matthew's omission of the woes: "Matthew is more concerned in the Sermon on the Mount to develop the positive theme of the content of the righteousness demanded of the disciples; woes against others are more appropriate, in Matthew's present arrangement, in the later discourse in ch. 23."[22] Another reason appears when we compare Matthew's beatitudes with Luke's. Luke has preserved the four second-person Q beatitudes and to these correspond the four second-person Q woes. Matthew, on the other hand, has preserved eight third-person beatitudes and only one of the second-person Q beatitudes. The Q woes therefore would not correspond well to Matthew's beatitudes either in number or style. This lack of correspondence may have made the Q woes unattractive to Matthew.

---

20. Kloppenborg Verbin, *Excavating Q*, 100.

21. Joseph A. Fitzmyer, *The Gospel according to Luke: A New Translation with Introduction and Commentary* (AB 28–28A; 2 vols.; Garden City, N.Y.: Doubleday, 1981, 1985), 1:627.

22. Tuckett, "Beatitudes," 199 n. 27. For this view, Tuckett cites Schürmann and Frankemölle.

ANOTHER FOLLOWER (LUKE 9:61–62)

The next material that we will consider occurs in the Q section on following Jesus. Here both Evangelists include two dialogues between Jesus and prospective followers. Luke also has a third in Luke 9:61–62.

In the first dialogue (Matt 8:19–20/Luke 9:57–58), the two Evangelists have close to the same wording, an indication that both drew this from Q. In the second (Matt 8:21–22/Luke 9:59–60), Luke's version of the saying has a three-part structure: Jesus speaks, the would-be follower replies, then Jesus replies. Matthew's version has a two-part structure: the would-be follower speaks, and Jesus replies. Since both Matthew and Luke have the two-part structure in the first dialogue, it is likely that Matthew preserved the original structure, which Luke modified in the second dialogue. Apart from this Lukan modification, Matthew and Luke have substantially the same wording in the second dialogue, except that they differ in their placement of Jesus' command "Follow me" and that Luke has an additional command: "but you go proclaim the kingdom of God."

The third dialogue (Luke 9:61–62) occurs in Luke but not in Matthew. Critics sometimes attribute it to L.[23] However, it has such affinities in structure and wording with the two preceding dialogues that it more likely came from Q.[24] It exhibits the same two-part structure and the same style as the two preceding dialogues. The would-be follower proclaims "I will follow you" (ἀκολουθήσω σοι) as in the first dialogue. As in the second, he is "another" (ἕτερος) who addresses Jesus as "Master" (κύριε) and asks to first be allowed (πρῶτον ἐπίτρεψόν μοι) to deal with a matter at home. If this dialogue did stand in Q, then Matthew omitted it. Allison suggests that "Matthew's propensity to abbreviate" might have moved him to omit it.[25]

FRIEND AT NIGHT (LUKE 11:5–8)

The third uniquely Lukan passage is the parable "Friend at night" in Luke 11:5–8. Since this occurs only in Luke, it could be attributed to L.[26] It includes one stylistic feature that occurs elsewhere in both Q and L. This is a rhetorical question introduced by the phrase "Who among you," which introduces a hypothetical situation (Luke 11:5). This same construction appears in Epicte-

---

23. E.g., Manson, *Sayings*, 72; Fitzmyer, *Luke*, 1:833.

24. Paffenroth, *Story of Jesus*, 45–46. Schürmann ("Sprachliche Reminiszenen," 121) attributes 9:60b–62 to Q, but on questionable grounds.

25. Allison in Davies and Allison, *Matthew*, 2:40 n. 112.

26. Fitzmyer, *Luke*, 2:910; Paffenroth, *Story of Jesus*, 46–47

tus.[27] It occurs elsewhere in the New Testament only in Q and L (B.34). A similar phrase does occur in John 8:46 and in the Hebrew Bible (Isa 42:23; 50:10; Hag 2:3), but there it introduces a real, not a hypothetical, situation.

A second feature occurs elsewhere in Q but not in L. This parable shares the term χρῄζω ("to have need") with the Q pericope "Do not worry" (Matt 6:32/Luke 12:30). This term occurs nowhere else in the Gospels and only twice elsewhere in the New Testament (B.35).[28]

David Catchpole gives a further reason for assigning this parable to Q.[29] He argues that the saying "Ask, seek, knock" (Matt 7:7–8/Luke 11:9–10), which immediately follows this parable in Luke, originally formed the conclusion of the parable. The saying provides the moral that the parable lacks, while the parable provides the context for asking, seeking, and knocking that the saying lacks. If the two passages originally constituted a single pericope, then both must have stood together in Q, as they do in Luke.[30]

It seems likely, therefore, that this parable did stand in Q. Matthew adopted only the conclusion "Ask, seek, knock" for the Sermon on the Mount and omitted the parable, presumably because its narrative form did not fit well with the other material in the Sermon.

Hear and Do (Luke 11:27–28)

A fourth Lukan passage that may come from Q is the anecdote "Hear and do" in Luke 11:27–28. For two reasons, we can infer that this came from Q.[31] First, this anecdote, though brief, shares two features of style and theme with other Q material: a blessing, which occurs in several other Q passages (B.15), and the theme of hearing and doing the word, which occurs in the Q pericopes "Lord, Lord" and "Two houses" (B.26).

---

27. Kloppenborg, *Formation of Q*, 219; Frans Neirynck, "Luke 14,1–6: Lukan Composition and Q Saying," in *Der Treue Gottes trauen: Beiträge zum Werk des Lukas: Für Gerhard Schneider* (ed. Claus Bussmann and Walter Radl; Freiburg: Herder, 1991), 243–63, esp. 257.

28. This link is pointed out by David Catchpole, "Q and 'The Friend at Midnight' (Luke xi. 5–8/9)," *JTS* NS 34 (1983): 407–24, esp. 422.

29. Ibid., 416–19.

30. Kloppenborg (*Formation of Q*, 203 n. 132) cites Gospel of Thomas 92 as evidence that the imperative in "Ask, seek, knock" needed no such context. However, Catchpole's argument is based not on necessity but on plausibility.

31. *Contra* Fitzmyer, *Luke*, 2:926–27, who assigns this pericope to L. Paffenroth tentatively assigns the pericope to L while recognizing the possibility that it came from Q (*Story of Jesus*, 47).

Second, the position of the anecdote in Luke, following the Q version of the Beelzebul debate, also suggests that it came from Q. Table 5.3 shows this passage and related material.

TABLE 5.3. BEELZEBUL DEBATE IN MARKAN SOURCE AND Q

	Matthew PMkA	Mark PMkA/B	Luke PMkB	Matthew Q	Luke Q
Mute demoniac	(12:22–23)	—	—	(12:22–23)	11:14
By Beelzebul	(12:24)	3:22	—	(12:24)	11:15
Satan divided	(12:25–26)	3:23–26	—	(12:25–26)	11:17–18
Jewish exorcists				12:27–28	11:19–20
Strong man	12:29	3:27	—	—	11:21–22
With or against				12:30	11:23
Hear and do	12:46–50	3:31–35	8:19–21	—	11:27–28

In table 5.3, three columns on the left show the Markan version of the Beelzebul debate. This is followed in all three Gospels by the Markan version of the anecdote "Hear and do." The last two columns of the table show the Q version of the Beelzebul debate. Parentheses indicate where Matthew has conflated his sources.

In Luke this is followed by a second version of the anecdote "Hear and do." While the two versions of this anecdote differ considerably, they both declare that those who hear and do the word of God are more blessed than Jesus' physical kin. These are apparently two different developments of the same original anecdote, which at some early stage of the tradition was attached to the Beelzebul debate. If so, the two versions of the anecdote must have come from the same sources as the two versions of the Beelzebul debate, that is, from the Markan source and Q, respectively.

Luke, who usually avoids doublets, in this case retained both the Markan version and the Q version of the anecdote. Matthew, however, omitted the Q version, presumably to avoid this doublet.

AGAINST GREED (LUKE 12:15) AND RICH FOOL (LUKE 12:16–21)

Luke's section on possessions (Luke 12:13–34) includes two further pericopes unique to Luke that probably came from Q: the warning "Against greed" in Luke 12:15 and the story of the rich fool in Luke 12:16–21.

This section begins with an introduction consisting of two parts: an anecdote in which Jesus denies that he is a divider (Luke 12:13–14), and a

warning against greed (Luke 12:15). Schürmann[32] and others think that both
the anecdote and the warning stood in Q, Kloppenborg thinks that the anecdote probably did,[33] while Fitzmyer finds it farfetched to think that either
did.[34] What, then, can we infer from the criterion of style and theme? The
anecdote (Luke 12:13–14) has no stylistic or thematic affinities with Q. We
therefore have no reason to assign it to that source. However, the warning in
Luke 12:15 expresses the theme that life consists of more than possessions, a
theme that recurs later in the same section, in the Q pericope "Do not worry"
(Matt 6:25b/Luke 12:23). It is reasonable to think, therefore, that Luke 12:15
stood in Q as the introduction to this complex of sayings.

Following this introduction is a second pericope unique to Luke, the
story of the rich fool (Luke 12:16–21). While Fitzmyer assigns this story to
L,[35] Schürmann[36] and Kloppenborg[37] think that it came from Q. The criterion of style and theme supports the latter view. This story has two stylistic or
thematic features in common with Q. First, the motif of gathering wheat into
a granary (Luke 12:18) links this story to the same motif in two other Q pericopes: the pericope "Do not worry" (Matt 6:26/Luke 12:24), which occurs in
the same section, and the pericope "Wheat and chaff" (Matt 3:12/Luke 3:17).
Second, the term "treasure up," θησαυρίζω (Luke 12:21), links this story to the
only other occurrence of this term in the Gospels, the Q pericope on storing
up treasure in heaven (Matt 6:19, 20; not Luke 12:33). These two features of
the story of the rich man suggest that it is from Q.

This conclusion is supported by the expression "for this reason," διὰ
τοῦτο (Matt 6:25a/Luke 12:22), at the beginning of the following Q pericope,
"Do not worry." In Luke, this expression links this pericope back to the story
of the rich fool. The same expression in Matthew probably served the same
function in Q but lost that function when Matthew omitted the story of the
rich fool.[38]

PROPHET'S FATE (LUKE 13:31–33)

The next passage that we will consider is the pericope "Prophet's fate" in Luke
13:31–33, in which Pharisees warn Jesus that Herod wants to kill him. Because

---

32. Schürmann, "Sprachliche Reminiszenzen," 119–20, 125.
33. Kloppenborg Verbin, *Excavating Q*, 100.
34. Fitzmyer, *Luke*, 2:968.
35. Ibid., 2:971.
36. Schürmann, "Sprachliche Reminiszenzen," 119–20.
37. Kloppenborg Verbin, *Excavating Q*, 100.
38. Schürmann, "Sprachliche Reminiszenzen," 119.

only Luke includes this, it is usually assigned to L.[39] However, it contains three significant features of style and theme that identify it as Q material. First, the sentence "it is not acceptable for a prophet to perish outside of Jerusalem" (Luke 13:33) expresses the theme of rejected or persecuted prophets (B.17). This "Deuteronomistic" theme is so typical of Q that Jacobson identified it as the theological basis for the literary unity of Q.[40] Elsewhere in Q it occurs in the blessing on the persecuted (Matt 5:11–12/Luke 6:22–23), the pericope "Children in the market" (Matt 11:16–17/Luke 7:31–35), the section on seeking signs (Matt 12:38–42/Luke 11:16, 29–32), the discourse against Pharisees (Matt 23:29–36/Luke 11:47–51), the pericope "Deserted house" (Matt 23:37/ Luke 13:34), and the Q eschatological discourse (Luke 17:25).

Second, this passage uses the distinctive imperative "go tell," πορευθέντες εἴπατε (Luke 13:32), which agrees closely with a similar imperative, "go report," πορευθέντες ἀπαγγείλατε, in the Q pericope "John's question" (Matt 11:4/Luke 7:22; B.27). Third, the expression "today and tomorrow," σήμερον καὶ αὔριον (Luke 13:32, 33), occurs elsewhere in the New Testament only in the Q pericope "Do not worry" (Matt 6:30/Luke 12:28) and in James 4:13 (B.40).

These three distinctive features of style and theme shared with Q strongly suggest that this pericope on the fate of a prophet also came from Q. In Luke this pericope immediately precedes the Q lament for Jerusalem (Matt 23:37–39/Luke 13:34–35), and both pericopes probably stood together in Q as well. Both condemn Jerusalem for rejecting or killing prophets, and the latter threatens that God would abandon the Jerusalem temple. It is likely that Matthew moved the latter (Matt 23:37–39) to the end of his discourse against Pharisees so that its prediction of the temple's abandonment would precede the prediction of its destruction (Matt 24:1–2). In so doing, he apparently found no place in that discourse for the former pericope, "Prophet's fate," and so omitted it.

ON MAMMON (LUKE 16:1–13)

The last two passages that we will consider occur in the same context: Luke's section on "mammon" or the proper use of money (Luke 16:1–13). This section includes three pericopes. The third of these has a parallel in Matthew and is generally assigned to Q (Matt 6:24/Luke 16:13). The first two are unique to

---

39. E.g., Fitzmyer, Luke, 2:1028; Paffenroth, Story of Jesus, 58.
40. Jacobson, First Gospel, 72–76.

Luke and generally assigned to L.[41] However, several facts suggest that these too may have come from Q.

The first pericope in this section, the story of the fired manager, begins in Luke 16:1, but where it ends is disputed. Scholars have variously judged the story to extend through 16:7, 16:8a, 16:8b, or 16:9.[42] The question has been complicated by the assumption that Jesus must have spoken some form of this story, presumably in a less-developed form than that in which it now appears. We can bypass that complication by simply asking in what form Luke received the story. Since 16:9 could not have circulated as an independent saying, but depends on 16:4 in the story, and since we have no stylistic reason to think that Luke created 16:9,[43] the story as Luke received it must have extended through that verse. The remaining two sayings could stand independently of the story and therefore probably did not form part of it. Thus this section consists of three distinct pericopes: "Fired manager" (Luke 16:1–9), "Faithful in little" (Luke 16:10–12), and "Two masters" (Luke 16:13).

Features of style and theme suggest that all three pericopes came from Q. First, this section is unified by the Aramaic term "mammon," which occurs in all three pericopes (Luke 16:9; 16:11; 16:13/Matt 6:24; B.53). It seems unlikely that Luke would find three separate pericopes circulating independently that each contained this unusual term. Since it appears nowhere else in the New Testament, its presence in these three pericopes suggests that they were conceived as a unit from the beginning and came to Luke in the same source. Clearly, the third pericope came from Q, since it occurs in both Matthew and Luke in almost identical wording (Matt 6:24/Luke 16:13). If Luke found all three pericopes together in the same source, then the first two pericopes must have come from Q as well.

A second stylistic feature confirms this conclusion. The theme of a "prudent" (φρόνιμος) manager in the story of the fired manager (Luke 16:1, 3, 8) occurs elsewhere only in the Q pericope on faithful or unfaithful slaves (B.46). Third, the theme of being "faithful" (πιστός) in the saying "Faithful in little" (Luke 16:10, 11, 12) occurs elsewhere in the Synoptics only in two Q pericopes (B.45): the pericope on faithful or unfaithful slaves (Matt 24:45/ Luke 12:42), and the parable of pounds (Matt 25:21/Luke 19:17).

These stylistic observations indicate that the section as a whole came from Q. While Luke preserved all three pericopes, Matthew picked out the saying on two masters (Matt 6:24) and moved it to the Sermon on the Mount

---

41. Fitzmyer, *Luke*, 2:1095; Paffenroth, *Story of Jesus*, 60–61.

42. Fitzmyer, *Luke*, 2:1096–97.

43. Ibid., 2:1105.

to add to a section on possessions there (Matt 6:19–34). He omitted the other two sayings, possibly because they did not fit in the Sermon. Another reason may also explain Matthew's omission. Many interpreters of the parable of the fired manager have found it odd that Jesus would commend the discredited manager. Matthew may have been one of the first to feel dubious about using an unrighteous character as a positive example. Such doubts might explain his decision to leave the story out of his Gospel.

ON READINESS

The pericope "On readiness" (Matt 24:42–44/Luke 12:35, 39–40) includes material unique to Matthew that probably came from Q as well as material unique to Luke that probably came from Q (table 5.4).

TABLE 5.4. ON READINESS

	Didache 16:1 Q?	Matthew 24:42–44 Q	Luke 12:35, 39–40 Q
Keep watch	16:1a	24:42a	—
Unknown time	—	24:42b	—
Loins and lamps	16:1b	—	12:35
Unexpected thief	—	24:43	12:39
Be ready	16:1c	24:44	12:40

As table 5.4 shows, elements of the same pericope occur in Matthew, Luke, and Didache 16:1. Since Matthew and Luke both include the elements "Unexpected thief" and "Be ready," at least these two elements came from Q.

While Luke lacks a parallel to Matthew 24:42 and Matthew lacks a parallel to Luke 12:35, the Didache attests to both of these elements. Though it is possible that the Didache drew 16:1a from Matthew and 16:1b from Luke, it is more likely that both came from the same source as 16:1c, that is, that all three elements came from Q. If so, both Matthew 24:42 and Luke 12:35 came from Q.

Neither Luke nor the Didache includes a parallel to the second part of Matthew 24:42. However, since both parts are attested together in a Markan version of this saying (Matt 25:13; Mark 13:33), both parts probably belong to the Q version.

In this instance, three different documents preserve different parts of the same Q pericope. Matthew 24:42 is Q material unique to Matthew, while Luke 12:35 is Q material unique to Luke.

Conclusion

As we have seen, several passages unique to Matthew or Luke share distinctive features of style and theme with Q material. In Matthew, these include the pericope "On words" (Matt 12:33–37/Luke 6:45), the parables unique to Matthew in Matthew 13 (Matt 13:24–30, 36b–52), and the saying "Keep watch" (Matt 24:42). In Luke, they include the pericopes "Woes on rich" (Luke 6:24–26), "Another follower" (Luke 9:61–62), "Friend at night" (Luke 11:5–8), "Hear and do" (Luke 11:27–28), "Against greed" (Luke 12:15), "Rich fool" (Luke 12:16–21), "Loins and lamps" (Luke 12:35), "Prophet's fate" (Luke 13:31–33), "Fired manager" (Luke 16:1–9), and "Faithful in little" (Luke 16:10–12). While we cannot claim certainty, the chances are good that these came from Q.

6

THE ORIGINAL ORDER OF Q

As we saw in chapter 3, the core of Q consists of a sequence of material that has essentially the same order in Matthew as in Luke. If the rest of the double tradition that we have examined also stood in Q, then it too once probably had the same order in the copies of Q known to Matthew and Luke. Since it has no such common order in its present state, presumably one Evangelist or the other altered the original order of the material.

Most scholars agree that Luke preserved the original order of Q better than Matthew.[1] I will not repeat the arguments for that view here, but take as a working hypothesis that Luke generally followed the order of Q. In some instances Matthew conflated Q with the Markan material and may have altered the order of the Q material to do so. In other instances, Matthew probably took material from its position in Q in order to incorporate it into one of his major discourses. In a few cases, Luke too probably relocated material. Table 6.1 shows the Q material that we have identified. With a few exceptions it is given in Luke's order. I have not included the discourse "On confession" (table 4.1) since this probably circulated independently of Q.

TABLE 6.1. PRESUMED ORDER OF Q

	Matthew Q/M	Luke Q/L
John appears	3:5b	3:2b–3a
Coming wrath	3:7–10	3:7–9
Greater one	3:11–12	3:16–17
Jesus' baptism	3:16–17	3:21–22
Jesus' temptation	4:1–11a	4:1b–13

1. E.g., Streeter, *Four Gospels*, 273–75; Taylor, "Order of Q"; idem, "Original Order of Q"; Kloppenborg, *Formation of Q*, 64–80; Kloppenborg Verbin, *Excavating Q*, 88–91.

Beatitudes	5:2–12	6:20–23
Woes on rich		6:24–26
Nonresistance	5:38–42	→ 6:29–30
Golden rule	7:12	→ 6:31
Love enemies	5:43–48	6:27–28, 32–36
Do not judge	7:1–2	6:37–38
Blind lead blind	15:14b	6:39
Mote and beam	7:3–5	6:41–42
Tree and fruit	7:15–20	6:43–44
Lord, Lord	7:21	6:46
Two houses	7:24–27	6:47–49
Jesus ends words	7:28a	7:1a
Centurion's boy	8:5–10, 13	7:1b–10
John's question	11:2–6	7:18–23
Jesus on John	11:7–11	7:24–28
Children in market	11:16–19	7:31–35
On following	8:19–22	9:57–60
Another follower		9:61–62
Pray for workers	9:37–38	10:2
Mission charge	10:9–15	10:4–12
Woes on cities	11:20–24	10:13–15
Father and son	11:25–27	10:21–22
Blessed eyes	13:16–17	10:23–24
Lord's prayer	6:9–13	11:1–4
Friend at night		11:5–8
Ask, seek, knock	7:7–8	11:9–10
Good gifts	7:9–11	11:11–13
Beelzebul debate	12:22–30	11:14–23
Hear and do		11:27–28
On words	12:33–37	→ 6:45
Seeking signs	12:38–42	11:29–32
Return of spirit	12:43–45	→ 11:24–26
Lamp on stand	5:15	11:33
Lamp of body	6:22–23	11:34–36
Weeds in wheat	13:24–30	
Weeds explained	13:36b–43	
Three parables	13:44–50	

New and old	13:51–52	
On Pharisees	23:23–36	11:39–51
Unforgivable sin	12:32	12:10
Against greed		12:15
Rich fool		12:16–21
Do not worry	6:25–33	12:22–31
On treasure	6:19–21	12:33b–34
On readiness	24:42–44	12:35, 39–40
Faithful or not	24:45–51	12:42–46
Signs of times	16:2–3	12:54–56
Agree on way	5:25–26	12:57–59
Narrow gate	7:13–14	13:23–24
Don't know you	7:22–23	13:25–27
Sons excluded	8:11–12	13:28–29
Last first	20:16	13:30
Prophet's fate		13:31–33
Deserted house	23:37–39	13:34–35
Man with dropsy	12:10c, 11	14:1–6
Great supper	22:1–14	14:15–24
Spoiled salt	5:13b	14:34–35
Lost sheep	18:12–13	15:3–7
Fired manager		16:1–9
Faithful in little		16:10–12
Two masters	6:24	16:13
Law until John	11:12–13	16:16
Law to remain	5:18	16:17
On divorce	5:32	16:18
Offender's fate	18:7	17:1–2
Correct a brother	18:15	17:3
Forgive 7 times	18:21–22	17:4
Effective faith	17:20b	17:5–6
Eschatology	24:26–41	17:22–37
Parable of pounds	25:14–30	19:12–27
12 thrones	19:28b	22:28–30

While Matthew has reordered the Q material considerably, Luke too has probably relocated a few passages, which are indicated in table 6.1 by an arrow and smaller font. These relocations include the following passages.

1. First, Luke has taken the the pericope on nonresistance (Luke 6:29–30) and the golden rule (Luke 6:31) and inserted them into the pericope "Love enemies" (Luke 6:27–28, 32–36). That Luke's order is secondary here is shown by the fact that it breaks the connection between the command to "Love your enemies" (Luke 6:27) and the justification for that command (Luke 6:32–33).

2. Second, Luke has moved Luke 6:45 to the Q sermon. Matthew includes the Q pericope "On words" (Matt 12:33–37), of which Luke preserves only two elements (Luke 6:45ab). These elements appear in Luke's Sermon on the Plain, but not in Matthew's Sermon on the Mount. Since it would be contrary to Matthew's presumed editorial practice to move material out of one of his major discourses, it is unlikely that this pericope originally stood in the Q sermon. Matthew therefore probably retains it in its original order in the sequence of Q. Luke moved two elements of it from that position in order to join them to the similar pericope on tree and fruit in the Q sermon (Luke 6:43–44; cf. Matt 7:18, 16).

3. Third, it was probably Luke who moved "Return of spirit" (Matt 12:43–45/Luke 11:24–26) from its original position in the common order. He placed it with the Beelzebul debate, probably because both passages address the theme of exorcism.

Table 6.1 includes four Q passages that both Matthew and Luke may have relocated. Two of these are the sayings "Spoiled salt" and "On divorce." These appear in the Sermon on the Mount in Matthew (Matt 5:13b; 5:32), while Luke has them later (Luke 14:34–35; 16:18). In Matthew these sayings have probably been added to the Sermon, so that Matthew does not preserve their original positions in Q. In these cases, however, Luke may not either. Luke has conflated both of these Q sayings with their parallels in Mark (Mark 9:50a/Luke 14:34–35 and Mark 10:11–12/Luke 16:18). The position of the Q sayings in Luke is determined by the order of their Markan parallels with which they are conflated. Hence Luke may not preserve the original order of Q in either case. It is thus possible that neither Matthew nor Luke kept these sayings in their original positions in the sequence of Q. I have included them in Luke's order for lack of a better option.

The third such passage is the saying "Blind lead blind." In Luke, this occurs in the Q sermon (Luke 6:39). However, this position may not be original, since the saying interrupts the connection between the two pericopes on judging[2] and precedes another saying that Luke has interpolated into that context from the discourse "On confession" (Luke 6:40; see ch. 4). Furthermore, if the saying stood in the Q sermon, then Matthew must have removed

---

2. Manson, *Sayings*, 57.

it from there, contrary to his normal practice. Matthew has not preserved the saying in its original position either but has inserted it into a passage that he shares with Mark (15:14b). The original position of the saying in Q therefore remains uncertain. Again I have included it in Luke's order for lack of a better option.

The fourth such passage is the golden rule (Matt 7:12/Luke 6:31). Luke has inserted this into the pericope "Love enemies," where it did not originally belong (see above). Matthew has combined the Q version with the M version at Matthew 7:12. This position probably represents the order of M but may not represent the order of Q. For lack of a better option, I have included the saying following the pericope on nonresistance.

At this point I have not attempted to distinguish between Q and passages in M or L that overlap with Q. Hence in Table 6.1 the headings "Q/M" and "Q/L" leave open the possibility that some of the material in the table came from M or L instead of Q.

7

CAUSES OF VERBAL DISAGREEMENT IN Q PARALLELS

If Q was a single unified source, then we might expect Matthew and Luke generally to agree in wording when they use it. Yet when we examine the wording of the double tradition in Matthew and Luke, we find that they sometimes agree closely in wording and sometimes hardly at all. This variation in the degree of verbal agreement has been the primary basis for the theory that Q consisted of multiple sources or existed in more than one version. In the present chapter, we will examine such extremes in verbal agreement and consider several explanations that might account for them.

VERBAL AGREEMENT IN Q

Much of Q manifests one of two extremes of verbal agreement: Matthew and Luke agree in wording to either a very high degree or a very low degree. We begin by identifying passages of both kinds.

With respect to the first extreme, Kloppenborg identifies seven pericopes that "display a very high degree of verbatim agreement," such that one must conclude that Q "had documentary form":[1]

Two masters (Matt 6:24/Luke 16:13)
Return of spirit (Matt 12:43–45/Luke 11:24–26)
Woes on cities (Matt 11:20–24/Luke 10:13–15)
Wheat and chaff (Matt 3:12/Luke 3:17)
Jewish exorcists etc. (Matt 12:27–32/Luke 11:19–23)
Deserted house (Matt 23:37–39/Luke 13:34–35)
Coming wrath (Matt 3:7–10/Luke 3:7–9)

---

1. John S. Kloppenborg, "Variation in the Reproduction of the Double Tradition and an Oral Q?" *ETL* 83 (2007): 53–80, esp. 53.

Allison similarly identifies eight Q passages where Matthew and Luke have such close "word for word correspondence" that both must have drawn upon the same written source.[2] Three of these duplicate Kloppenborg's list ("Coming wrath," "Woes on cities," "Deserted house"), leaving five additional passages:

Mote and beam (Matt 7:3–5/Luke 6:41–42)
Ask, seek, knock (Matt 7:7–11/Luke 11:9–13)
Jesus on John (Matt 11:4–11/Luke 7:22–28)
Father and son (Matt 11:25–27/Luke 10:21–22)
Faithful or not (Matt 24:45–51/Luke 12:42b–46)

Dunn gives a similar list of passages where "the wording is so close" that the most obvious explanation is that Matthew and Luke depended on the same literary source:[3] Several of these passages duplicate items in the list of either Kloppenborg or Allison ("Jesus on John," "Father and son," "Return of spirit," "Deserted house," "Faithful or not"), leaving two additional passages:

On following (Matt 8:19b–22/Luke 9:57b–60a)
Children in market (Matt 11:16–19/Luke 7:31–35)

Dunn also gives another list of passages in the Sermon on the Mount with a high degree of closeness in wording.[4] Several of these passages duplicate items that we have already mentioned ("Two masters"; "Mote and beam"; "Ask, seek, knock"), leaving four additional passages:

Lamp of body (Matt 6:22–23/Luke 11:34–36)
Do not worry (Matt 6:25–34/Luke 12:22–32)
Do not judge (Matt 7:1–2/Luke 6:37a, 38b)
Golden rule (Matt 7:12/Luke 6:31)

While we can agree that most of these passages exhibit close to identical wording, I will omit several that also have significant differences in wording. (1) We can accept all of Kloppenborg's examples except the fifth. This passage actually includes three segments: "Jewish exorcists" (Matt 12:27–28/Luke

---

2. Allison in Davies and Allison, *Matthew*, 1:116.
3. Dunn, *Jesus Remembered*, 234 n. 255.
4. Ibid., 231 n. 246.

11:19–20), "Strong man" (Matt 12:29/Luke 11:21–22), and "With or against" (Matt 12:30/Luke 11:23). In the second of these, Matthew follows Mark instead of Q. I therefore leave out this segment and include the other two. (2) The passage "Ask, seek, knock" has significant difference in wording in the last part, which is actually a separate pericope (Matt 7:9–11/Luke 11:11–13). We can, however, accept the first part (Matt 7:7–8/Luke 11:9–10). (3) In the pericope "Lamp of body," Luke 11:36 has no parallel in Matthew. (4) In the pericope "Do not worry," the two Gospels have several significant differences in wording. (5) In the pericope "Do not judge," Luke shows significant divergence in wording in Luke 6:37b–38b. And (6) the "Golden rule" differs significantly in Matthew and Luke. Omitting these passages leaves fifteen passages identified by Kloppenborg, Allison and/or Dunn.

To these fifteen passages we can add four others that exhibit a similarly high degree of agreement in wording: "Pray for workers," "On words," "Something more," and "Unexpected thief." Table 7.1 shows all of the high-agreement passages that we have identified.

TABLE 7.1. HIGH DEGREE OF VERBAL AGREEMENT IN Q

	Matthew	Luke
Coming wrath	3:7–10	3:7–9
Wheat and chaff	3:12	3:17
Mote and beam	7:3–5	6:41–42
Jesus on John	11:7–11	7:24–28
Children in market	11:16–19	7:31–35
On following	8:19–22	9:57–60
Pray for workers	9:37–38	10:2
Woes on cities	11:20–24	10:13–15
Father and son	11:25–27	10:21–22
Ask, seek, knock	7:7–8	11:9–10
Jewish exorcists	12:27–28	11:19–20
With or against	12:30	11:23
On words	12:34b–35	→ 6:45
Something more	12:41–42	11:31–32
Return of spirit	12:43–45	→ 11:24–26
Unexpected thief	24:43–44	12:39–40
Faithful or not	24:45–51	12:42–46
Deserted house	23:37–39	13:34–35
Two masters	6:24	16:13

With respect to the opposite extreme, Kloppenborg cites three passages where "there is low agreement":[5]

Parable of pounds (Matt 25:14–30/Luke 19:12–27)
Great supper (Matt 22:1–14/Luke 14:16–24)
Divided house (Matt 10:34–36/Luke 12:51–53)

Dunn also identifies a number of Q passages where Matthew and Luke differ in wording, to such a degree that he thinks they relied not on a common written source but on common oral tradition:[6]

Centurion's boy (Matt 8:5–13/Luke 7:1–10)
Lord's prayer (Matt 6:7–15/Luke 11:1–4)
Spoiled salt (Matt 5:13/Luke 14:34–35)
Agree on way (Matt 5:25–26/Luke 12:57–59)
Nonresistance (Matt 5:39b–42/Luke 6:29–30)
On treasure (Matt 6:19–21/Luke 12:33–34)
Narrow gate (Matt 7:13–14/Luke 13:24)
Two houses (Matt 7:24–27/Luke 6:47–49)
Divided house (Matt 10:34–36/Luke 12:51–53)
Love Jesus more (Matt 10:37/Luke 14:26)
Take up cross (Matt 10:38/Luke 14:27)
Correct a brother (Matt 18:15/Luke 17:3)
Forgive 7 times (Matt 18:21–22/Luke 17:4)
Great supper (Matt 22:1–14/Luke 14:15–24)

From these lists, I omit "Centurion's boy," "Lord's prayer," "Agree on way," and "On treasure," because all of these show substantial verbal agreement between Matthew and Luke in part of the pericope. I omit "Spoiled salt" because Luke's version represents not simply Q, but the Q version conflated with the Markan version. I also omit "Divided house," "Love Jesus more," and "Take up cross," because these come from the discourse "On confession," which probably did not form part of Q (see ch. 4). Omitting these leaves seven passages. To these seven, we can add eighteen others that have a similarly low degree of verbal agreement. Table 7.2 shows all of the low-agreement passages that we have identified.

---

5. Kloppenborg, "Variation," 55.
6. Dunn, *Jesus Remembered*, 212–15, 226–28, 231–38.

TABLE 7.2. LOW DEGREE OF VERBAL AGREEMENT IN Q

	Matthew	Luke
Beatitudes	5:2–12	6:20–23
Nonresistance	5:38–42	6:29–30
Love enemies	5:43–48	6:27–28, 32–36
Tree and fruit	7:15–20	6:43–44
Lord, Lord	7:21	6:46
Two houses	7:24–27	6:47–49
Jesus ends words	7:28a	7:1a
On Pharisees	23:23–36	11:39–51
Signs of times	16:2–3	12:54–56
Narrow gate	7:13–14	13:24
Don't know you	7:22–23	13:26–27
Last first	20:16	13:30
Man with dropsy	12:10c, 11	14:5
Great supper	22:1–14	14:15–24
Lost sheep	18:12–13	15:3–7
Law until John	11:12–13	16:16
Law to remain	5:15	16:17
Offender's fate	18:7	17:1–2
Correct a brother	18:15	17:3
Forgive 7 times	18:21–22	17:4
Effective faith	17:20b	17:5–6
Days will come	24:26–27	17:22–25
Days of Noah	24:37–39	17:26–30
Taken or left	24:40–41	17:34–35
Parable of pounds	25:14–30	19:12–27

For the material in table 7.1, Matthew and Luke have the same sentences in the same order with much the same wording. They do have minor differences of wording in some of this material, but none significant enough to obscure the essential agreement between Matthew and Luke. For the material in table 7.2, Matthew and Luke may not even have the same sentences, much less the same wording. They do have minor agreements of wording in some of this material, but none significant enough to obscure the essential difference between Matthew and Luke.

Not all of the Q material falls into one of the two extremes represented by tables 7.1 and 7.2. In some pericopes, Matthew and Luke have more of a mixture of agreement and disagreement in wording. Table 7.3 shows these passages.

TABLE 7.3. MIXED VERBAL AGREEMENT IN Q

	Matthew	Luke
John appears	3:5b	3:2b–3a
Greater one	3:11–12	3:16–17
Jesus' baptism	3:16–17	3:21–22
Jesus' temptation	4:1–11a	4:1b–13
Golden rule	7:12	6:31
Do not judge	7:1–2	6:37–38
Blind lead blind	15:14b	6:39
Centurion's boy	8:5–10, 13	7:1b–10
John's question	11:2–6	7:18–23
Mission charge	10:9–15	10:4–12
Blessed eyes	13:16–17	10:23–24
Lord's prayer	6:9–13	11:1–4
Good gifts	7:9–11	11:11–13
Beelzebul debate	12:22–26	11:14–15, 17–18
Sign of Jonah	12:38–40	11:16, 29–30
Lamp on stand	5:15	11:33
Lamp of body	6:22–23	11:34–36
Unforgivable sin	12:32	12:10
Do not worry	6:25–33	12:22–31
On treasure	6:19–21	12:33–34
Agree on way	5:25–26	12:57–59
Sons excluded	8:11–12	13:28–29
Spoiled salt	5:13	14:34–35
On divorce	5:32	16:18
12 thrones	19:28b	22:28–30

EXPLANATIONS FOR THE VARIATION

Tables 7.1, 7.2, and 7.3 illustrate the wide degree of variation in verbal agreement between Matthew and Luke in the double tradition. Kloppenborg identifies six different models for explaining such variation.[7] These boil down to three basic explanations: different recensions or translations of Q, changes by the Evangelists, or use of other sources or traditions that overlapped with Q.

For Matthew and Luke to produce the high degree of verbal agreement evident in the pericopes in table 7.1, three conditions had to be met: both Evangelists used the same version of Q; neither Evangelist made major changes to Q; and neither Evangelist used other sources or traditions than Q. For Matthew and Luke to produce the low degree of verbal agreement in table 7.2 or the mixed agreement in table 7.3, one or more of these conditions must not have been met. The Evangelists must have used different recensions or translations of Q, one or both of the Evangelists must have made major changes to Q, or they must have used other sources or traditions in addition to Q. We will examine each of these alternatives.

DIFFERENT RECENSIONS OR TRANSLATIONS OF Q

One explanation for the lack of verbal agreement in Q parallels is that Matthew and Luke used different recensions[8] or translations[9] of Q. I discussed the theory of different recensions (Q^{Matt} and Q^{Luke}) in chapter 2. It would explain why Matthew and Luke differ in wording in much of Q. However, if these recensions differed so widely in some Q material, then why in other Q material did they have almost identical wording? The theory does not explain why the Q material shows such wide variation in verbal agreement. It simply pushes the problem back to a stage prior to the Evangelists. A similar explanation posits two different translations of an originally Aramaic Q. In chapter 2, I discussed the versions of this theory offered by Bussman, Bergemann, and Casey, giving a critique of each.

CHANGES BY THE EVANGELISTS

If Matthew and Luke used a single version of Q exclusively for the double tradition, then no further explanation is needed for the material in table 7.1. However, the material in tables 7.2 and 7.3 does require a further explanation. The most common explanation is that one or both Evangelists changed Q. They might have done so either unintentionally (through lapses of memory

---

7. Kloppenborg, "Variation," 56–63.
8. Ibid., 58.
9. Ibid., 59–61.

in copying) or intentionally (through purposeful redaction). No doubt both explanations contributed to the variation in wording, but it is doubtful that either could account for all of it.

The appeal to memory must explain why the Evangelists had such good memory for the passages in table 7.1 but such poor memory for the passages in table 7.2. Kloppenborg raises the possibility that Matthew relied on memory for Q sayings that he inserted into another context, but finds that such sayings do not exhibit a consistently lower level of agreement with Luke. He concludes that "reliance on memory can at best be a partial explanation of the phenomenon of high variation."[10]

The appeal to redaction faces a similar problem. Clearly the Evangelists did edit their sources in places. The problem is to explain why the Evangelists would have redacted the material in table 7.1 hardly at all but the material in table 7.2 so thoroughly that hardly any wording remains in common. Is it plausible that one or both of the Evangelists would have treated their source in such an inconsistent manner? Kloppenborg Verbin assumes so. He has drawn on Morgenthaler's statistics to show five ranges of verbatim agreement between Matthew and Luke in the Q material: 0–19%, 20–39%, 40–59%, 60–79%, and 80–98%. He thinks that this is what one ought to expect if Matthew and Luke independently redacted the same version of Q.[11] However, such statistics can be misleading, since different causes might produce a mixture of agreement and disagreement. Kloppenborg Verbin assumes that such mixture arose as the Evangelists redacted the same version of Q. However, such mixture could also arise if one Evangelist combined or conflated Q with a parallel source. Thus Morgenthaler's statistics do not necessarily support the interpretation that Kloppenborg Verbin gives them.

If the Evangelists did use the Q source in an inconsistent manner, why would they have done so? Kloppenborg seeks to shed light on this question by surveying the way other ancient writers treated their sources.[12] He identifies three scribal activities in which ancient writers drew on earlier sources: composing, compiling, and copying.

1. At the more creative end of the scale, historians and teachers drew on earlier sources in composing their own works. As examples of Greek and Hebrew historians, Kloppenborg cites Diodorus Siculus, Josephus, the author of *1QapGen ar*, and Pseudo-Philo. As an example of a Jewish teacher, he cites Sirach. These composers generally paraphrased and expanded their sources,

---

10. Ibid., 58.
11. Kloppenborg Verbin, *Excavating Q*, 63.
12. Kloppenborg, "Variation," 63–80.

though occasionally one might copy some lines of the source verbatim, as when Diodorus used Ephorus as a source. Kloppenborg concludes that "Matthew and Luke are dramatically out of step" with such composers since the Evangelists exhibit so much verbatim agreement:

> Were Matthew and Luke using Q (or Mark) as Diodorus, Josephus, *1QapGen ar* or Ps-Philo used their sources, we should expect almost no verbatim agreement, since *both* would sometimes paraphrase generously and, because they would have done so independently, the likelihood of coincidental agreement in *not* changing Q would be exceedingly low.[13]

Despite finding that Matthew and Luke were not using their sources like ancient composers, Kloppenborg still assumes that they *were* composing and that their paraphrasing of Q would account for the low-agreement pericopes in Q. He denies that these should be explained by appealing to oral tradition as Dunn and Mournet do. However, Kloppenborg's examples seem to point to a more obvious and natural conclusion: namely, that the Evangelists were *not* composing. As Kloppenborg recognizes, the Evangelists are "dramatically out of step" with the ancient composers that he cites. Diodorus incorporates verbatim citations into his own descriptions, but none of these composers take entire pericopes in nearly identical wording out of their sources without adding their own composition. In doing so, the Evangelists were clearly not composing like other ancient authors.

2. At the less creative end of the scale, scribes in the shops of booksellers would also use a source as they worked from an exemplar in making copies of literary works. In this process, "the ideal of copying was naturally an error-free and unadulterated copy of the exemplar."[14] Clearly Matthew and Luke were doing more than copying, since their work involved combining more than one source.

3. If Matthew and Luke were not using their sources like composers or copyists, what were they doing? Between these two ends of the scale of creativity stood another scribal activity, that of compilation, "where predecessor documents were taken over nearly unchanged and extra materials simply interpolated and appended to a core."[15] Kloppenborg gives three examples of ancient works that illustrate compilation. (1) The scribe of *QpaleoExod*[m] (4Q22), a scroll of Exodus from Qumran, compiled this work by inserting into the text of Exodus parallel pericopes from Deuteronomy, other passages

---

13. Ibid., 73–74.
14. Ibid., 77.
15. Ibid.

from Deuteronomy, and even pericopes from other contexts in Exodus. (2) Fragments of *Serek hayachad* (S) from Qumran represent various stages in the development of 1QS, the community rule. "This development included expansion of a core of materials, the introduction of other versions of penal rules, and the addition of materials not intrinsically related to that core."[16] (3) Both the Doctrina Apostolorum and the Didache incorporate the Jewish "Two Ways" document. In the Didache, the Two Ways document has been expanded by sayings of Jesus and supplemented with various instructions relating to church life. In all three cases of compilation, the scribes took over the texts that they were copying with minimal changes of wording.

The work of Matthew and Luke corresponds more closely to the scribal activity of compilation than to composition. They took various sources and traditions, including the Markan source, Q, M in the case of Matthew, and L in the case of Luke, and combined these into a new whole. No doubt they exercised a measure of creativity as editors in doing so. However, as Kloppenborg acknowledges, "Matthew and Luke come closer to the wooden copying techniques of *Serek haYachad* than they do to the practices of other historians or biographers."[17] If so, then we would expect the Evangelists to take over their sources with minimal changes of wording like other ancient compilers. Clearly they did so with respect to the passages listed in table 7.1. What calls for explanation, then, is not the common wording in these passages, but the variations in wording seen in the passages in tables 7.2 and 7.3.[18]

From this survey of ancient scribal practice, we can infer that the Evangelists functioned more as compilers and editors than as composers. If so, then ancient composition does not provide an accurate model for explaining the high degree of variation in wording between Matthew and Luke in using Q. We must explain such variation as a result of their work as compilers and editors. Such work involved combining more than one source, and this plurality of sources brings us to the next explanation.

OVERLAPPING SOURCES OR TRADITIONS

A third explanation is that the Evangelists knew alternative versions of some Q pericopes. These may have come from written sources that overlapped with Q, such as Mark, or M and L if these were documents.[19] Or they may have

---

16. Ibid., 75.
17. Ibid., 77.
18. *Contra* Kloppenborg, ibid., 63, 80.
19. Ibid., 59.

come from oral tradition if they were not,[20] or from reoralizations of material from a written source.[21] This explanation has promise. If Matthew and Luke were functioning essentially as compilers, combining different sources into a new whole, then they would often be faced with decisions about how to create some sort of unity out of the diversity of their sources. In some cases, it is clear that these sources overlapped, and combining such overlaps would have affected the wording of the individual sources. In other cases, putting the material from one source into the context of another source might also require some rewording. This explanation, therefore, deserves further exploration. At least three different sources or traditions included material that overlapped with Q: the Markan source, M, and L. In the rest of this chapter, I will examine an overlap from each of these three sources to see what effect each had on the wording of Q.

COMBINATION OF Q WITH THE MARKAN SOURCE

Fortunately, we have known examples of overlaps with Q in the Synoptic tradition that we can examine. I refer to the Mark/Q overlaps, where the Markan source and Q included the same pericope. In some cases, the Evangelists kept the overlaps separate. For example, Matthew includes the pericope "Seeking signs" twice but keeps the Markan version in one position (Matt 16:1, 4; Mark 8:11–13) and the Q version elsewhere (Matt 12:38–40/Luke 11:16, 29–30). In other cases, one of the Evangelists conflated the two overlapping passages. Such an overlap occurs, for example, in the Beelzebul debate, where Matthew conflates the Markan version of the material with the Q version (Matt 12:22–30; Mark 3:22–27; Luke 11:14–23). I will examine this instance to see how such conflation affects the agreement of Matthew and Luke in the wording of the passage.

For the Markan material, I assume that Mark and Matthew shared a common source (Proto-Mark A) and that Mark and Luke shared a common source (Proto-Mark B). If we assumed that Matthew and Luke copied Mark, the conclusions relevant for Q would remain the same.

In the Beelzebul debate, Mark follows the Markan source, Luke follows Q, and Matthew combines Q with his Markan source (Proto-Mark A). Comparing Matthew and Luke in this material, we find the same three degrees of verbal agreement that we see in the Q material as a whole. First, when Mat-

---

20. Ibid., 56.
21. Ibid., 61–63, 79–80.

thew and Luke both follow Q they have almost identical wording, as shown in table 7.4.

TABLE 7.4. HIGH MATTHEW/LUKE AGREEMENT IN BEELZEBUL DEBATE

Matthew 12:27–28, 30 Q	Luke 11:19–20, 23 Q
12:27 And if I by Beelzebul cast out the demons, by whom do your sons cast them out? For this reason, they will be your judges.	11:19 But if I by Beelzebul cast out the demons, by whom do your sons cast them out? For this reason, they will be your judges.
28 But if by the Spirit of God I cast out the demons, then the kingdom of God has come to you.	20 But if by the finger of God I cast out the demons, then the kingdom of God has come to you.
30 One who is not with me is against me, and one who does not gather with me scatters.	23 One who is not with me is against me, and one who does not gather with me scatters.

Here Matthew and Luke simply reproduce their source, except that Matthew has apparently changed "finger" to "Spirit." This high degree of verbal agreement corresponds to what we find in the Q passages listed in table 7.1

Second, when Luke follows Q and Matthew follows the Markan source, they have hardly any wording in common (table 7.5).

TABLE 7.5. LOW MATTHEW/LUKE AGREEMENT IN BEELZEBUL DEBATE

Mark 3:27 PMkA/B	Matthew 12:29 PMkA	Luke 11:21–22 Q
		21 When the strong man fully armed guards his own courtyard, his belongings are in peace.
3:27 But no one can upon entering the house of the strong man loot his goods unless first he binds the strong man.	12:29 Or how can someone enter the house of the strong man and seize his goods unless first he binds the strong man?	22 But when one stronger than he comes against him and defeats him, he takes his armor on which he had relied
And then he will loot his house.	And then he will loot his house.	and distributes his spoil.

Here about the only wording that Matthew and Luke have in common is the word "strong man." This low degree of verbal agreement corresponds to what we find in the Q passages listed in table 7.2.

Third, where Matthew conflates the Markan source with Q, Matthew and Luke show a mixture of agreement and disagreement in wording (table 7.6).

TABLE 7.6. MIXED MATTHEW/LUKE AGREEMENT IN BEELZEBUL DEBATE

Mark 3:23b–26 PMkA/B	Matthew 12:25–26 Q, PMkA	Luke 11:17–18 Q
	12:25a εἰδὼς δὲ τὰς ἐνθυμήσεις αὐτῶν	11:17 αὐτὸς δὲ εἰδὼς αὐτῶν τὰ διανοήματα
3:23b ἔλεγεν αὐτοῖς·	εἶπεν αὐτοῖς·	εἶπεν αὐτοῖς·
πῶς δύναται σατανᾶς σατανᾶν ἐκβάλλειν;		
24 καὶ ἐὰν βασιλεία	πᾶσα βασιλεία	πᾶσα βασιλεία
ἐφ' ἑαυτὴν μερισθῇ,	μερισθεῖσα καθ' ἑαυτῆς	ἐφ' ἑαυτὴν διαμερισθεῖσα
οὐ δύναται σταθῆναι ἡ βασιλεία ἐκείνη·	ἐρημοῦται	ἐρημοῦται
25 καὶ	25b καὶ	καὶ
	πᾶσα πόλις	
ἐὰν οἰκία	ἢ οἰκία	οἶκος
ἐφ' ἑαυτὴν μερισθῇ,	μερισθεῖσα καθ' ἑαυτῆς	ἐπὶ οἶκον
οὐ δυνήσεται ἡ οἰκία ἐκείνη σταθῆναι.	οὐ σταθήσεται.	πίπτει.
26 καὶ εἰ ὁ σατανᾶς	26a καὶ εἰ ὁ σατανᾶς	18 εἰ δὲ καὶ ὁ σατανᾶς
[cf. 23b: σατανᾶν ἐκβάλλειν]	τὸν σατανᾶν ἐκβάλλει,	
ἀνέστη		
ἐφ' ἑαυτὸν καὶ ἐμερίσθη,	ἐφ' ἑαυτὸν ἐμερίσθη·	ἐφ' ἑαυτὸν διεμερίσθη,
οὐ δύναται στῆναι	26b πῶς οὖν σταθήσεται ἡ βασιλεία αὐτοῦ;	πῶς σταθήσεται ἡ βασιλεία αὐτοῦ;
ἀλλὰ τέλος ἔχει.		

The middle column of the table shows Matthew's conflated account, while the columns to left and right show the versions of Mark and Luke, respectively.

In Matthew 12:25a and 26b, Matthew agrees with Luke more closely than with Mark, and hence must be following Q. In Matthew 12:25b–26a, Matthew agrees more closely with Mark than with Luke, and hence must be following Proto-Mark A. Matthew's redaction would consist primarily of changing διανοήματα to ἐνθυμήσεις (unless Luke did the reverse) and adding πᾶσα πόλις. This mixture of agreement and disagreement with Luke corresponds to what we find in the Q passages listed in table 7.3.

If we did not have Mark and we compared Matthew and Luke in the Beelzebul debate, we might suppose that one Evangelist or the other redacted the material much more heavily than is actually the case. Since we do have Mark, we can see that most of Matthew's differences from Luke's wording occurred when Matthew was following an alternative version of the material in an overlapping source. The Beelzebul debate thus suggests a model for explaining much of the variation in verbal agreement in the Q parallels. When Matthew and Luke both follow Q, they have much the same wording. When one Evangelist followed Q and the other followed another source, they have little wording in common. When one Evangelist followed Q and the other conflated Q with another source, they have a mixture of agreement and disagreement in wording. While this model will not account for all of the verbal variation in Q parallels, it will account for a large part of it, as we shall see.

COMBINATION OF Q WITH M

What sources, then, besides Mark, overlapped with Q? The most likely candidates are M (Matthew's special material) and L (Luke's special material).

Critics generally agree that Matthew knew material besides that which came from his Markan source or Q, but they disagree as to whether this "M" material came from a written source, oral tradition, or a combination of written source(s) and oral tradition.[22] Whether oral or written, it occasionally overlapped with Q, as the following example shows.

A saying about trees and their fruit occurred in several different versions. It occurs three times in Matthew and once in Luke (table 7.7).

---

22. Streeter, *Four Gospels*, 150, 198, 238–65, 281–85; Manson, *Sayings*, 21–26; Allison in Davies and Allison, *Matthew*, 1:121–27. For an attempt to distinguish M from Matthean redaction, see Stephenson H. Brooks, *Matthew's Community: The Evidence of His Special Sayings Material* (JSNTSup 16; Sheffield: Sheffield Academic Press, 1987). For a survey of scholarly views on M, see Paul Foster, "The M-Source: Its History and Demise in Biblical Scholarship," in *New Studies in the Synoptic Problem* (ed. Paul Foster, Andrew Gregory, John S. Kloppenborg, and Joseph Verheyden; Leuven: Peeters, forthcoming).

TABLE 7.7. TREE AND FRUIT

Matt 7:17, 20 M Positive	Matt 12:33 Q Positive	Matt 7:18, 16a Q Negative	Luke 6:43–44a Q Negative
17 Thus every healthy tree bears good fruits, but the rotten tree bears bad fruits.	33 Either make the tree good and its fruit good, or make the tree rotten and its fruit rotten.	→18 A healthy tree cannot bear bad fruits, nor can a rotten tree bear good fruits.	43 There is no good tree bearing rotten fruit, nor again a rotten tree bearing good fruit.
20 So then, by their fruits you will know them.	For by the fruit the tree is known.	16a By their fruits you will know them.	44a For every tree by its own fruit is known.

This saying consists of two parts: a premise that the quality of the tree determines the quality of the fruit and a conclusion that a tree is therefore known by its fruit. It occurs in both a positive and a negative form. In the positive form, the premise states what kind of fruit a tree can or should bear; in the negative, it states what kind of fruit it cannot bear. The positive form is shown in the first two columns of table 7.7; the negative, in the last two columns.

Luke's one version of the saying occurs in the Q sermon and can therefore be ascribed to Q. In Matthew's sermon, two of Matthew's versions have been combined (table 7.8).

TABLE 7.8.TREE AND FRUIT IN Q SERMON

Matthew 7:15, 17, 20 M	Matthew 7: 18, 16 Q	Luke 6:43–44 Q
15 Beware of false prophets, who come to you in sheep's clothing but within are ravening wolves.		
17 Thus every healthy tree bears good fruits, but the rotten tree bears bad fruits.	18 A healthy tree cannot bear bad fruits, nor can a rotten tree bear good fruits.	6:43 For there is no good tree bearing rotten fruit nor again a rotten tree bearing good fruit.
20 So then, by their fruits you will know them.	16a By their fruits you will know them.	44a For every tree by its own fruit is known.

	16b Do they gather grapes from thorns, or figs from thistles?	44b For they do not gather figs from thorns or pick grapes from a bramble bush.

The first Matthean version in table 7.8 includes a warning against false prophets, has a positive version of the tree and fruit saying, and lacks the saying on gathering fruit from thorns. In all three of these respects it differs from the Q version in Luke. The second Matthean version lacks the warning against false prophets, has a negative version of the tree and fruit saying, and includes the saying on gathering fruit from thorns. In all three of these respects it resembles the Q version in Luke. We can infer therefore that the second Matthean version came from Q.

Scholars disagree on the source of the first Matthean version (Matt 7:15, 17, 20). Manson recognizes that Matthew 7:15–20 is a combination of Q and M.[23] In contrast, Brooks[24] and Allison[25] attribute 7:15–20 to Q plus Matthean redaction. For two reasons, it is more likely that 7:15, 17, 20 came from M. First, 7:17, 20 is a doublet of the Q saying in 7:18, 16a. If a Gospel includes the same pericope twice, it is usually because the pericope occurred in two of the Gospel's sources, as when Matthew includes the pericope on seeking signs from both the Markan source (Matt 16:1, 4) and Q (Matt 12:38–40). In the present case, Matthew includes the same pericope twice, once from Q and once from a source unique to Matthew, that is, from M. And if the doublet in 7:17, 20 came from M, then 7:15, to which it is attached, also probably came from M. Second, this conclusion accords better with the view that the Evangelists functioned more as compilers than as composers who freely created new material. If we ascribed the material in the first column of table 7.8 to Matthew, then we would have to suppose that he composed more material here than he received from Q and that most of what he composed simply repeated the Q material.

More likely, then, Matthew combined the Q material with partially overlapping material from M. In so doing, he moved the premise of the Q version (Matt 7:18) from its original position in Q, apparently so that it would stand by the corresponding premise in the M version (Matt 7:17).[26] Here the act of

---

23. Manson, *Sayings*, 23, 175.

24. Brooks, *Matthew's Community*, 93–94.

25. Allison in Davies and Allison, *Matthew*, 1:694.

26. Allison gives a different reason for the transposition (Davies and Allison, *Matthew*, 1:706).

combining Q with M affected the order of Q. Matthew favored the order of M and adapted the Q material to M.

The wording of the two versions confirms that Matthew favored M here. In combining the Q version with the M version, Matthew assimilated the wording of Q to the wording of the M version. A comparison of the three versions reveals that Matthew's Q version differs in wording from Luke's Q version but agrees in wording with the M version, as table 7.9 shows.

TABLE 7.9. COMPARISON OF WORDING

Matthew M	Matthew Q	Luke Q
healthy tree	healthy tree	good tree
bad fruits	bad fruits	rotten fruit
rotten tree	rotten tree	rotten tree
good fruits	good fruits	good fruit
by their fruits you will know them	by their fruits you will know them	every tree by its own fruit is known
—	grapes from thorns	figs from thorns
—	figs from thistles	grapes from a bramble bush

If Matthew preserved the original wording of Q, then we would have to assume that M and Q shared much the same wording and that Luke for some unknown reason decided to revise the Q version. It is more likely that Luke better preserves the original wording of Q since then we have an explanation for the changes to Q. If Luke better preserves Q, then the M version and the Q version differed in wording, and Matthew assimilated the wording of Q to the wording of M. It is possible that Matthew changed the saying on grapes and figs (Matt 7:16b) in a similar way to match the wording of an M version that he omitted.

This example shows how incorporating Q into the context of M could affect both the order and the wording of Q in Matthew. If we did not have the M version, we might think that Matthew or Luke revised the Q version by freely paraphrasing it.

COMBINATION OF Q WITH L

Critics generally agree that Luke knew material besides that which came from his Markan source or Q.[27] It is less certain whether this "L" material came from a written source, oral tradition, or a combination of written source(s) and oral tradition. Whether oral or written, L is an extensive body of material, constituting about a third of Luke. It would not be surprising therefore if it occasionally overlapped with Q. I give one example of such an overlap here.

In the pericope "Do not judge" (Matt 7:1–2/Luke 6:37–38), Luke includes twice as much material as Matthew, some of which is repetitive (table 7.10).

TABLE 7.10. DO NOT JUDGE

Matt 7:1–2 Q	Luke 6:37a, 38c Q	Luke 6:37b–38b L
7:1 Do not judge, so that you will not be judged.	6:37a And do not judge, and you will not be judged.	6:37b And do not condemn, and you will not be condemned.
2a For by the judgment with which you judge, you will be judged.	—	37c Acquit, and you will be acquitted.
2b And by the measure with which you measure, it will be measured to you.	38c For by the measure with which you measure, it will be measured back to you.	38ab Give, and it will be given to you; good measure, pressed down, shaken together, overflowing, will they give into your lap.

The first column of table 7.10 shows Matthew's version of this material. The second column shows the material in Luke that agrees closely in wording with that in Matthew. Because of the close agreement in wording, we can identify the first two columns as Q material.

The third column shows material in Luke that differs from Matthew. Some scholars regard this as Q material,[28] but its absence from Matthew speaks against this assessment. Others regard it as Lukan redaction.[29] For two reasons, it is more likely that it came from Luke's special material. First, it is difficult to see why Luke would have created Luke 6:37b since it simply restates Luke 6:37a. It appears instead that Luke has included two different

---

27. Fitzmyer, *Luke*, 1:82–85; Paffenroth, *Story of Jesus*, seeks to distinguish between L and Lukan redaction.

28. Manson, *Sayings*, 55; Allison in Davies and Allison, *Matthew*, 1:667–68.

29. E.g., Fitzmyer, *Luke*, 1:641.

versions of the same saying, one from Q (Luke 6:37a) and one from material unique to Luke (Luke 6:37b). If that is the case, then Luke 6:37c and 6:38ab probably are also L versions of the corresponding Q sayings. Thus Q and L have parallel versions of the same pericope, which included two sayings on judging and one on measuring. Second, this conclusion accords better with the view that the Evangelists functioned more as compilers than as composers who freely created new material. If we ascribed the material in the third column of table 7.10 to Luke, then we would have to suppose that he composed more material here than he received from Q.

While both Matthew and Luke have the first saying, "Do not judge" (μὴ κρίνετε) from Q, Luke also includes the parallel "Do not condemn" (μὴ καταδικάζετε) from L. The L version says the same thing as the Q version but substitutes "condemn" for "judge." By including both versions, Luke creates a doublet.

The second saying in Q, preserved in Matthew 7:2a but not in Luke, differs from the second saying in L, preserved in Luke 6:37c. Both sayings, however, continue the theme of the first saying. In Q the second saying states that how one judges determines how one will be judged. This is a general principle that could apply to either a favorable or an unfavorable judgment. The corresponding saying in L envisions only the case of a favorable judgment: it exhorts one to give a favorable judgment of acquittal in order to receive the same.

The third pair of sayings differ in a similar manner. In Q, the third saying states that the measure one gives will determine the measure one receives. This again is a general principle that could apply to either a generous measure or an ungenerous measure. The corresponding saying in L envisions only the case of a generous measure: it exhorts one to give generously in order to receive back "good measure."

In combining Q with L, Luke included the entire pericope from L. It stands between the first and third sayings of Q, where it replaces the second Q saying. In this example of overlapping traditions, the wording of Q is not changed in either Matthew or Luke. However, in Luke, Q is augmented with a parallel version from L, which replaces part of the Q material.

CONCLUSION

The large amount of verbatim agreement between Matthew and Luke suggests that they functioned primarily as compilers and editors. What requires explanation, then, is any passage where they substantially disagree in wording.

With respect to Q, we have seen that differences in wording arose as the Evangelists combined different sources. These Evangelists had inherited a variety of sources and traditions that they wished to combine into some sort of a unified whole, and this task required a measure of editorial creativity. Major adaptations might be required when they combined more than one version of the material or when they incorporated material from one source into the context of another.

While other types of editorial revision undoubtedly contributed to differences in wording as well, we will focus in the next several chapters on those places where the Evangelists combined Q with other sources. Specifically, we have seen that changes to the wording of a Q passage could take place when the Evangelists combined Q with the Markan source, when Matthew combined Q with M, or when Luke combined Q with L. We will give further examples of these types of changes in the next three chapters.

8

Combination of Q with the Markan Source

We are now ready to survey the Q material with the purpose of understanding why Matthew and Luke so frequently differ in wording in Q parallels. In the present chapter, we examine one cause of such differences: the Evangelists often combined Q with the Markan source. We examined one instance of such combination in chapter 7 (tables 7.4–6). In the present chapter, we will examine others. These include cases where an Evangelist has conflated Q with the Markan source, has inserted a Q passage into a Markan context, or has assimilated the wording of Q to an overlap from the Markan source. I will examine these in the order in which they occur in Luke. I will not consider the mission charge, which I will examine in chapter 10.

In discussing the Markan material, I presuppose the theory that Mark and Matthew shared Proto-Mark A, while Mark and Luke shared Proto-Mark B.[1] If we assumed that Matthew and Luke used Mark, the conclusions that are relevant for Q would remain the same.

The Beginning of Q

The beginning of Q overlaps considerably with the beginning of the Markan source. Here Matthew and Luke independently conflated their two sources or inserted Q material into a Markan context. As we would expect, they exhibit a mixture of agreement and disagreement in wording in this material.

John Appears (Matt 3:5b/Luke 3:2b–3a)

The beginning of Q is disputed.[2] I suggest that it began with the appearance of John, as in table 8.1.

---

1. Burkett, *From Proto-Mark to Mark*.

2. E.g., Jacobson, *First Gospel*, 80; David R. Catchpole, "The Beginning of Q: A Proposal," *NTS* 38 (1992): 205–21; Harry T. Fleddermann, "The Beginning of Q," in *Society of*

TABLE 8.1. JOHN APPEARS

Matthew 3:5b Q	Luke 3:2b–3a Q
—	3:2b The word of God came to John, the son of Zachariah, in the wilderness,
3:5b all the region of the Jordan	3a and he came into all the region of the Jordan.

The first non-Markan material common to Matthew and Luke is the phrase "all the region of the Jordan" (Matt 3:5b/Luke 3:3a). Matthew inserted this non-Markan phrase into a Markan sentence (Matt 3:5a, 6), where it did not originally belong (cf. Mark 1:5). Since it could not have stood by itself, when we find it integrated into a complete sentence in Luke 3:2b–3a, we have reason to believe that Luke preserves it in its original context. The phrase in Matthew (πᾶσα ἡ περίχωρος τοῦ Ἰορδάνου) matches the corresponding phrase in Luke 3:3 (πᾶσαν [τὴν] περίχωρον τοῦ Ἰορδάνου) except for its grammatical case, which Matthew adapted to the Markan sentence into which he inserted it. We can infer therefore that both Matthew and Luke drew this material from Q.[3] Changes to the wording occurred when Matthew dropped the first part and adapted the second part to a context in Mark.

If this analysis is correct, then Q began by implicitly identifying John as a prophet. In Luke 3:2b, the phrase "the word of God came" is a typical formula used in the Hebrew Bible to describe the divine inspiration of a prophet:

- "The word of Yahweh came to Ezekiel the son of Buzi the priest in the land of the Chaldeans" (Ezek 1:3);
- "The word of Yahweh came to Jonah the son of Amittai" (Jonah 1:1);
- "The word of Yahweh came to Zechariah the son of Berechiah" (Zech 1:1; cf. Isa 38:4; Jer 1:2; Hos 1:1; Joel 1:1; Mic 1:1; Zeph 1:1; Hag 1:1).

Biblical Literature 1985 Seminar Papers (Missoula, Mont.: Scholars Press, 1985), 153–59; James M. Robinson, "The Incipit of the Sayings Gospel Q," *RHPR* 75 (1995): 9–33; Frans Neirynck, "The First Synoptic Pericope: The Appearance of John the Baptist in Q?" *ETL* 72 (1996): 41–74.

3. James M. Robinson assumes that Luke 3:2 stood in Q ("Basic Shifts in German Theology," *Interpretation* 16 [1962]: 76–97, esp. 83). Kloppenborg Verbin and the International Q Project have included portions of Luke 3:2b–3a in Q, "albeit in a highly lacunary form" (Kloppenborg Verbin, *Excavating Q*, 95).

This implicit identification of John as a prophet corresponds to the explicit depiction of John later in Q (Matt 11:9/Luke 7:26). It also serves as an appropriate introduction to the Q material that immediately follows (Matt 3:7–10/Luke 3:7–9): John, the prophet to whom the word of God comes, immediately delivers that word in the form of a prophetic threat of judgment and call to repentance. Luke 3:2b–3a thus provides a suitable beginning for Q.

One could infer that the beginning of Q also included the quotation of Isaiah 40:3 (Matt 3:3/Luke 3:4), since Matthew and Luke agree against Mark in placing this quotation after the appearance of John rather than before. There is a good reason, however, for thinking that it did not stand in Q. The phrase that more certainly comes from Q, "all the region of the Jordan," comes before the quotation in Luke, but after in Matthew. One can see this in table 1.2 in chapter 1. Thus the two items do not have a common sequence in Matthew and Luke. This fact suggests that they came from different sources, which Matthew and Luke combined differently. While the phrase "all the region of the Jordan" came from Q, the quotation of Isaiah 40:3 came from the Markan source.[4]

GREATER ONE (MATT 3:11/LUKE 3:16)

In John's prediction of the "Greater one" (Matt 3:11/Luke 3:16), Q overlapped with the Markan source. Table 8.2 delineates the sources for this pericope.

TABLE 8.2. GREATER ONE

Matthew 3:11–12 Q	Mark 1:7–8 PMkA/B	Luke 3:16–17 Q, {PMkB}
	1:7 And he preached saying,	16 John replied, saying to all,
11 "I baptize you in water for repentance,		"I baptize you in water,
but the one coming after me is more powerful than me, and I am not worthy to bear his sandals.	"The one more powerful than me comes after me, and I am not worthy to kneel and undo the strap of his sandals.	{"but the one more powerful than me comes, and I am not worthy to undo the strap of his sandals.}

4. In my theory, Matthew would have found it in Proto-Mark A, Luke in Proto-Mark B, and Mark in both. Apparently Matthew and Luke have preserved the original order of Proto-Mark in placing the quotation after the appearance of John, while Mark has moved it from its original position (Burkett, *From Proto-Mark to Mark*, 101).

	8 I baptize you in water,	
He will baptize you in Holy Spirit	but he will baptize you in Holy Spirit."	He will baptize you in Holy Spirit
and fire.		and fire.
12 Wheat and chaff		17 Wheat and chaff

In this pericope, Matthew and Luke exhibit a mixture of agreement and disagreement in wording, which often indicates that one of them has conflated Q with another source. In this case, Luke has conflated Q with the Markan source. Where Matthew and Luke agree against Mark, they have almost identical wording, which indicates that both used Q here. Where they disagree with each other, Luke agrees with Mark, an indication that he also used his version of the Markan source (Proto-Mark B). In the third column, braces enclose Luke's material that agrees with Mark.

The Q version, preserved in Matthew and less fully in Luke, differed in several respects from the Markan version. It had the clause "I baptize you in water" before the prediction of the one to come instead of after. It referred to Jesus as "the one coming" instead of as "the one more powerful than me." It had John profess himself unworthy "to bear his sandals" instead of "to undo the strap of his sandals." It included the words "and fire," which the Markan source lacked, and it concluded with the saying "Wheat and chaff," also absent from the Markan source.

In this passage, Luke's conflation of Q with the Markan source accounts for the differences in wording between Matthew and Luke. They agree in wording when both follow Q but disagree when Luke switches to Proto-Mark B.

Jesus' Baptism (Matt 3:16–17/Luke 3:21–22)

Scholars have debated whether or not Q contained an account of Jesus' baptism. In chapter 3, we saw good reason to think that it did,[5] since the Q temptation narrative seems to presuppose the baptismal scene, specifically Jesus' reception of the Spirit and identification as the son of God. Furthermore, in the baptism story, Matthew and Luke show several divergences from Mark, in some of which they agree against Mark. Using these divergences as a guide, we can distinguish the non-Markan material from the Markan, as shown in table 8.3.

---

5. *Contra* Kloppenborg, *Formation of Q*, 84–85; *Excavating Q*, 93.

TABLE 8.3. JESUS' BAPTISM

Matthew 3:13, 16–17 Q {PMkA}	Mark 1:9–11 PMkA/B	Luke 3:21–22 Q {PMkB}
	1:9 And it happened	3:21 {It happened}
3:13 Then	in those days	
		when all the people were baptized
{Jesus comes from Galilee to the Jordan to John to be baptized by him.}	that Jesus came from Nazareth of Galilee and was baptized in the Jordan by John.	
16 When Jesus was baptized,		and Jesus was baptized
		and was praying,
{immediately he came up from the water.}	10 And immediately on coming up from the water,	
And behold the heavens were opened to him,	he saw the heavens torn	that heaven opened,
and {he saw} the Spirit of God {descending} as if a dove and coming upon him.	and the Spirit as a dove descending to him.	22 and the Holy Spirit descended in bodily appearance as a dove upon him,
17 And there was a voice from the heavens, saying, "This is my beloved son, with whom I am pleased."	11 And a voice came from the heavens: "You are my beloved son; with you I am pleased."	{and a voice came from heaven: "You are my beloved son; with you I am pleased."}

As the table shows, Matthew followed Proto-Mark A for the words in braces, where Matthew agrees with Mark. Likewise, Luke followed Proto-Mark B for the words in braces, where Luke agrees with Mark. The remaining material in these two Gospels is shown in table 8.4.

TABLE 8.4. DIFFERENCES FROM MARK IN THE BAPTISM STORY

Matthew Q	Luke Q
	3:21 ἐν τῷ βαπτισθῆναι ἅπαντα τὸν λαὸν
3:16 βαπτισθεὶς δὲ ὁ Ἰησοῦς	καὶ Ἰησοῦ βαπτισθέντος
	καὶ προσευχομένου
καὶ ἰδοὺ	
ἠνεῴχθησαν [αὐτῷ] οἱ οὐρανοί	ἀνεῳχθῆναι τὸν οὐρανὸν
	22 καὶ καταβῆναι
[τὸ] πνεῦμα [τοῦ] θεοῦ	τὸ πνεῦμα τὸ ἅγιον
	σωματικῷ εἴδει
ὡσεὶ περιστερὰν	ὡς περιστερὰν
[καὶ] ἐρχόμενον	
ἐπ᾽ αὐτόν	ἐπ᾽ αὐτόν
17 καὶ ἰδοὺ φωνὴ ἐκ τῶν οὐρανῶν λέγουσα· οὗτός ἐστιν ὁ υἱός μου ὁ ἀγαπητός, ἐν ᾧ εὐδόκησα.	

Luke's version of the baptism differs almost completely from that of Mark, except for the voice from heaven, and Matthew's differs considerably as well. Where they differ from Mark, Matthew and Luke have a few agreements. Both describe the act of Jesus' baptism with an aorist passive participle. Both describe the heavens as "opened" rather than as "torn." Both describe the Spirit coming "upon" Jesus rather than "to" him. These agreements against Mark suggest that both Matthew and Luke used Q as well as their respective Markan sources. Matthew alone uses third person instead of second person in quoting the voice from heaven. If this distinctive wording did not come from Matthean redaction, it may have come from Q. In the material that we can identify as Q, Matthew and Luke have little verbatim agreement, probably because one or both found it necessary to reword Q in order to conflate it with the Markan version.

JESUS TESTED (MATT 4:1/LUKE 4:1B–2A)

The temptation narrative in the double tradition begins with an introduction that overlaps with Mark (table 8.5).

TABLE 8.5. JESUS TESTED

Matthew 4:1 Q, {PMkA}	Mark 1:12–13a PMkA/B	Luke 4:1b–2a Q, {PMkB}
4:1 Then Jesus	1:12 And immediately	4:1b {And}
	the Spirit	
was led	drives him out	he was being led
{into the wilderness}	into the wilderness.	
by the Spirit		in the Spirit
	13a And he was	
	in the wilderness	{in the wilderness
	forty days	2a forty days
to be tempted	being tempted	being tempted}
by the devil.	by Satan.	by the devil.

Mark has the Spirit "drive" Jesus and designates his opponent as "Satan." From conflating his sources, he duplicates "into the wilderness" from Proto-Mark A (shared with Matthew) and "in the wilderness" from Proto-Mark B (shared with Luke).[6]

Matthew, in contrast, has Jesus "led" by the Spirit and designates his opponent as "the devil." For the words in braces ("into the wilderness"), Matthew agrees with Mark and hence may have followed their common source Proto-Mark A, unless Q also included this phrase.

Luke agrees partly with Mark and partly with Matthew. For the words in braces, Luke agrees with Mark and hence followed Proto-Mark B. In the remaining material, Luke agrees with Matthew in having Jesus "led" by the Spirit and in designating Jesus' opponent as "the devil."

In the non-Markan material, Matthew and Luke have the following wording:

ἀνήχθη ὑπὸ τοῦ πνεύματος πειρασθῆναι ὑπὸ τοῦ διαβόλου (Matt)
ἤγετο   ἐν τῷ πνεύματι   ὑπὸ τοῦ διαβόλου (Luke)

This agreement against Mark is close enough in wording to indicate that both Evangelists used Q here.[7] Their differences in wording probably resulted from

---

6. Burkett, *From Proto-Mark to Mark*, 124.

7. For the reconstruction by the International Q Project, see Shawn Carruth and James M. Robinson, *Q 4:1–13, 16: The Temptations of Jesus; Nazara* (ed. Christoph Heil;

redaction by one Evangelist or the other. Thus their differences in this passage arose partly because of redaction but primarily because both combined Q with the Markan source.

OTHER Q SAYINGS IN A MARKAN CONTEXT

After the initial section on John and Jesus, Q includes a number of other sayings that are affected, especially in Matthew, by a Markan parallel or context.

BLIND LEAD BLIND (MATT 15:14B/LUKE 6:39)

The saying "Blind lead blind" in both Matthew and Luke uses the same substantives and verbs in the same order: τυφλὸς τυφλὸν ὁδηγεῖν (ὁδηγῇ,) ἀμφότεροι εἰς βόθυνον (ἐμ)πεσοῦνται. Furthermore, the term βόθυνον occurs elsewhere in Q (Matt 12:11). The saying in both Gospels therefore probably came from Q.[8]

In Luke this saying occurs in the Q sermon (Luke 6:39), but Matthew has it later in a context shared with Mark (Matt 15:14b). Its position in Mathew is not original. Its position in Luke may not be either since the saying interrupts the connection between the two pericopes on judging[9] and precedes another saying that Luke has interpolated into that context from the discourse "On confession" (Luke 6:40; see ch. 4). Furthermore, if the saying stood in the Q sermon, then Matthew must have removed it from there, contrary to his normal practice. The original position of the saying in Q therefore remains uncertain.

The saying in Matthew takes the form of a conditional sentence, while in Luke it consists of two questions. This difference in wording probably arose when Matthew adapted the saying to the Markan context into which he inserted it. Allison suggests that Matthew changed its original interrogative form because "Matthew's Jesus is not asking a question but passing a judgment."[10]

BLESSED EYES (MATT 13:16–17/LUKE 10:23–24)

While Luke keeps the Q pericope "Blessed eyes" in a Q context (Luke 10:23–24), Matthew has inserted it into the Markan parable discourse (Matt

Documenta Q; Leuven: Peeters, 1996), 1–96; Robinson et al., *Critical Edition of Q*, 22–23; idem, *Sayings Gospel Q*, 78–79.

8. Fitzmyer, *Luke*, 1:627; Kloppenborg, *Formation of Q*, 181–82.

9. Manson, *Sayings*, 57.

10. Allison in Davies and Allison, *Matthew*, 2:533.

13:16–17). Matthew and Luke have close agreement in wording in the last verse of this pericope (Matt 13:17/Luke 10:24). The same was probably true originally for the first verse as well (Matt 13:16/Luke 10:23b), but Matthew has apparently adapted it to the Markan context in which he placed it. Luke's version blesses the disciples' eyes because of *what* they see, while Matthew's blesses them because they *do* see. Matthew has assimilated the Q saying to the context of the Markan discourse (Matt 13:13–15; Mark 4:12), which concerns those who do not see.[11]

BEELZEBUL DEBATE (MATT 12:22–30/LUKE 11:14–23)

The Beelzebul debate represents another overlap of Q with the Markan source. I gave a partial analysis of this in chapter 7 (tables 7.4–6).

Only the Q version included the pericopes "Jewish exorcists" (Matt 12:27–28/Luke 11:19–20) and "With or against" (Matt 12:30/Luke 11:23). Matthew and Luke give these pericopes in almost the same wording (table 7.4).

Where the Markan source and Q overlapped, Matthew knew both versions. Such overlaps occurred in three places: the introduction (Matt 12:22–24), "Satan divided" (Matt 12:25–26), and "Strong man" (Matt 12:29).

1. In the introduction to the debate (Matt 12:22–24), Jesus heals a mute man possessed by a demon and is then accused of casting out demons by Beelzebul. Luke too includes all of this (Luke 11:14–15), while Mark includes only the accusation (Mark 3:22). We would expect Matthew's version of this introduction to be a conflation of Proto-Mark A, shared with Mark, and Q, shared with Luke, yet in this pericope Matthew has little wording in common with either Mark or Luke. At least part of the reason for this difference is that in Matthew, the healing of a mute man, common to all versions of the introduction, has been conflated with the healing of a blind man, and Matthew's inclusion of this extra element has affected the wording of the passage.

2. In the pericope "Satan divided" (table 7.6), Mark and Luke have hardly any wording in common since Mark follows the Markan source while Luke follows Q. Matthew shares some wording with Mark and some wording with Luke, an indication that Matthew conflated the Markan source with Q.

3. In the pericope "Strong man" (table 7.5), Matthew agrees closely in wording with Mark, while agreeing hardly at all with Luke. We can infer

---

11. So Allison: Matthew has assimilated Matthew 13:16 to Matthew 13:15, "with the result that there is a shift from the content of what is seen (cf. Luke) to the topic of perception itself" (Davies and Allison, *Matthew*, 2:395).

therefore that Matthew followed the Markan source here (Matt 12:29; Mark 3:27) without using the very different Q version seen in Luke 11:21–22.

Matthew and Luke thus show a mixture of agreement and disagreement in wording in this passage: agreement where they both follow Q, disagreement where Matthew follows the Markan source or his special material.

SEEKING SIGNS (MATT 12:38–40/LUKE 11:16, 29–30)

Matthew included the pericope "Seeking signs" twice, but kept the Markan version in one position (Matt 16:1, 4; Mark 8:11–13) and the Q version elsewhere (Matt 12:38–40). Luke conflated the two versions where the Q version stood in Q (Luke 11:16, 29–30). Both versions include a request for a sign and Jesus' refusal to give a sign, and the Q version includes the exception of the sign of Jonah as well.

1. Matthew's Q version begins with a request for a sign (Matt 12:38). For some reason, Luke inserted this request into the preceding pericope, the Beelzebul debate, at Luke 11:16. Table 8.6 shows both versions.

TABLE 8.6. REQUEST FOR A SIGN

Matthew 12:38 Q	Luke 11:16 PMkB
Then they replied to him,	
some of the scribes and Pharisees,	Others, though,
	testing,
saying, "Teacher, we wish from you	
a sign	a sign out of heaven
to see."	were seeking from him.

Matthew and Luke have very little wording in common in this saying because, while Matthew's version came from Q, Luke's came from the Markan source. In Luke 11:16, the terms "testing," "out of heaven," and "were seeking from him" have no parallel in Matthew's Q version but are found in the Markan version in Mark 8:11 and Matthew 16:1.[12]

2. Table 8.7 shows Jesus' refusal to give a sign.

---

12. Luke added 11:16 "as a foreshadowing of 11:29" using a phrase from Mark 8:11: Fitzmyer, *Luke*, 2:918.

TABLE 8.7. SIGN DENIED

Matthew 16:4 PMkA	Mark 8:12 PMkA/B	Matthew 12:39 Q	Luke 11:29 Q, {PMkB}
An evil and adulterous generation	Why does this generation	An evil and adulterous generation	{This generation} is an evil generation.
seeks for a sign.	seek a sign?	seeks for a sign.	It {seeks} a sign.
	Amen I say to you,		
And no sign will be given to it	if a sign will be given to this generation.	And no sign will be given to it	And no sign will be given to it
except the sign of Jonah.		except the sign of Jonah the prophet.	except the sign of Jonah.

The first two columns of table 8.7 show the Markan version in Matthew and Mark, respectively. The third column shows Matthew's Q version, while the fourth shows Luke's conflated version.

Matthew has standardized the two versions, in this case assimilating the Markan version to the wording of Q.[13] Luke has followed Q in the second half of the verse but has conflated Q with the Markan version in the first half. The term "this generation" is from the Markan source, while "an evil generation" comes from Q. By including both, Luke has doubled the word "generation," which occurs only once in either of his sources. The verb "seeks" (ζητεῖ) comes from the Markan source, for which the Q version in Matthew has ἐπιζητεῖ.

3. The Q version continues with the "Sign of Jonah" (Matt 12:40/Luke 11:30). In this pericope, Matthew and Luke differ widely in wording. Luke's version states that the Son of Man will be a sign to this generation just as Jonah was a sign to the Ninevites. Matthew's version makes explicit the parallel between Jesus and Jonah: the Son of Man will be in the heart of the earth for three days and three nights, just as Jonah was in the belly of the fish for that length of time. Critics generally agree that Luke preserves the more original form of Q.[14] Matthew has redacted it to make explicit his interpretation

---

13. Allison in Davies and Allison, *Matthew*, 2:577, 583.

14. Manson, *Sayings*, 89–90; Fitzmyer, *Luke*, 2:931; Allison in Davies and Allison, *Matthew*, 2:351–52.

of the saying as a reference to Jesus' resurrection. The alternative, that the reference to Jesus' resurrection stood in Q, seems less likely, since then it is difficult to see why Luke would omit it.

To summarize: in this pericope, differences between Matthew and Luke in wording had three causes. In the first part, Matthew followed Q, while Luke followed the Markan version. In the second part, Matthew followed Q while Luke conflated Q with the Markan version. In the third part, Matthew edited the saying to express his interpretation of it as a reference to Jesus' resurrection.

Unforgivable Sin (Matt 12:32/Luke 12:10)

In Matthew 12:31–32, Matthew has conflated two distinct versions of the saying on the unforgivable sin: one shared with Mark from the Markan source, and one shared with Luke from Q (see table 1.1). Table 8.8 shows the Q version.

Table 8.8. Unforgivable Sin

Matthew 12:32 Q	Luke 12:10 Q
32a καὶ ὃς ἐὰν εἴπῃ λόγον κατὰ τοῦ υἱοῦ τοῦ ἀνθρώπου, ἀφεθήσεται αὐτῷ·	12:10 καὶ πᾶς ὃς ἐρεῖ λόγον εἰς τὸν υἱὸν τοῦ ἀνθρώπου, ἀφεθήσεται αὐτῷ·
32b ὃς δ᾽ ἂν εἴπῃ κατὰ τοῦ πνεύματος τοῦ ἁγίου, οὐκ ἀφεθήσεται αὐτῷ	τῷ δὲ εἰς τὸ ἅγιον πνεῦμα βλασφημήσαντι οὐκ ἀφεθήσεται.

Matthew and Luke agree on the words λόγον, ἀφεθήσεται αὐτῷ, and οὐκ ἀφεθήσεται. Their differences in wording can be attributed to Matthew's editing, some of which follows Mark. Luke introduces the two clauses with different forms of the pronoun and uses different verbs: πᾶς ὃς ἐρεῖ and τῷ δὲ βλασφημήσαντι. Matthew standardized both the pronoun and the verb: ὃς ἐὰν εἴπῃ and ὃς δ᾽ ἂν εἴπῃ. His choice of pronoun follows Mark 3:29: ὃς δ᾽ ἄν.[15] While Luke uses the preposition εἰς with the accusative for εἰς τὸν υἱὸν τοῦ ἀνθρώπου, and Luke agrees with Mark on using the same preposi-

---

15. For a different conclusion, see the reconstruction of the International Q Project: Paul Hoffmann et al., *Q 12:8–12: Confessing or Denying; Speaking against the Holy Spirit; Hearings before Synagogues* (ed. Christoph Heil; Documenta Q; Leuven: Peeters, 1997), 427–568; Robinson et al., *Critical Edition of Q*, 308–11; idem, *Sayings Gospel Q*, 118–19.

tion for εἰς τὸ ἅγιον πνεῦμα, Matthew preferred κατά with the genitive for both.

SIGNS OF TIMES (MATT 16:2–3/LUKE 12:54–56)

The saying on discerning the times in Luke 12:54–56 has a remote parallel in Matthew 16:2–3. However, the latter is omitted by important manuscripts. The UBS text includes it in brackets with a certainty rating of "C." The International Q Project has collected the scholarly discussion of the text-critical issue and tentatively concluded that the saying is an original part of the Gospel of Matthew.[16]

Matthew and Luke have very different versions of the saying. The only common words are "the face" and "of the sky." The International Q Project tentatively assigns both versions to Q with a certainty rating of "C"[17] and reconstructs the presumed original form of the Q saying.[18] Other critics think that the two versions came from different sources but disagree on what the sources were. Manson regarded the Matthean version as an interpolation and ascribed Luke's version to Q.[19] Fitzmyer assigns Luke's version to L.[20] Allison theorizes that Matthew's text came from M, while Luke's came from L or Q.[21]

If Matthew's saying is part of the original text, Matthew inserted it into a Markan context, the pericope on seeking a sign (Matt 16:1, 4; Mark 8:11–13). Since we have seen other instances where Matthew inserted a Q saying into a Markan context, Matthew's version probably came from Q. Whether the context in Mark affected the wording of Matthew's Q version is unclear.

In Luke's version, the plural "hypocrites" (Luke 12:56) occurs elsewhere in Luke only in the L story of the crippled woman (Luke 13:15). Luke's version therefore probably came from L. Thus Matthew and Luke differ in wording because they used different versions of the saying and also perhaps because Matthew inserted it into a Markan context.

---

16. Albrecht Garsky et al., *Q 12:49–59: Children against Parents; Judging the Time; Settling out of Court* (ed. Shawn Carruth; Documenta Q; Leuven: Peeters, 1997), 162–76.

17. Ibid., 177–85.

18. Ibid., 186–268; Robinson et al., *Critical Edition of Q*, 388–91; idem, *Sayings Gospel Q*, 126–29.

19. Manson, *Sayings*, 16, 121.

20. Fitzmyer, *Luke*, 2:999.

21. Allison in Davies and Allison, *Matthew*, 2:577.

Spoiled Salt (Matt 5:13b/Luke 14:34–35)

A saying on spoiled salt occurred in both the Markan source and Q. Matthew has the Q version, Mark has the Markan version, and Luke has conflated the two (table 8.9).

Table 8.9. Spoiled Salt

Matthew 5:13b Q	Mark 9:50a PMkA/B	Luke 14:34–35b Q, {PMkB}
	9:50 Salt is good;	14:34 {So salt is good;}
5:13b but if the salt becomes insipid, with what will it be salted?	but if the salt becomes unsalty, with what will you season it?	but if even the salt becomes insipid, with what will it be {seasoned}?
It is no longer good for anything		35a It is fit for neither soil nor manure.
except to be cast out		35b They cast it out.
and trampled by people.		

The third column of table 8.9 gives Luke's conflated version of the saying while the other two columns show the sources that he conflated, as these appear in Matthew and Mark, respectively. For the most part, Luke followed the wording of Q, but the words in braces show influence from the source that he shared with Mark, i.e. Proto-Mark B.

In the Q material, Luke agrees in wording with Matthew almost completely in Luke 14:34b, but differs in 14:35. The common wording in 14:34b indicates that they drew this from their common source Q. The expression "cast out" (ἐκβάλλειν ἔξω) also identifies Q as the source of this saying (B.49; cf. B.51, B.52). The phrase "and trampled by people" in Matthew arose from assimilation of Q to its context in M, as we will see in chapter 9. Thus while Matthew's divergences from Q came from integrating Q into M, those in Luke came from combining Q with the parallel Markan version.

Law to Remain (Matt 5:18/Luke 16:17)

Matthew and Luke share a Q saying on the continuing validity of the Law (Matt 5:18/Luke 16:17). The Markan source included a similar saying (Matt 24:35; Mark 13:31; Luke 21:33). While Luke kept the Q saying in its Q context, Matthew moved it to follow another saying on the enduring validity of the Law (Matt 5:17) in the Sermon on the Mount.

In the Q version of the saying, Matthew and Luke have little wording in common. The main reason seems to be that Matthew has assimilated the wording of the Q version to Matthew 24:34, a saying that precedes the Markan version in 24:35 (table 8.10).[22]

TABLE 8.10. LAW TO REMAIN

Matthew 24:34 PMkA	Matthew 5:18 Q	Luke 16:17 Q
Amen, I say to you that	Amen, for I say to you,	
	until (ἕως ἄν) the sky and the earth pass away,	It is easier for the sky and the earth to pass away
this generation	one yod or one stroke	than for one stroke
will not pass away	will not pass away	to fall
	from the Law	from the Law.
until (ἕως ἄν) all these things happen.	until (ἕως ἄν) all happens.	

The last two columns of table 8.10 show the Q version in Matthew and Luke, respectively. The first column shows Matthew 24:34 from the Markan source. This verse apparently provided the basic structure for Matthew 5:18, including the "Amen" clause in the first row of the table, the form with "until" in the second row, the verb "will not pass away" in the fourth row, and the phrase "until all happens" in the last row. It appears then that Luke better preserves the Q form of the saying, while Matthew has assimilated it to a parallel from the Markan source.

ON DIVORCE (MATT 5:32/LUKE 16:18)

The saying on divorce occurs four times in the Synoptics. Table 8.11 shows the different versions of it.

---

22. John P. Meier, *Law and History in Matthew's Gospel: A Redactional Study of Mt. 5:17–48* (AnBib 71; Rome: Biblical Institute Press, 1976), 62–63.

TABLE 8.11. ON DIVORCE

Matthew 19:9 PMkA	Mark 10:11–12 PMkA/B	Luke 16:18 PMkB, {Q}	Matthew 5:32 M, {Q}
			31 It was said, whoever divorces his wife, let him give her a certificate of separation.
19:9a But I say to you that			5:32a But I say to you that
b whoever divorces his wife	10:11a Whoever divorces his wife	16:18a {Everyone who divorces his wife}	{b everyone who divorces his wife}
c except for unchastity			c except by reason of unchastity
d and marries another	b and marries another	b and marries another	
e commits adultery.	c commits adultery	c commits adultery.	d makes her become adulterous.
	d against her.		
	12 And if she who has divorced her husband marries another, she commits adultery.	d And if the woman divorced from her husband marries, she commits adultery.	e And whoever marries a divorced woman commits adultery.

The first three columns of the table show the saying as it occurs in all three Synoptics in the same place in the Markan outline. The last column shows Matthew's M version.

M includes a series of antitheses, and the saying on divorce in the last column of table 8.11 is an essential part of the third. However, critics disagree as to whether this antithesis formed an original member of that series.[23] Some think that Matthew created the third antithesis out of a Q saying.[24] Others ascribe the antithesis to M,[25] and since we have no evidence that Matthew

---

23. Allison in Davies and Allison, *Matthew*, 1:505–506.
24. Brooks, *Matthew's Community*, 33–36; Allison in Davies and Allison, *Matthew*, 1:528.
25. E.g., Manson, *Sayings*, 23, 157.

expanded the antitheses, this seems most likely. However, since part of it (Matt 5:32b) agrees with Luke 16:18a, it is probable that Matthew conflated a Q version with M. Since the phrase "except by reason of unchastity" (Matt 5:32c) has no parallel in Luke, it could be from either Matthean redaction[26] or M. Matthew 5:32de could be from either M or Q.

Thus the Q version began with "Everyone who divorces his wife" (Matt 5:32b/Luke 16:18a) and may have continued with "makes her become adulterous. And whoever marries a divorced woman commits adultery" (Matt 5:32de).

In Matthew 19:9 in the first column, Matthew agrees with Mark in 19:9bde, but with M (Matt 5:32) in 19:9ac. Matthew has thus revised the Markan version in light of the M version.

In Luke 16:18 in the third column, Luke agrees with Mark in Luke 16:18bcd, an indication that he followed the Markan version for most of the saying. In Luke 16:18a, Luke agrees with Matthew 5:32b, an indication that both also knew a Q version.

Thus while Matthew conflated the Q version with M, Luke conflated it with the Markan version. Such conflation accounts for the differences between Matthew and Luke in the wording of the saying.

OFFENDER'S FATE (MATT 18:7/LUKE 17:1–2)

Matthew knew two versions of the saying "Offender's fate," one shared with Mark and one from Q (table 8.12).

TABLE 8.12. OFFENDER'S FATE

Mark 9:42	Matthew 18:6, 7 {Q}	Luke 17:1b–2 Q
9:42 And whoever causes one of these little ones who believe in me to apostatize, it is better for him if a donkey's millstone is put around his neck and he is thrown into the sea.	18:6 Whoever then causes one of these little ones who believe in me to apostatize, it is preferable for him that a donkey's millstone be hung around his neck and that he be drowned in the depth of the sea.	

---

26. Allison in Davies and Allison, *Matthew*, 1:528.

	{7 Woe to the world from apostasies.	
	For it is necessary for apostasies to come,	17:1b It is unavoidable for apostasies not to come,
	but woe to the person through whom the apostasy comes.}	but woe through whom it comes.
		2 It is more to his advantage if a millstone is put around his neck and he is cast into the sea than that he cause one of these little ones to apostatize.

In this saying, Luke best preserves the Q version. For the sake of clarity, I will designate the first part of this as "a" (Luke 17:1b) and the second part as "b" (Luke 17:2). The version in Mark paralleled only part "b" (Mark 9:42). Matthew combined the two versions. He started with part "b" from the Markan source (Matt 18:6) and then added part "a" from Q (Matt 18:7b). In this way he reversed the order of the Q saying. He probably made this reversal intentionally, to position the expression "little ones" in 18:6 near the references to children in 18:2–5.

Matthew also made some stylistic improvements. He changed the awkward double negative of Q ("it is unavoidable for apostasies not to come") to a less cumbersome positive statement ("it is necessary for apostasies to come"). He also corrected the overly condensed Q version ("but woe through whom it comes") to a more grammatical statement: "but woe *to the person* through whom *the apostasy* comes." The statement that introduces Matthew's Q saying, "Woe to the world from apostasies" (Matt 18:7a), may have come from Q or from Matthew.

In this case, the differences in wording in the Q parallels arose because Matthew replaced part of Q with the Markan version and improved the wording of the rest.

EFFECTIVE FAITH (MATT 17:20B/LUKE 17:5–6)

The saying on effective faith occurs four times in the Synoptics (table 8.13).

TABLE 8.13. EFFECTIVE FAITH

Mark 11:23 Fig tree	Matthew 21:21 Fig tree	Matthew 17:20b Q	Luke 17:5–6 Q
			17:5 And the apostles said to the Lord, "Impart faith to us." 6 The Lord said,
11:23 Amen I tell you that	21:21 Amen I tell you,	17:20b For amen I tell you,	
	if you have faith and do not doubt,	if you have faith like a mustard seed,	If you have faith like a mustard seed,
	not only will you do this thing of the fig tree, but also		
whoever says to this mountain, "Be picked up and thrown into the sea,"	if you say to this mountain, "Be picked up and thrown into the sea,"	you will say to this mountain, "Move from here to there,"	you would say to this mulberry tree, "Be uprooted and be planted in the sea,"
and does not doubt in his heart, but believes that what he says happens,			
he will have it.	it will happen.	and it will move.	and it would obey you.

The first two columns of the table show the version of the saying that Mark and Matthew, respectively, have in the story of the cursed fig tree. The last two columns show the Q version in Matthew and Luke, respectively.

Matthew has attached the Q version to the end of a Markan passage about failed exorcisms (Matt 17:19–20a; Mark 9:28). The only verbatim agreement it has with Luke's Q version is the phrase "faith like a mustard seed." The difference in wording is due to the fact that Matthew has standardized his two versions of the saying. Both begin like the Markan version ("Amen I tell you"), both make the saying a conditional sentence like the Q version ("if you have faith"), and both use the example of a mountain like the Markan version. Thus Matthew has partially assimilated the Q saying to the Markan version (and vice versa), causing the Q saying to diverge from its original wording, which lacked "For amen I tell you" and used a mulberry tree as an example.

HERE OR THERE (MATT 24:26/LUKE 17:23)

The saying "Here or there" also occurs four times in the Synoptics (table 8.14).

TABLE 8.14. HERE OR THERE

Mark 13:21 PMkA	Matthew 24:23 PMkA	Matthew 24:26 Q	Luke 17:23 Q
13:21 And then if someone says to you,	24:23 Then if someone says to you,	24:26 So if they say to you,	17:23 And they will say to you,
"Look, here is the Christ;	"Behold, here is the Christ,"	"Behold, he is in the wilderness,"	"Behold, there"
		do not go out;	
look, there,"	or "Here,"	"Behold, in the private chambers,"	or "Behold, here."
			Do not go forth;
do not believe.	do not believe.	do not believe.	do not pursue.

The first two columns of the table show the Markan version of the saying, while the last two columns show the Q version.

Matthew has assimilated the Q version to the Markan version at the beginning (the conditional "if") and the end ("do not believe"). In between, he has added "in the wilderness" and "in the private chambers." These were originally simply "here" or "there," as the agreement of Mark and Luke's Q version show. It is not clear whether Q had both imperatives at the end (as in Luke) or one after each "behold" clause (as in Matthew). In any case, Matthew's version has diverged from the wording of Q through a combination of redaction and assimilation to the Markan version.

TWELVE THRONES (MATT 19:28B/LUKE 22:28–30)

The final item of Q in Luke's order is the saying "Twelve thrones" (table 8.15).

TABLE 8.15. TWELVE THRONES

Matthew 19:28b Q	Luke 22:28–30 Q, {L}
19:28b you who have followed me,	22:28 You are the ones who have remained with me
	in my trials.
	{29 And I bequeath to you, just as my Father bequeathed to me, a kingdom 30 so that you may eat and drink at my table in my kingdom.}
in the rebirth, when the Son of Man sits on his throne of glory,	
you too will sit on twelve thrones judging the twelve tribes of Israel.	And you will sit on thrones judging the twelve tribes of Israel.

Since the versions of Matthew and Luke have little wording in common, and neither occurs in a Q context, Streeter assigned them to M and L, respectively.[27] Manson followed suit.[28] However, the two versions show fairly close agreement in wording in the first and last rows of the table, an indication that both Evangelists took this material from Q.[29] These parallels at beginning and end probably constitute the original extent of the Q saying.[30]

Matthew has inserted the saying into a Markan context, the pericope on riches and rewards (Matt 19:23–28a, 29–30 parr). To adapt the saying to this context, Matthew probably changed the verb at the beginning to "follow" (contrast Luke: "remain") so that it would correspond to the verb in Peter's question: "we have followed you" (Matt 19:27). Matthew also added references to "the rebirth" and the glorious throne of the Son of Man to clarify when the disciples would receive their reward. The latter reference recalls the M pericope of the judgment of the nations (Matt 25:31).

Luke has conflated the Q saying with a saying in which he bequeaths the kingdom to his disciples (Luke 22:29–30a). This would have come from either

---

27. Streeter, *Four Gospels*, 288.

28. Manson, *Sayings*, 216.

29. Fitzmyer, *Luke*, 2:1412–13; Allison in Davies and Allison, *Matthew*, 3:39, 55.

30. So the International Q Project: Paul Hoffman with Stefan H. Brandenburger, Ulrike Brauner, and Thomas Hieke, *Q 22:28, 30: You Will Judge the Twelve Tribes of Israel* (ed. Christoph Heil; Documenta Q; Leuven: Peeters, 1999); Robinson et al., *Critical Edition of Q*, 558–61; idem, *Sayings Gospel Q*, 150–51.

Lukan redaction or L.[31] The International Q Project regards it as the former.[32] However, the latter is more likely since the saying exhibits the same theme as another L saying: "Do not fear, little flock, because the Father has agreed to give you the kingdom" (Luke 12:32).

CONCLUSION

In the material that we have examined in this chapter, Matthew and Luke combine two overlapping sources, the Markan source and Q. Both use their sources as compilers, not as composers. They do not compose new material, nor do they paraphrase their sources. Where both follow Q, they usually have close to identical wording.

Some differences in wording arose as Matthew in particular edited the Q material. He did so in order to improve the language, to clarify it by interpreting what seemed unclear, and in one case, to provide an exception to the ruling on divorce.

More often, differences in wording arose as the Markan source influenced the wording of Q. This occurred where the Markan source overlapped with Q, or when Matthew placed Q in a Markan context. Such influence took several forms. a) One Evangelist or the other sometimes conflated Q with the Markan material, producing a mixture of agreement and disagreement in the resultant saying. b) Matthew in particular sometimes inserted Q material into a Markan context. In such cases, Matthew usually adapted the wording of the Q material to the Markan context in which he placed it. c) Matthew sometimes preserved a doublet of Q and the Markan source. In such cases, he usually standardized the wording, assimilating the wording of Q to the Markan version and vice versa.

---

31. Fitzmyer, *Luke*, 2:1413.

32. Hoffman et al., *Q 22:28, 30*, 289–95.

9

COMBINATION OF Q WITH M

In the preceding chapter, we examined one cause of differences in wording between Matthew and Luke in Q parallels. In the present chapter, we examine another: Matthew often combined Q with M. We have already observed one instance of this in chapter 7 (tables 7.7–9).

Scholars who adopt the Two-Document hypothesis and related theories generally agree that Matthew had access to material other than his Markan source and Q. Streeter and others thought that this "M" material exhibited a unified Judaistic perspective.[1] Allison and others regard M not as a unified composition, but as a plurality of sources, oral and/or written.[2]

Whatever our view of M, it has its own distinctive language. One example is the expression "Father who is in the heavens," which is a characteristic feature of the M material (Matt 5:16; 5:45; 6:1; 6:9; 7:21; 16:17; 18:10, 14, 19). This expression is sometimes regarded as a creation of Matthew. However, its presence in Mark 11:25 shows that Matthew did not create it.[3] It is a pre-Matthean expression that Matthew particularly favored.

As we shall see, Matthew often knew an M parallel to the Q material. In such cases, he favored M over Q. Matthew also frequently combined Q with M, usually inserting Q material into an M context. In such cases, he generally assimilated the wording of Q to the language of its M context. In the present chapter, we will examine such combination of Q with M in the Sermon on the Mount, the discourse on community relations, the discourse against Pharisees, and the eschatological discourse. Another example may occur in the mission charge, which we will examine in chapter 10.

---

1. Streeter, *Four Gospels*, 150, 198, 238–65, 281–85; cf. Manson, *Sayings*, 21–26.

2. Allison in Davies and Allison, *Matthew*, 1:121–27. For an attempt to distinguish M from Matthean redaction, see Brooks, *Matthew's Community*. For a survey of scholarly views on M, see Foster, "The M-Source."

3. This conclusion stands if Mark did not use Matthew, as I have argued elsewhere: Burkett, *From Proto-Mark to Mark*, 43–59.

Sermon on the Mount

Beatitudes (Matt 5:2–12/Luke 6:20–23)

Both Matthew's Sermon on the Mount and Luke's Sermon on the Plain begin with a series of blessings or beatitudes (table 9.1).

Table 9.1. Beatitudes

	Matthew M	Matthew Q	Luke Q
Poor	5:3	—	6:20b
Grieving	5:4		
Meek	5:5		
Hungry	5:6	—	6:21a
Weeping		—	6:21b
Merciful	5:7		
Pure	5:8		
Peacemakers	5:9		
Persecuted	5:10	5:11–12	6:22–23

Luke has preserved four second-person beatitudes. Since Matthew includes the fourth of these, it came from a source common to Matthew and Luke, that is, from Q. If Luke's fourth beatitude came from Q, it is likely that his first three did as well.[4]

Matthew has eight third-person beatitudes, along with one of the second-person beatitudes from Q. It is not likely that he created the third-person beatitudes, since then it would be difficult to explain why the eighth one forms a doublet with his one second-person beatitude (table 9.2).

---

4. The members of the International Q Project assign Luke's first two second-person beatitudes (i.e., Luke 6:20b, 21a) to Q; but for the third beatitude, they convert Matthew 5:4 from third to second person and assign that to Q. For their rationale, see Thomas Hieke, *Q 6:20–21: The Beatitudes for the Poor, Hungry, and Mourning* (Documenta Q; Leuven: Peeters, 2001).

TABLE 9.2. BLESSING ON THE PERSECUTED

Matthew 5:10 M	Matthew 5:11–12 Q
Blessed	11 Blessed
	are you when they insult you
are those persecuted	and persecute (you)
	and speak every sort of evil against you [lying]
on account of righteousness,	on account of me.
	Rejoice and be glad,
because theirs is the kingdom of the heavens.	because your reward is great in the heavens;
	12 for thus they persecuted the prophets who were before you.

Since Matthew included the second-person beatitude on the persecuted from Q (Matt 5:11–12), he had no reason to create a shorter third-person version as well (Matt 5:10).[5] In fact, it is more likely that the third-person version is the more original, since it has the same two-member form as all the other beatitudes. By contrast, the form of the second-person Q version is anomalous, suggesting that it has been expanded from a more original two-member form. The fact that Matthew includes the same beatitude twice in different forms suggests that he found them in two different sources. And if Matthew did not create the third-person beatitude in 5:10, he probably did not create the other third-person beatitudes either but found them in his special material M.[6]

Streeter theorized that M contained only four third-person beatitudes (Matt 5:7–10). Matthew took the four beatitudes from Q, changed the person and modified the wording to create the remaining third-person beatitudes.[7] However, this would not explain why Matthew would change the person in

---

5. Allison theorizes that Matthew created 5:10 "in order to bring the total number of beatitudes to a multiple of 3" (Davies and Allison, *Matthew*, 1:431). This theory is unpersuasive, since it does not explain why Matthew would create a beatitude that repeated one that he already had.

6. Allison traces four of the beatitudes in Matthew (5:5, 7, 8, 9) to a pre-Matthean source but designates this as Q^{Mt} rather than M (Davies and Allison, *Matthew*, 1:434–36). For reasons that I have already discussed, I have not adopted the distinction between Q^{Mt} and Q^{Lk}.

7. Streeter, *Four Gospels*, 250, 251–52. Streeter regards the blessing on the meek (Matt 5:5) as an interpolation.

three of the Q beatitudes (Matt 5:3, 4, 6/Luke 6:20b, 21b, 21a) but not in the fourth (Matt 5:11–12). The one beatitude that Matthew more certainly took from Q (Matt 5:11–12) he left in the second person. This fact suggests that the beatitudes that are not in the second person did not come from Q. It is more likely, then, that all of the third-person beatitudes came from M.

These observations indicate that M and Q preserved two distinct versions of the beatitudes. Four of the beatitudes in M overlapped with the four in Q. This overlap indicates that both versions developed from an earlier archetype. The Q version may better preserve the number of beatitudes, while M preserves a more original form of the beatitude on persecution, which in Q has been expanded beyond its original two-member form.

In the one Q beatitude that they share, Matthew and Luke have very little wording in common, as table 9.3 shows.

TABLE 9.3. YOU PERSECUTED

Matthew 5:11–12 Q	Luke 6:22–23 Q
5:11 μακάριοί ἐστε ὅταν	6:22 μακάριοί ἐστε ὅταν
	μισήσωσιν ὑμᾶς οἱ ἄνθρωποι
	καὶ ὅταν ἀφορίσωσιν ὑμᾶς
ὀνειδίσωσιν ὑμᾶς	καὶ ὀνειδίσωσιν
καὶ διώξωσιν	
καὶ εἴπωσιν πᾶν πονηρὸν καθ' ὑμῶν	καὶ ἐκβάλωσιν τὸ ὄνομα ὑμῶν ὡς πονηρὸν
[ψευδόμενοι]	
ἕνεκεν ἐμοῦ.	ἕνεκα τοῦ υἱοῦ τοῦ ἀνθρώπου·
12 χαίρετε	23 χάρητε
	ἐν ἐκείνῃ τῇ ἡμέρᾳ
καὶ ἀγαλλιᾶσθε,	καὶ σκιρτήσατε,
ὅτι	ἰδοὺ γὰρ
ὁ μισθὸς ὑμῶν πολὺς	ὁ μισθὸς ὑμῶν πολὺς
ἐν τοῖς οὐρανοῖς·	ἐν τῷ οὐρανῷ·
οὕτως γὰρ ἐδίωξαν τοὺς προφήτας τοὺς πρὸ ὑμῶν.	κατὰ τὰ αὐτὰ γὰρ ἐποίουν τοῖς προφήταις οἱ πατέρες αὐτῶν.

In this beatitude, Matthew and Luke have verbatim agreement in only three phrases: "Blessed are you when," "they insult," and "your reward is great." Elsewhere they disagree. If both versions originally came from Q, then the wording has been revised by one or both of the Evangelists. The International Q Project makes Luke responsible for most of the revision.[8] While Luke probably did revise the saying, we can also see a reason why Matthew would revise it. As table 9.1 illustrates, Matthew here gave preference to M. He took M as his primary source for the beatitudes, using Q merely as a supplement for the one anomalous beatitude. Is it possible that this preference for M might extend not only to the content of M but also to the language of M? In three cases, it does seem that Matthew assimilated the language of the Q beatitude to the language of the parallel M beatitude (Matt 5:10). The verb διώκω ("persecute") appears twice in Matthew's Q beatitude (Matt 5:11, 12) but not at all in Luke's. While this word occurs once elsewhere in Q in the required sense (Matt 23:34/Luke 11:49), it is somewhat more common in M (Matt 5:10; 5:44; 10:23), and it occurs in the context under discussion in the parallel M beatitude. It appears then that Matthew twice assimilated the language of the Q beatitude to that of the M beatitude that precedes it. As a third instance, Matthew also assimilated the singular "heaven" of Q to the plural "heavens" of the M beatitude (Q Matt 5:12; cf. M Matt 5:10).

The beatitudes are the first instance in Matthew where we find a Q saying inserted into an M context. As we proceed, we will see other instances of the same pattern: where Matthew has inserted a Q saying into an M context, the Q saying has little wording in common with Luke's version and exhibits signs of assimilation to the language of its M context.

SALT AND LIGHT (MATT 5:13B/LUKE 14:34–35; MATT 5:15/LUKE 11:33)

In the section on salt and light in the Sermon on the Mount, Matthew has inserted two Q pericopes into a pericope from M (table 9.4).

TABLE 9.4. SALT AND LIGHT

Matthew 5:13a, 14, 16 M	Matthew 5:13b, 15 Q	Luke 14:34–35b; 11:33 Q, {PMkB}
5:13a You are the salt of the earth.		14:34 {So salt is good;}
	5:13b But if the salt becomes insipid, with what will it be salted?	but if even the salt becomes insipid, with what will it be {seasoned}?

8. Robinson et al., *Critical Edition of Q*, 50–53; idem, *Sayings Gospel Q*, 82–83.

	It is no longer good for anything	35 It is fit for neither soil nor manure.
	except to be cast out	They cast it out.
	and trampled by people.	
14 You are the light of the world. A city set on a hill cannot be hidden.		
	15 Nor do they light a lamp	11:33 No one kindling a lamp
	and put it under the basket,	puts it in a hidden place [or under the basket],
	but on the lampstand,	but on the lampstand
	and it shines for all those in the house.	so that those going in may see the light.
16 Thus let your light shine before people so that they may see your good deeds and glorify your Father who is in the heavens.		

The first column of table 9.4 shows the material unique to Matthew in this section. Manson assigns this to M.[9] Both Brooks and Allison assume that this material is Matthean redaction except for 14b, which they assign to Q or M, respectively.[10] Two observations support the view that this material came from M. With the two Q sayings removed, what remains in the first column of table 9.4 constitutes a self-sufficient unit of thought on salt and light. Furthermore this unit exhibits not only thematic but also stylistic unity, employing second-person direct address in contrast to the third-person speech of the two Q sayings. These features of the material suggest that it had an independent existence as a unit before the two Q sayings were inserted into it. The best explanation therefore is that it came from Matthew's special material M.

The middle column of the table shows two Q sayings, one on salt and one on light, which Matthew has incorporated into the M paragraph at the

9. Manson, *Sayings*, 152. Manson's further suggestion, that the rest of this section (Matt 5:13bc, 15) is also from M, is less persuasive.

10. Brooks, *Matthew's Community*, 90–91; Allison in Davies and Allison, *Matthew*, 1:470–71.

appropriate places. The third column shows Luke's parallel Q sayings. Both Evangelists have revised Q here.

1. In the first Q saying, "Spoiled salt," Luke agrees in wording with Matthew almost completely in Luke 14:34b, but differs in 14:35. The common wording in 14:34b indicates that both Evangelists drew this from their common source Q. The expression "cast out" (ἐκβάλλειν ἔξω) also identifies Q as the source of this saying (B.49; cf. B.51, B.52). For the most part, Luke followed the wording of Q, but the words in braces show influence from the source that he shared with Mark, i.e. Proto-Mark B (see table 8.9).

Apart from the words in braces, the differences in wording between Matthew and Luke can be ascribed to the fact that Matthew has inserted the Q saying into an M context (between Matt 5:13a and 5:14) and assimilated the wording of Q to this new context. The phrase "and trampled by people," which Matthew has added to Q, shows two signs of such assimilation. First, the term "trampled" (καταπατεῖσθαι) anticipates the same term in the saying "Dogs and swine" (Matt 7:6) shortly afterward in the M material. Second, the collective expression "people" (οἱ ἄνθρωποι), while not unique to M, is especially favored by that material[11] and appears in this context in Matthew 5:16.

2. In the second Q saying, "Lamp on stand," one textual variant calls for comment. In Luke 11:33c, the phrase "or under the basket" stands in some manuscripts of Luke but not others and is included in brackets in the Nestle/Aland and United Bible Society texts. It probably resulted when a scribe assimilated Luke to Matthew.

In the Q version of the saying, Matthew and Luke have little wording in common, except for the phrase "but on the lampstand." Matthew's "under the basket (μόδιον)" probably preserves Q, in agreement with Mark 4:21. Luke redacted to avoid this expression in the Q saying as well as in his version of the Markan saying (Luke 8:16). Other differences in wording are due to the fact that Matthew has inserted the Q saying into an M context (between Matt 5:14 and 5:16). Matthew adapted it to that context at the beginning, where "Nor" continues the negative in Matthew 5:14b, and at the end, where "it shines" picks up the verb of Matthew 5:16a.

In these two sayings, then, Luke's wording diverged from Q when he combined Q with the Markan source or redacted the saying. Matthew's divergences arose because Matthew assimilated the wording of the Q sayings to the wording of their context in M.

---

11. Matt 5:16, 19; 6:1, 2, 5, 14, 15, 16, 18; 10:17; 19:12; 23:5, 7.

LAW TO REMAIN (MATT 5:18/LUKE 16:17)

The Sermon on the Mount continues with a distinctive section generally known as the "antitheses" (Matt 5:17–48), a construction of M that Matthew has occasionally augmented with Q material. Matthew 5:17–20 forms an introduction to these antitheses. Into this introduction from M, Matthew has inserted 5:18, the Q saying "Law to remain" (table 9.5).

TABLE 9.5. LAW TO REMAIN

Matthew 5:17, 19 M, {R}	Matthew 5:18 Q	Luke 16:17 Q
5:17 Do not think that I came to abolish the Law {or the prophets}. I came not to abolish but to {fulfill}.		
	5:18 Amen, for I say to you,	
	until the sky and the earth pass away,	17 It is easier for the sky and the earth to pass away
	one yod or one stroke will not pass away from the Law	than for one stroke to fall from the Law.
	until all happens.	
19 So whoever relaxes one of the least of these commandments and teaches people to do so will be called least in the kingdom of the heavens.		

Manson, Meier, Brooks, and Allison all regard Matthew 5:19 as pre-Matthean. All but Brooks take 5:17 as pre-Matthean also, though it is likely that the phrase "or the prophets" and other aspects of the saying are Matthean redaction.[12] The saying originally expressed the enduring validity of the Law,

---

12. Manson, *Sayings*, 23; Meier, *Law and History*, 82–85, 101; Brooks, *Matthew's Com-*

but Matthew redacted it to include his favorite theme of Jesus as the fulfill-
ment of prophecy.

Into this M context, Matthew has inserted the Q saying in Matthew 5:18.
This saying serves to agree with and confirm the preceding saying on the
enduring validity of the Law (Matt 5:17) but is unnecessary to the sense of the
context. When it is removed (as in the first column of the table), the connection between 5:17 and 5:19 becomes clearer, and the sense of the M context
remains intact: Jesus did not come to abolish the Law, so it must be kept.
Luke's parallel to Matthew 5:18 also probably came from Q, rather than L,
since it is one of three sayings (Luke 16:16–18) that interrupt the L material,
separating the parable of the rich man and Lazarus (Luke 16:19–31) from its
introduction (Luke 16:14–15).

In their respective versions of the Q saying, Matthew and Luke have very
little agreement in wording. They have a few of the same root words (heaven,
earth, stroke, pass away, the Law) but no verbatim agreement. It is likely that
Luke better preserves the Q version, while Matthew has assimilated it to the
Markan saying in Matthew 24:34, as I have shown previously (see table 8.10).
This assimilation produced the "Amen" clause in 5:18a, the form with "until"
in 5:18b, the verb "will not pass away" in 5:18c, and the phrase "until all happens" in 5:18d. This assimilation, at least the phrase "until all happens," served
to adapt 5:18 to Matthew's redaction of 5:17. The redactional elements "or the
prophets" and "fulfill" in 5:17 and the redactional phrase "until all happens"
in 5:18 all formed part of Matthew's redactional theme of Jesus as the fulfill-
ment of prophecy.

Agree on Way (Matt 5:25–26/Luke 12:57–59)

The first antithesis, "Against anger" from M (Matt 5:21–22), is augmented
by the M pericope "Be reconciled" (Matt 5:23–24).[13] It is augmented further by the pericope "Agree on way" (Matt 5:25–26), which has a parallel in
Luke 12:57–59. In the first part of this pericope (Matt 5:25/Luke 12:57–58),
Matthew and Luke have only a few words in common: "your adversary," "on
the way," "lest," "you," "the judge," and "into jail." In the second part (Matt
5:26/Luke 12:59), they have essentially the same sentence: "I tell you, you will
not get out of there until you repay the last (*quadrans/lepton*)." This common

---

munity, 25–30; Allison in Davies and Allison, *Matthew*, 1:482–84, 495 (assigns 5:17–19 to
Q[Mt]).

13. That Matthew 5:21–24 came from M is agreed upon by Manson, *Sayings*, 23;
Brooks, *Matthew's Community*, 30–33; and Allison in Davies and Allison, *Matthew*, 1:126,
504–505.

wording indicates that at least the second part of the saying came from Q. It was probably Luke who changed *quadrans* to *lepton*, which is the smaller coin, to emphasize the need to pay even the least amount.[14]

Most critics assume that the first part of the saying came from Q as well.[15] If so, it is difficult to determine whether Matthew or Luke better preserves the wording of Q.[16] The alternative would be to suppose that Luke drew the whole saying from Q, while Matthew drew the first part from M and the second part from Q.

In any case, the saying occurs in Matthew in an M context following the M material in the first antithesis (Matt 5:21–24). If Matthew drew this saying from Q, he inserted it into an M context. He probably adapted the order of the clauses to this setting. Luke has the temporal clause ("as you are going") before the imperative of the main clause ("make an effort to be reconciled"). Matthew probably reversed the order to bring the imperative ("be in agreement with your adversary") closer to the similar imperative ("be reconciled with your brother") in the preceding M material (Matt 5:24).

AGAINST DIVORCE (MATT 5:32/LUKE 16:18)

The third antithesis consists of the saying against divorce. I previously discussed this saying in chapter 8 (see table 8.11), and here I simply summarize that discussion. Luke conflated the Q version with the Markan version (Luke 16:18). Matthew knew a parallel version from the third antithesis of M (Matt 5:32) and followed this, possibly modifying it with the phrase "everyone who divorces his wife" (Matt 5:32b) from Q. Thus the wording of the saying differs in Matthew and Luke because Matthew followed M while Luke conflated Q with the Markan version.

AGAINST RESISTANCE AND HATE (MATT 5:38–48/LUKE 6:27–36)

The fifth antithesis is a pericope against resisting evil (Matt 5:38–42), and the sixth is a pericope against hating one's enemy (Matt 5:43–48). Luke has parallels to both antitheses, but inserts the first (Luke 6:29–30) within the second (Luke 6:27–28, 32–36). Matthew probably preserves the more original order

---

14. Garsky et al., *Q 12:49–59*, 409–13; Allison in Davies and Allison, *Matthew*, 1:521.

15. E.g., Manson, *Sayings*, 122, 155; Fitzmyer, *Luke*, 2:1001; Allison in Davies and Allison, *Matthew*, 1:519.

16. Allison in Davies and Allison, *Matthew*, 1:519. For the reconstruction of the Q saying by the International Q Project, see Garsky et al., *Q 12:49–59*, 271–415; Robinson et al., *Critical Edition of Q*, 392–99; idem, *Sayings Gospel Q*, 128–29.

of the material.[17] That Luke's order is secondary here is shown by the fact that it breaks the connection between the command to "Love your enemies" (Luke 6:27) and the justification for that command (Luke 6:32–33).

    1. Table 9.6 shows the fifth antithesis in Matthew and its parallel in Luke.

TABLE 9.6. AGAINST RESISTANCE

Matthew 5:38–42 M	Luke 6:29–30 Q
5:38 You have heard that it was said, "An eye for an eye and a tooth for a tooth." 39a But I say to you not to resist the evil one.	
39b But whoever slaps you on the right cheek, turn the other to him also.	6:29a To the one who hits you on the cheek, provide the other also.
40 And to the one who wishes to go to court with you and take your tunic, leave him your cloak also.	29b And from the one who is taking your cloak, do not withhold your tunic either.
41 And whoever compels you to go one mile, go with him two.	
42a Give to the one who asks you,	30a Be giving to everyone who asks you,
42b and do not turn away the one who wishes to borrow from you.	30b and from the one taking what is yours, do not ask for it back.

According to one perspective, Matthew created the fifth antithesis out of a Q pericope.[18] According to a second perspective, the fifth antithesis stood in M (Matt 5:38–39a, 41), but Matthew augmented it with a pericope from Q (Matt 5:39b–40, 42).[19]

A third alternative seems more likely: that Matthew found the fifth antithesis already in M and used it instead of the parallel Q version seen in Luke. Several observations suggest that Matthew's version came from M, not from Q. First, all of the previous antitheses came from M, a fact that creates a *prima facie* presumption that this one did as well. Second, since Matthew 5:41 has

---

17. *Pace* Kloppenborg, *Formation of Q*, 174; Allison in Davies and Allison, *Matthew*, 1:539.

18. E.g., Brooks, *Matthew's Community*, 40–41; Allison in Davies and Allison, *Matthew*, 1:122, 504–5.

19. Manson, *Sayings*, 23, 159.

no parallel in Luke, it is more likely that it came from M than from Q.[20] If so, it testifies along with Matthew 5:38–39a to the existence of a fifth antithesis in M. Third, Matthew and Luke do not have precise parallels even in the material where they overlap. Where Matthew imagines a lawsuit (Matt 5:40), Luke thinks of robbery (Luke 6:29b); where Matthew pictures borrowing (Matt 5:42b), Luke pictures theft (Luke 6:30b).[21] Fourth, even in the overlapping material, Matthew and Luke have little wording in common. Common wording consists of σε, τὴν σιαγόνα, καὶ τὴν ἄλλην, καὶ, σου, καὶ, and αἰτοῦντί σε. Otherwise the two versions disagree. The cumulative weight of these observations makes it likely that Matthew and Luke preserve two different versions of the pericope, from M and Q respectively.

2. Table 9.7 shows the sixth antithesis in Matthew and its parallel in Luke.

TABLE 9.7. AGAINST HATE

Matthew 5:43–48 M	Luke 6:27–28, 32–36 Q, {L, R}
5:43 You have heard that it was said, "Love your neighbor and hate your enemy."	
44a But I say to you,	6:27a But to you who hear I say,
44b love your enemies	27b love your enemies;
	do well to those who hate you.
	28 Bless those who curse you;
44c and pray for those who persecute you	pray for those who abuse you.
45 so that you may become sons of your Father who is in the heavens, because he causes the sun to rise on evil and good, and he sends rain on righteous and unrighteous.	
46 For if you love those who love you, what reward do you have?	32 If you love those who love you, what credit is it to you?

---

20. Allison ascribes Matthew 5:41 to Q and thinks that Luke may have omitted it "because of his general tendency to exonerate the Romans" (Davies and Allison, *Matthew*, 1:547). However, since the saying is absent from Luke, we have no evidence that Luke even knew it. Furthermore, it contains no feature of style or theme that identifies it as Q material.

21. Fitzmyer, *Luke*, 1:639; Allison in Davies and Allison, *Matthew*, 1:544–46, 548.

Do not even the tax collectors do the same?	For even the sinners love those who love them.
47 And if you greet your brothers only, what more do you do?	33 And if you do good to those who do good to you, what credit is it to you?
Do not even the Gentiles (ἔθνικοι) do the same?	Even the sinners do the same.
	{L 34 And if you lend to those from whom you hope to get it back, what credit is it to you? Even sinners lend to sinners so that they may get back the equivalent.}
	35a But love your enemies 35b and do good
	35c {R and lend expecting nothing back},
	35d and your reward will be great.
	35e and you will be sons of the Most High, 35f because he is kind to the ungracious and evil.
48 So you will be perfect as your heavenly Father is perfect.	36 Be compassionate just as your Father is compassionate.

The second column of table 9.7 shows Luke's version of the pericope. Most of this came from Q. The clause "your reward will be great" (Luke 6:35d) links this passage stylistically to the Q version of the beatitudes, where the same wording occurs (Matt 5:12/Luke 6:23). In Luke 6:32b and 33b, the passage probably referred originally to "tax collectors" and "sinners" as elsewhere in Q (Matt 11:19/Luke 7:34), but Luke apparently standardized both terms as "sinners."[22]

In addition to the Q material, Luke also includes material from L or Lukan redaction. In the Q material, the conditional sentences "if you love" and "if you do good" (Luke 6:32a, 33a) correspond to the preceding imperatives "love" and "do good" (Luke 6:27). In contrast, the conditional sentence "if you lend" (Luke 6:34) lacks a preceding imperative, an indication that it did not originally belong with the Q material. Luke apparently added this material on lending (Luke 6:34, 35c), probably from L. This conclusion is confirmed by the fact that Matthew lacks a parallel for this material.

---

22. Fitzmyer, *Luke*, 1:640; Allison in Davies and Allison, *Matthew*, 1:557–58.

The first column of table 9.7 shows Matthew's version of the pericope. According to one view, Matthew took this from Q, composing 5:43 in order to turn the Q pericope into the sixth antithesis.[23] According to another view, Matthew's version represents an M parallel to the Q version in Luke.[24] The latter view seems more likely for several reasons. First, all of the previous antitheses came from M, a fact that creates a *prima facie* presumption that this one did as well. Second, in this pericope the clause, "but I say to you" (Matt 5:44a), a feature of the antithesis form, has a parallel in Luke (Luke 6:27a). This fact shows that Matthew did not create it.[25] The evidence indicates therefore that Matthew found this antithesis already in M. Third, Matthew's version of the material differs in wording and order from Luke's Q version to such a degree that there is little reason to assign it to Q.

Fourth, Matthew's version exhibits numerous stylistic features of M: the term "persecute" (Matt 5:44c), which occurs elsewhere in M (Matt 5:10; 10:23); the expression "your Father who is in the heavens" (Matt 5:45), a typical feature of M (Matt 5:16; 6:1; 6:9; 7:21; 16:17; 18:10, 14, 19); the expression "have a reward" (Matt 5:46a), which occurs elsewhere in the Gospels only in M (Matt 6:1, 2, 5, 16); the term ἐθνικός for "Gentile" (Matt 5:47b), which also occurs elsewhere in the Gospels only in M (Matt 6:7; 18:17); the pairing of "tax collectors" with "Gentiles" (Matt 5:46b, 47b), another feature unique to M (Matt 18:17); and the term "brother" for a member of the community (Matt 5:47a), a frequent stylistic trait in M (Matt 5:22, 22, 23, 24; 18:15, 15, 21, 35; 25:40; 28:10). While some of these occur in other sources as well, the combination of so many stylistic features of M in such a brief compass indicates that this passage represents an M parallel to Q.

A fifth observation confirms that Matthew and Luke preserve independent versions of this material. Both Matthew's M version and Luke's Q version independently combine two originally distinct pericopes. The first of these is shown in table 9.8.

---

23. E.g., Fitzmyer, *Luke*, 1:627; Brooks, *Matthew's Community*, 41–42; Allison in Davies and Allison, *Matthew*, 1:122, 504–5, 549.

24. E.g., Manson, *Sayings*, 161.

25. *Pace* Allison in Davies and Allison, *Matthew*, 1:550–51.

TABLE 9.8. LOVE ENEMIES

Matthew 5:43–44b, 46–47 M	Luke 6:27, 32–33, 35abd Q
5:43 You have heard that it was said, "Love your neighbor and hate your enemy."	
44a But I say to you,	6:27 But to you who hear I say,
44b love your enemies	love your enemies;
	do well to those who hate you.
46 For if you love those who love you, what reward do you have?	32 If you love those who love you, what credit is it to you?
Do not even the tax collectors do the same?	For even the sinners love those who love them.
47 And if you greet your brothers only, what more do you do?	33 And if you do good to those who do good to you, what credit is it to you?
Do not even the Gentiles (ἔθνικοι) do the same?	Even the sinners do the same.
	35 But love your enemies and do good… and your reward will be great.

The right-hand column of table 9.8 shows Luke's Q version of this pericope. This version is unified by the paired verbs "love" and "do well," which are repeated three times. At the beginning they appear as imperatives: "love your enemies" and "do well to those who hate you" (Luke 6:27bc). They are repeated in two corresponding hypothetical questions: "if you love" (Luke 6:32) and "if you do good" (Luke 6:33). A final exhortation repeats the initial imperatives: "love your enemies" and "do good" (Luke 6:35).

Matthew's M version lacks this symmetrical repetition of the same two verbs. It has a few phrases of verbatim agreement with Luke's: namely, ἀγαπᾶτε τοὺς ἐχθροὺς ὑμῶν, τοὺς ἀγαπῶντας ὑμᾶς, and τὸ αὐτὸ ποιοῦσιν. Otherwise the two versions differ in wording. The motivation for proper behavior in Matthew is "reward" (Matt 5:46a) or doing "more" (Matt 5:47a), while in Luke it is "credit" (Luke 6:32a, 33a), though "reward" also appears in 6:35. Matthew uses "tax collectors" and "Gentiles" (Matt 5:46b, 47b) as negative examples, while Luke uses "sinners" (Luke 6:32b, 33b). Matthew hypothesizes greeting one's brothers only (Matt 5:47a), while Luke hypothesizes doing good to those who do good to you (Luke 6:33a).

In both Matthew and Luke, this pericope is conflated with similar material that was probably once a separate pericope (table 9.9).

TABLE 9.9. BLESS CURSERS

Matthew 5:44c–45, 48 M	Luke 6:28, 35e-36 Q
—	28 Bless those who curse you,
44c and pray for those who persecute you	pray for those who abuse you,
45 so that you may become sons of your Father who is in the heavens,	35e and you will be sons of the Most High,
because he causes the sun to rise on evil and good, and he sends rain on righteous and unrighteous.	35f because he is kind to the ungracious and evil.
48 So you will be perfect as your heavenly Father is perfect.	36 Be compassionate just as your Father is compassionate.

Several considerations suggest that this pericope originated separately from the pericope "Love enemies," with which it is conflated. First, each pericope standing alone is complete without the other. Second, the verbs "bless" and "pray" (Luke 6:28) are superfluous in the first Q pericope, which repeats the verbs "love" and "do well" three times, but they form a fitting introduction to the second pericope. Third, the second pericope provides a different motivation for practicing benevolence toward enemies than the first: not "reward" or "credit," but following God's example as sons of God. Fourth, the two pericopes are combined differently in Matthew than in Luke. Matthew 5:45 comes before the rhetorical questions in "Love enemies," while its parallel in Luke 6:35ef comes after.

The evidence indicates therefore that M and Q contained parallel versions of three distinct pericopes in this section: one on nonresistance (Matt 5:38–42/Luke 6:29–30), one on loving enemies (Matt 5:43–44b, 46–47/Luke 6:27, 32–33, 35abd), and one on blessing enemies (Matt 5:44c–45, 48/Luke 6:28, 35e-36). M and Q independently conflated the last two of these, probably because they were so similar in thought. Luke took the Q version of this conflated passage (Luke 6:27-28, 32–33, 35abd-36) and inserted into it the first pericope (Luke 6:29–30), the golden rule (Luke 6:31) and further material from L (Luke 6:34, 35c), thus carrying the conflation further.

LORD'S PRAYER (MATT 6:9–13/LUKE 11:1–4)

After the antitheses, the Sermon on the Mount continues with a section on devotions (Matt 6:1–18), which includes the Lord's prayer (Matt 6:9–13). This prayer has scholars divided on the question of whether it stood in

Q.[26] Scholars also debate whether Luke's introduction to the prayer came from Q or from Luke.[27] Some critics have thought that Matthew and Luke found the prayer in the written sources M and L, respectively.[28] Others similarly believe that the Evangelists received it through oral tradition from two different church communities that knew it in two different versions.

For two reasons, it seems likely that Luke's version stood in Q. First, in Luke the prayer belongs to a complex of sayings on the topic of prayer (Luke 11:1–13), a type of organization that appears to be typical of Q. Second, the prayer shares two features of style and theme with Q. One of these, the theme of the kingdom of God, while not unique to Q, is a significant theme in Q (B.16). The other shared theme occurs in Luke's introduction to the prayer (Luke 11:1), which refers to John's disciples (B.25). While this theme is not unique to Q either, it does occur in Q in the pericope "John's question" (Matt 11:2/Luke 7:18). Thus Luke's version of the prayer, including the introduction, is organizationally and thematically consistent with Q.

It is more difficult to determine whether Matthew's version came from Q or M. In places it has the same wording as Luke's. They have verbatim agreement in Matthew 6:9c, 10a, 11a, and 13a. Minor differences appear in Matthew 6:11b and 6:12. The major differences are the additional elements in Matthew's version. Whereas the prayer in Luke addresses God simply as "Father," in Matthew it addresses him as "Our Father who is in the heavens." In addition, Matthew's version includes two petitions that are lacking in Luke (Matt 6:10b; 6:13b).

Significantly, all of these additional elements in Matthew's version exhibit typical features of M. The expanded address of the prayer, "Our Father who is in the heavens," is a typical feature of M (Matt 5:16; 5:45; 6:1; 7:21; 16:17; 18:10, 14, 19). A second feature of M is seen in the first additional petition: "May your will be done, as in heaven so on earth" (Matt 6:10b). This expresses the theme of "the will" of the father, a theme found several times elsewhere in M (Matt 7:21; 18:14; 21:31).[29] A third feature occurs in the second extra petition: "Deliver us from the evil one" (Matt 6:13b). The expression "the evil one" is unique to Matthew among the Synoptics, and in several instances probably represents M (Matt 5:37; 5:39).

---

26. Shawn Carruth and Albrecht Garsky, *Q 11:2b–4* (ed. Stanley D. Anderson; Documenta Q; Leuven: Peeters, 1996), 19–33.

27. Ibid., 51–69.

28. Streeter, *Four Gospels*, 277; Manson (tentatively), *Sayings*, 23, 27, 167, 265.

29. It also occurs in a passage common to Matthew and Mark (Matt 12:50; Mark 3:35).

This comparison suggests that a form of the prayer similar to the Q version in Luke was expanded with typical features of the M material to produce the version found in Matthew. Either the Evangelist Matthew himself assimilated the prayer to the concerns of M, or he found this expanded version already in M. While we cannot rule out the possibility that Matthew himself assimilated the prayer to M, it is perhaps more likely that the prayer reflects the liturgical practice of the community from which Matthew drew the M material.

This conclusion is consistent with the fact that the prayer occurs in Matthew in an M context. The M framework into which it fits consists of a series of admonitions concerning devotions that should be kept secret: secret righteousness (Matt 6:1), secret charity (Matt 6:2–4), secret prayer (Matt 6:5–6), and secret fasting (Matt 6:16–18). This series is interrupted after the paragraph on secret prayer by the insertion of three further pericopes on prayer. The first of these is M material (Matt 6:7–8), and the second, the Lord's prayer (Matt 6:9–13), probably is as well. The third (Matt 6:14–15) is either from a source that Matthew shared with Mark (Mark 11:25) or from an M parallel to the pericope in that source.

GOLDEN RULE

Following Matthew's order brings us at this point to the golden rule (Matt 7:12), which Luke places earlier in the sermon (Luke 6:31). Both Matthew and Luke include a positive version of the rule. Didache 1:2 has a negative version of this saying taken from one of its sources, the Jewish "Two Ways" tractate.[30] Matthew's wording resembles Luke's version in some respects, but in other respects resembles the version of the saying in the Didache (table 9.10).

TABLE 9.10. GOLDEN RULE

Didache 1:2 Two Ways	Matthew 7:12 M	Matthew 7:12 Q	Luke 6:31 Q
πάντα δὲ ὅσα ἐὰν	πάντα οὖν ὅσα ἐὰν	—	καὶ καθὼς
θελήσῃς	θέλητε	θέλητε	θέλετε
μὴ γίνεσθαί σοι	—	ἵνα ποιῶσιν ὑμῖν οἱ ἄνθρωποι	ἵνα ποιῶσιν ὑμῖν οἱ ἄνθρωποι

---

30. A reconstruction of the Two Ways document is given by Huub van de Sandt and David Flusser, *The Didache: Its Jewish Sources and Its Place in Early Judaism and Christianity* (CRINT 3/5; Assen: Van Gorcum; Minneapolis: Fortress, 2002), 112–39.

		οὕτως	
καὶ σὺ	καὶ ὑμεῖς		
ἄλλῳ μὴ ποίει	—	ποιεῖτε αὐτοῖς	ποιεῖτε αὐτοῖς
		—	ὁμοίως
	οὗτος γάρ ἐστιν ὁ νόμος καὶ οἱ προφῆται.		

The first two columns of table 9.10 show the negative version in the Didache and the corresponding material in Matthew's version. The last two columns show the Q version in Luke and the corresponding material in Matthew's version. In the first row of text, Matthew agrees with the Two Ways version. In the next row, Matthew's θέλητε combines the subjunctive of the Two Ways version with the plural of the Q version. In the third row, Matthew agrees with the Q version. Likewise in the fourth row, Matthew's οὕτως probably reflects the ὁμοίως at the end of the Q version. In the fifth row, Matthew agrees with the Two Ways version but again adapts this to the plural of the Q version. In the sixth row, Matthew agrees with the positive formulation of the Q version rather than the negative formulation of the Two Ways version. In the final row, the concluding sentence agrees with neither version.

From this comparison, we can infer that Matthew conflated two different versions of the saying: one similar to the Two Ways version in the Didache and one from Q. Since the former version is unique to Matthew in the Synoptics, by definition it belongs to his special material M. A line (—) in table 9.10 indicates material that Matthew omitted in combining the two versions.

The M version in Matthew resembles the Two Ways version in the Didache. However, it is not necessary to suppose that it came from the Didache. It may have come directly from the Two Ways tractate or from some other Jewish source. The golden rule circulated widely in Jewish tradition in a variety of formulations.[31] The concluding statement of the M version, that the golden rule sums up the Law and the prophets, resembles a similar interpretation of the golden rule attributed to Rabbi Hillel (b. Shab. 31a).

One observation suggests that Matthew found the M version of the saying in a written source. The Q version in Luke occurs after the pericope on nonresistance, and this may reflect its original position in the Q document. Matthew has moved the Q version to a later position in the sermon. If Matthew received the M saying from oral tradition, it would have occupied no

---

31. Allison in Davies and Allison, *Matthew*, 1:686–87.

fixed position in a document. Therefore Matthew probably would have left the Q version in place and conflated the M version with it at that position. The fact that he moved the Q version out of its place suggests that the M version had a fixed place in a document parallel to Q and that Matthew moved the Q version to conflate it with the M version at that position. If so, it would seem that Matthew was inserting Q material into an M document rather than vice-versa. Such a procedure corresponds with what we observed previously in the sermon, where Matthew tends to favor M over Q.

NARROW GATE (MATT 7:13–14/LUKE 13:24)

Table 9.11 shows Matthew's saying "Narrow gate" with its parallel in Luke.

TABLE 9.11. NARROW GATE

Matthew 7:13b–14 M	Matthew 7:13a Q	Luke 13:24 Q/L
	7:13a Enter through the narrow gate, because	13:24a Strive to enter through the narrow door, because
	—	24b many, I tell you, will seek to enter and will not be able.
13b Wide the gate and spacious the path that leads to destruction, and many are they who enter through it.		
14 How narrow the gate and restricted the path that leads to life, and few are they who find it.		

Allison cites several theories about the relation between Matthew 7:13–14 and Luke 13:24, but leaves the question open.[32] Streeter is probably correct that Matthew has conflated a Q saying on the narrow gate (Matt 7:13a) with an M saying about the wide and narrow paths (Matt 7:13b–14).[33]

---

32. Ibid., 1:695.
33. Streeter, *Four Gospels*, 283–84.

Matthew 7:13–14 occurs in the Sermon on the Mount in an M context, between the golden rule (Matt 7:12) and the warning against false prophets (Matt 7:15). This saying consists of two parts. The first (Matt 7:13a) has a parallel in Luke 13:24, except that where Luke refers to "the narrow door," Matthew refers to "the narrow gate." Luke knew both a Q and an L version of this saying, as we will see in chapter 10 (table 10.11).

The second part of the Matthean saying (Matt 7:13b–14) has no parallel in Luke and therefore probably came from M rather than Q. It refers to the two ways or paths, the path to destruction and the path to life, a common theme in Jewish tradition.[34] Matthew took the first part of the narrow gate saying from Q and attached it as an introduction to the two ways saying from M.

The differences in wording between Matthew and Luke in this pericope thus have two causes. Matthew affixed the first part of the Q saying to an M saying, while Luke knew an L version of the saying as well as Q.

Tree and Fruit (Matt 7:16, 18–19/Luke 6:43–44)

In chapter 7, we discussed the saying on tree and fruit as an example of a Q saying that Matthew assimilated to M (tables 7.7–9). As we saw, Matthew combined a Q version (Matt 7:18, 16) with an M version (Matt 7:15, 17, 20), assimilating the wording of Q to that of M. This assimilation accounts for most of the differences in wording between Matthew and Luke's Q version. Matthew changed "good tree" in Q to "healthy tree" in order to match M. For the same reason, he changed "rotten fruit" to "bad fruits," "good fruit" to "good fruits," and "every tree by its own fruit is known" to "by their fruits you will know them." In all these respects, Matthew assimilated the Q version to the language of M. It is possible that Matthew changed the saying on grapes and figs (Matt 7:16b) in a similar way to match an M version that he omitted.

The threat of burning a bad tree in Matthew 7:19 occurs in identical wording in a saying of John the Baptist in Q (Matt 3:10b/Luke 3:9b). Either Matthew added this saying from Q to the pericope on tree and fruit, or a previous editor had already added it to M.

Doing the Word (Matt 7:21, 24–28a/Luke 6:46–7:1)

The Q sermon ends with three pericopes: the saying "Lord, Lord" (Matt 7:21/Luke 6:46), the parable of the two houses (Matt 7:24–27/Luke 6:47–49), and

---

34. Allison gives examples of the two ways theme in Judaism and elsewhere (Davies and Allison, *Matthew*, 1:695–96.

the concluding formula (Matt 7:28a/Luke 7:1a). In all of this material, Matthew and Luke show very little agreement in wording.

1. Table 9.12 compares the two versions of the saying "Lord, Lord."

TABLE 9.12. LORD, LORD

Matthew 7:21 M	Luke 6:46 Q
Not everyone who says to me "Lord, Lord" will enter the kingdom of the heavens,	Why do you call me "Lord, Lord"
but the one who does the will of my Father who is in the heavens.	and not do what I say?

Here the two Gospels share only the double vocative "Lord, Lord."

Luke preserves the more original version of the saying. Originally this saying introduced the parable of the two houses that follows it. Both the saying and the parable had the same message: do what Jesus said to do. Luke has retained this message in both parts. In Matthew, however, only the parable preserves this message. The introductory saying has a somewhat different message: do the will of the Father in heaven.

One way to account for Matthew's divergence in wording is to suppose that Matthew has substantially revised Q, which Luke has better preserved.[35] An alternative is that Matthew followed M rather than Q.[36] Matthew's version contains several characteristic features of M, including the expression "the will" of the father (Matt 6:10; 18:14; 21:31) and the designation of God as the "Father who is in the heavens" (Matt 5:16; 5:45; 6:1; 6:9; 16:17; 18:10, 14, 19). The theme of entering the kingdom of heaven occurs in various sources, including M (Matt 5:20). Furthermore, while Matthew has the saying in third person, Luke has it in second person. We saw the same difference in the beatitudes, where the third-person language came from M, while second-person language was used by Q. While we cannot rule out the possibility that Matthew assimilated the wording of the Q saying to the style of M, the number of features typical of M in this brief saying makes it more likely that Matthew found a version of the saying already in M.

---

35. Kloppenborg, *Formation of Q*, 185; Allison in Davies and Allison, *Matthew*, 1:694.

36. Manson, *Sayings*, 176.

2. The same lack of agreement also characterizes the pericope that comes next, the parable of the two houses (table 9.13).

TABLE 9.13. TWO HOUSES

Matthew 7:24–27 M?	Luke 6:47–49 Q
24 Everyone then who	47 Everyone
	coming to me and
listens to these my words	listening to my words
and does them	and doing them,
	I will show you whom he is like.
will be likened to a prudent man	48 He is like a person
who built his house	building a house
	who dug deeply and laid a foundation
on the rock.	on the rock.
25 And the rain came down and the rivers came and the winds blew	When a flood came,
and fell against that house,	the river burst against that house,
and it did not fall;	and it was not able to shake it
for it had been founded on the rock.	because it had been well built.
26 And everyone hearing	49 But one having heard
these my words	
and not doing	and not having done,
them	
will be likened to a foolish man,	is like a person
who built his house	having built a house
on the sand.	on the ground without a foundation.
27 And the rain came down and the rivers came and the winds blew	Against it the river burst,
and knocked against that house,	
and it fell.	and it fell over at once.
And its fall was great.	And the destruction of that house was great.

The structure of this parable is exactly the same in each Gospel: the corresponding clauses and phrases follow the same order in each Gospel. Yet Matthew and Luke have minimal verbatim agreement (πᾶς, μου, καὶ, αὐτούς, οἰκίαν, ἐπὶ τὴν πέτραν, τῇ οἰκίᾳ ἐκείνῃ, καὶ οὐκ, καὶ μὴ, οἰκίαν ἐπὶ τὴν, καὶ,

καὶ). It is possible that one or both of the Evangelists heavily revised the same Q version of this passage. The International Q Project adopts this view, attributing most of the revision to Luke.[37] It is also possible that one Evangelist or the other knew an alternate version of this passage in addition to the one from Q.

We find several typical features of M in Matthew's version. First, in Matthew the parable is narrated exclusively in the third person, while in Luke it is prefaced with direct address in second person: "I will show you whom he is like" (Luke 6:47). We saw the same difference in the beatitudes and the saying "Lord, Lord," and in each case ascribed the third-person language to M, or the influence of M, and the second-person language to Q. Second, Matthew's version exhibits two other stylistic features that elsewhere occur in M passages: the contrast between the "prudent" (Matt 7:24; cf. Matt 10:16; 25:2, 4, 8, 9) and the "foolish" (Matt 7:26; cf. Matt 5:22; 23:17, 19; 25:2, 3, 8).

It is likely that Luke drew his version from Q, which he may have revised. Matthew either assimilated the language of the Q version to M or found a parallel version already in M.

3. The conclusion of the Q sermon is shown in table 9.14.

TABLE 9.14. JESUS ENDS WORDS

Matthew 7:28a; 8:5a Q, {M?}	Luke 7:1 Q
{7:28a And it came to pass when Jesus finished these sayings,}	7:1 Once he completed all his words
	in the hearing of the people,
8:5a At his entering Capernaum,	he entered Capernaum.

Revision of Q by one or both of the Evangelists could account for the differences in wording here. The International Q Project finds the Q version preserved partially in Matthew and partially in Luke.[38] However, given the evidence for an M parallel in Matthew's version of the sermon, we cannot rule out the possibility that Matthew reflects M in 7:28a.

COMMUNITY RELATIONS

In the Matthean discourse on community relations (Matt 18:1–35), as in the

---

37. Robinson et al., *Critical Edition of Q*, 96–101; idem, *Sayings Gospel Q*, 90–91.
38. Robinson et al., *Critical Edition of Q*, 102–3; idem, *Sayings Gospel Q*, 90–91.

Sermon on the Mount, we find M parallels to Q, as well as Q material that Matthew inserted into an M context.

Lost Sheep (Matt 18:12–13/Luke 15:3–7)

One element of this discourse is the parable of the lost sheep (Matt 18:12–13). Matthew's version has only minimal wording in common with Luke's (Luke 15:3–7), such as "a hundred sheep" and "the ninety-nine." To account for the differences, Streeter and Manson theorized that Matthew's version came from M.[39] While this is possible, it might instead be a Q parable that Matthew inserted into an M context.

The parable stands between two passages unique to Matthew, 18:10 and 18:14. Manson assigned these to M,[40] while Allison attributes them to Matthean redaction.[41] Several observations support the view that they came from M. First, with the parable of the sheep removed, the two passages constitute a self-sufficient unit of thought on God's love for little ones:

> 10 See that you do not despise one of these little ones. For I say to you that their angels in the heavens at all times see the face of my Father in the heavens. 14 Thus there is no wish (will) before your Father in the heavens that one of these little ones should be lost.

This feature of the material suggests that these sentences had an independent existence as a unit before the parable of the sheep was inserted into it. Second, this unit contains at least two stylistic features of M: the expression "Father in the heavens" (Matt 5:16; 5:45; 6:1; 6:9; 7:21; 16:17; 18:19) and the theme of the Father's "will" (Matt 6:10b; 7:21; 21:31).

Third, there is one further reason to think that this paragraph stood in an earlier form of the discourse in M: it would explain why Matthew added the parable of the lost sheep to this discourse. The "little ones" here are Christian believers of lowly status, and the concern is that they should not be despised, driven away from the community, and lost. It was apparently the idea of being "lost" that caused Matthew to think of the parable of the lost sheep from Q and to insert it into this M context.

The integration of this Q parable into an M saying affected its wording. The parable, if Luke's version is any indication, originally concerned bringing repentant sinners back to the fold (Luke 15:7). Matthew removed any men-

---

39. Streeter, *Four Gospels*, 265; Manson, *Sayings*, 283.

40. Manson, *Sayings*, 207.

41. Allison in Davies and Allison, *Matthew*, 1:123; 2:752–53.

tion of sinners (Matt 18:13), so that the parable in its new context would refer to bringing back members of the community who had strayed. Matthew's differences from Luke in wording are magnified by the fact that Luke's version of the parable probably came from L, as we will discuss in chapter 10.

ON OFFENSES (MATT 18:7, 15, 21–22; 17:20B/LUKE 17:1–6)

Matthew's discourse on community relations also includes several sayings that stand together in Luke (table 9.15).

TABLE 9.15. ON OFFENSES

	Mark	Matthew	Matthew Q/M	Luke Q
Offender's fate	9:42	18:6	18:7	17:1–2
Correct a brother			18:15	17:3
Forgive 7 times			18:21–22	17:4
Effective faith	11:23	21:21	17:20b	17:5–6

As the last column of the table shows, Luke included all four of these sayings together, presumably from Q. Matthew knew these from more than one source. The first Matthean column shows that the first and last sayings occurred in a source that Matthew shared with Mark.

The next Matthean column shows that Matthew had a parallel to Luke's Q version as well. An examination of the wording suggests that Matthew's parallel came from both Q and M. Matthew inserted the first and last saying of this series into Markan contexts, as we saw in chapter 8 (tables 8.12 and 8.13). Here we are concerned with the two middle sayings (Matt 18:15 and 18:21–22).

1. The first of these, "Correct a brother" (Matt 18:15) forms an integral part of the material in 18:15–17, the instruction on resolving a dispute with another church member (table 9.16)

TABLE 9.16. CORRECT A BROTHER

Matthew 18:15–17 M, {Q}	Luke 17:3 Q
	17:3 Be on your guard.
18:15 {If your brother sins} against you, go correct him	If your brother sins, rebuke him;
between you and him alone;	

if he listens to you, you have gained your brother.	and if he repents, forgive him.
16 But if he does not listen, take along with you one or two others so that "by the mouth of two or three witnesses every matter may be established."	
17 But if he refuses to listen to them, tell it to the church. And if he refuses to listen to the church too, let him be to you like the Gentile (ἐθνικός) and the tax collector.	

The relation between Matthew 18:15 and Luke 17:3 might be explained in one of two ways. Matthew may have taken the Q saying in Luke 17:3 and expanded it.[42] Alternatively, Luke 17:3 and Matthew 18:15–17 may have developed independently as two different instructions based on Jewish interpretation of Leviticus 19:17. Several such instructions have been preserved. Luke's version of the saying resembles that in *Testament of Gad* 6: "if anyone sins against you, speak to him peaceably.... If he confesses and repents, forgive him."[43] Matthew's version resembles the instructions in 1QS 5.24–6.1 and CD 9.2–8, which mandate that the offended party should reprove the offender and do so in the presence of witnesses before bringing the matter to the elders or the assembly.[44]

This previous history of Jewish interpretation makes it likely that Luke 17:3 and Matthew 18:15–17 developed independently. While Luke 17:3 came from Q, Matthew 18:15–17 came from M. In that case, Matthew 18:15–17 belonged to M before Matthew received it.[45] Matthew knew both the Q version and the M version and, though he gave preference to M, he may have taken the first phrase of 18:15 from Q.

Two stylistic features of Matthew 18:15–17 confirm that it came from M. The term ἐθνικός ("Gentile") occurs elsewhere in the Gospels only in M (Matt 5:47; 6:7). Similarly, the term ἐκκλησία ("church") occurs elsewhere in the Gospels only in another M passage (Matt 16:18).

---

42. Brooks, *Matthew's Community*, 100–103.

43. Translation from Fitzmyer, *Luke*, 2:1140.

44. The relevant texts are cited by David Catchpole, "Reproof and Reconciliation in the Q Community: A Study of the Tradition-History of Mt 18,15–17,21–22/Lk 17,3–4," *SNTU* 8 (1983): 79–90, esp. 81–82.

45. Manson, *Sayings*, 209. Allison also attributes the paragraph to a pre-Matthean source but identifies this as Q^{Mt} instead of M (Davies and Allison, *Matthew*, 2:781).

Matthew 18:15 says essentially the same thing as Luke 17:3, but its differences in wording relate it to the rest of the paragraph that follows. The phrase "between you and him alone" contrasts the first effort at correction with the later ones, which involve other people. Using the clause "if he listens to you," as opposed to "if he repents" in Luke, makes it possible to use the same verb for the cases where the brother does not respond to others. And the clause "you have gained your brother" provides a better contrast than "forgive him" in Luke to the alternative scenario in which the brother is lost.

2. Matthew has inserted the second of these sayings, "Forgive seven times" (Matt 18:21–22), into the same discourse between the M sayings on the community's authority (Matt 18:18–20)[46] and the M parable of the unforgiving slave (Matt 18:23–35).[47] It too has very little agreement in wording with the Q version in Luke 17:4 (ἑπτάκις, εἰς, αὐτῷ). It is either an M saying or a Q saying that Matthew revised when he embedded it in this M context. While Luke's Q version recommends forgiving the same offender seven times a day, Matthew's says not seven times but seventy-seven times. Both versions probably arose from a saying that recommended forgiving seven times, a number representing repeated forgiveness. Taking exception to this apparent limitation to seven, Q (or Luke) raised this to seven times "a day," while M (or Matthew) explicitly rejected the number seven, raising it to "seventy-seven."

LAST FIRST

After the discourse on community relations and before that on Pharisees, Matthew has inserted the Q saying "Last first" into an M context (table 9.17).

TABLE 9.17. LAST FIRST

Matthew 20:16 Q	Luke 13:30 Q/L
20:16 Thus shall be the last first and the first last.	30 And behold there are last who will be first and there are first who will be last.

---

46. Manson, (*Sayings*, 209) and Brooks (*Matthew's Community*, 104–7) assign Matthew 18:18–20 to M. Allison assigns only 18:19–20 to M (Davies and Allison, *Matthew*, 2:781).

47. Manson (*Sayings*, 207) and Allison (Davies and Allison, *Matthew*, 2:781, 794–95) both assign the parable to M. Streeter also thought that Matthew found this saying in M. He cites another version of it from the Gospel according to the Hebrews to show that it circulated in more than one version (*Four Gospels*, 281–82). However, the Hebrews version of the saying probably represents a conflation of Luke and Matthew.

Matthew and Luke have little wording in common here except for the key words "first" and "last."

Matthew attached the Q version of the saying to the end of the parable of the hired workers from M (Matt 20:1–15), adapting it to this context by adding "Thus" at the beginning. As we shall see in chapter 10, Luke knew an L version of this saying, and his version may have come from that source.

ON PHARISEES

In the discourse against Pharisees (Matt 23:1–36/Luke 11:37–54), we find a further overlap between Q and M. Table 9.18 shows the probable sources of this material.

TABLE 9.18. ON PHARISEES

	Matthew M	Luke Q	Luke L
Pharisee's dinner			11:37
Hand washing			11:38
Inside and out			11:39–41
Lawyer objects			11:45
Moses' seat	23:1–3		
Heavy burdens	23:4		11:46
To be seen	23:5		
Called rabbi	23:7b–12		
Kingdom locked	23:13		11:52
Proselytes, oaths	23:15–22		
On tithing	23:23	11:42	
Gnat and camel	23:24		
Inside and out	23:25–26	—	
Tombs/graves	23:27–28	11:44	
Prophets' tombs	23:29–32	11:47–48	
Brood of vipers	23:33		
Blood avenged	23:34–36	11:49–51	
Foes plot			11:53–54

The first part of Matthew's discourse (23:1–22) consists primarily of material unique to Matthew. Critics generally agree that this material came from M.[48] The source of the second part of Matthew's discourse (23:23–36) is less certain. This material has a Q parallel in Luke but generally disagrees with it in wording. Table 9.19 gives one example of this disagreement, the saying on whitewashed tombs or unmarked graves.

TABLE 9.19. TOMBS/GRAVES

Matthew 23:27–28	Luke 11:44
27 Woe to you, scribes and Pharisees, hypocrites, because you resemble whitewashed tombs,	44 Woe to you, because you are like unmarked graves,
which appear beautiful on the outside, but inside are full of the bones of dead people and of all uncleanness.	
28 So too, on the outside you appear righteous to people,	and the people walking on them do not know it.
but inside you are full of hypocrisy and lawlessness.	

Here Matthew and Luke do not even have the same sentences, much less the same wording. Such a low degree of agreement in wording also characterizes the rest of the Q material in this discourse. Verbatim agreement is limited to single words or brief phrases:

- Matt 23:23/Luke 11:42: οὐαὶ ὑμῖν, ὅτι ἀποδεκατοῦτε τὸ ἡδύοσμον, τὴν κρίσιν, ταῦτα δὲ ἔδει ποιῆσαι κἀκεῖνα μὴ
- Matt 23:25/Luke 11:39: τὸ ἔξωθεν τοῦ ποτηρίου, καθαρίζετε, ἔσωθεν, ἁρπαγῆς
- Matt 23:27/Luke 11:44: οὐαὶ ὑμῖν, ὅτι
- Matt 23:29/Luke 11:47: οὐαὶ ὑμῖν, ὅτι οἰκοδομεῖτε, τῶν προφητῶν
- Matt 23:34/Luke 11:49: διὰ τοῦτο, προφήτας, ἐξ αὐτῶν
- Matt 23:35/Luke 11:50–51a: αἷμα, ἐκκεχυμένον, ἀπὸ αἵματος Ἄβελ, ἕως αἵματος Ζαχαρίου, μεταξὺ
- Matt 23:36/Luke 11:51b: λέγω ὑμῖν

How should we explain this low degree of agreement in wording between Matthew and Luke? The International Q Project assumes that here Mat-

---

thew and Luke started from the same version of Q and created divergences in wording by redacting this common source.[49] This would mean that Matthew and/or Luke revised the entire discourse to such a degree that very little common wording remains. If, as I have argued, Matthew and Luke functioned primarily as compilers rather than composers, we would not expect either to paraphrase their source to this degree.

Other scholars account for the differences in wording by theorizing that Matthew's M material included the last part of the discourse as well as the first. In the last part, while Luke followed Q, Matthew conflated Q with M.[50] This theory would better account for the differences, with one qualification. If Matthew conflated a parallel version with Q, we would expect his conflated version to exhibit more of a mixture of agreement and disagreement with Luke, like that seen in table 7.6. In actuality, however, it almost always disagrees. One would have to say in that case that Matthew primarily used the M version rather than the Q version even in the last part of the discourse.

Stylistic considerations confirm this conclusion. The last part of Matthew's discourse includes numerous features of style and theme that are characteristic of M. For example, this part of the discourse includes four woes. Luke preserves the simpler form of Q: "Woe to you, Pharisees" or simply "Woe to you" (Luke 11:42, 44, 47). Matthew has a longer form, "Woe to you, scribes and Pharisees, hypocrites" (Matt 23:23, 25, 27, 29), which also appears in the purely M part of the discourse (Matt 23:13, 15). Other stylistic and thematic features of M include the term "mercy,"[51] the adjective "blind"[52] especially in the expression "blind guides,"[53] the expression "tombs" (τάφοι)[54] alongside "memorials" (μνημεῖα) from Q,[55] the verb "appear" (φαίνω) to express outward appearance,[56] the expression "lawlessness,"[57] the term "Gehenna,"[58] possibly the theme of floggings in synagogues,[59] and the theme of persecution from city to city.[60] Matthew uses the term "righteous" (δίκαιος) four times in

49. Robinson et al., *Critical Edition of Q,* 264–89; idem, *Sayings Gospel Q,* 112–15.

50. Streeter, *Four Gospels,* 253–54; Manson, *Sayings,* 96; Allison in Davies and Allison, *Matthew,* 3:265–66, 283–84.

51. Matt 23:23; cf. M? Matt 9:13a; 12:7.

52. Matt 23:26; cf. M Matt 23:17, 19.

53. Matt 23:24; cf. M Matt 23:16; cf. also Matt 15:14a.

54. Matt 23:27, 29; cf. M Matt 27:61, 64, 66; 28:1.

55. Matt 23:29/Luke 11:47; cf. Luke 11:44, 48 v.l.

56. Matt 23:27, 28; cf. M Matt 6:5, 16, 18.

57. Matt 23:28; cf. M Matt 24:12; cf. also Matt 7:23; 13:41.

58. Matt 23:33; cf. M Matt 5:22, 29, 30; 23:15.

59. Matt 23:34; cf. M? Matt 10:17.

60. Matt 23:34; cf. M Matt 10:23.

the last part of the discourse, none of which appear in Luke, in ways that are characteristic of M: in reference to the righteous person,[61] in the combination of "prophets" with "righteous persons,"[62] and in the expression "righteous blood."[63] Mathew uses the term "murder" twice (Matt 23:31, 35), where Luke uses "kill" or "perish" (Luke 11:47–48, 51). This term recalls the language of the commandment, "You shall not commit murder," which occurs elsewhere in M (Matt 5:21, 21). These numerous features of M in the last part of Matthew's discourse confirm that it came primarily from M.

In addition to the woes against Pharisees from Q, Luke included another set of woes from L (last column of table 9.18).[64] This pericope runs as follows: a Pharisee asks Jesus to dinner and is surprised that he does not wash his hands (Luke 11:37–38). Jesus replies with an accusation that Pharisees focus on the outside, not the inside (Luke 11:39–41). A lawyer objects that Jesus is maligning them as well (Luke 11:45). Jesus replies with two woes on the lawyers (Luke 11:46, 52). The scribes (lawyers?) and Pharisees take offense and begin to plot against Jesus (Luke 11:53–54).

Three features distinguish this pericope from the discourse in Q. (1) In Luke, it is addressed to "lawyers" instead of Pharisees, a term that occurs elsewhere in the Gospels only in L (Luke 11:45, 46, 52; cf. Luke 7:30; 10:25; 14:3). (2) The imperative "Give charity" is a characteristic of L (Luke 11:41; cf. Luke 12:33). (3) In Matthew, two components of this pericope (Matt 23:4, 13) occur not with the sayings that have a Q parallel (Matt 23:23–36), but with the sayings unique to M (23:2–5, 7b–22). If this pericope originally belonged with the Q sayings against Pharisees, it would be a striking coincidence that Matthew and Luke should independently distinguish it from Q in these ways. More likely, this pericope did not come from Q; part of one version came to Matthew in the M material, and a fuller version came to Luke from L. This would explain why Matthew's version occurs with the purely M material instead of the material that has a Q parallel. Luke took the version from L and combined it with the Q discourse against Pharisees.

One further observation concerns Luke's L version of the pericope. Jesus' first pronouncement in this pericope (Luke 11:39–41) parallels the saying "Inside and out" in the Q/M discourse (Matt 23:25–26), but lacks the woe form of this discourse. Luke included the version from L and omitted the Q parallel.

If these conclusions are correct, then the differences in wording in the discourse against Pharisees had two main causes. Matthew drew the discourse

---

61. Matt 23:28, 35; cf. M Matt 5:45; 25:37, 46; cf. Matt 13:43, 49.
62. Matt 23:29; cf. M Matt 10:41; cf. Q Matt 13:17 (not Luke 10:24).
63. Matt 23:35; cf. M Matt 27:4 "innocent blood" with variant "righteous blood."
64. So Manson, *Sayings*, 96.

primarily from M, though he also had a Q version for the second part of the discourse. Furthermore, Luke added to the Q material a discourse against lawyers from L.

Eschatology

While Luke kept the Q eschatological discourse separate (Luke 17:22–37), Matthew combined parts of it with the Markan discourse and M (Matt 24:26–27, 37–41). Table 9.20 shows the Q and M material.[65]

TABLE 9.20. ESCHATOLOGY

	Matthew M	Matthew Q	Luke Q
Days will come			17:22
Apostasy, hate	24:10–12		
Here or there		24:26	17:23
Like lightning		24:27	17:24
Rejection first			17:25
Eagles gather		24:28	
Sign, tribes	24:30ab		
Great trumpet	24:31b		
Days of Noah		24:37–39a	17:26–27
Days of Lot			17:28–29
So it will be		24:39b	17:30
No turning back			17:31
Lot's wife			17:32
Taken or left		24:40–41	17:34–35
Eagles gather			17:37

That Luke's version came from Q is shown by Luke 17:25: "First, though, he must suffer much and be rejected by this generation." Here the theme of the rejected prophet and the expression "this generation" are both characteristic features of Q (B.17; B.28). They suggest that this verse came from Q,

---

65. Allison finds pre-Matthean tradition in Matthew 24:10–12, 30a, 30b, and the trumpet in 31 and attributes this to a source common to Matthew and the Didache (Davies and Allison, *Matthew*, 3:327–28), in agreement with John S. Kloppenborg, "Didache 16.6–8 and Special Matthean Tradition," *ZNW* 70 (1979): 54–67.

even though Matthew lacks it. Likewise the theme of Lot's flight from Sodom and Gomorrah (Luke 17:28–32) is a feature of Q (B.33). It links this passage to the Q mission charge (Matt 10:15/Luke 10:12) and the Q pericope "Woes on cities" (Matt 11:20–24/Luke 10:13–15). These links to other Q passages confirm that Luke's version of the discourse came from Q.

Matthew took this discourse primarily from his Markan source and used M and Q merely to supplement it. This preference for Mark may account for the fact that Matthew does not include as much of Q here as Luke does. Matthew has parallels to only some of Luke's Q material.

In the Q material that they share, Matthew and Luke have enough wording in common to make it likely that they used the same source. In the Q saying "Here or there" (Matt 24:26/Luke 17:23), we have seen that Matthew assimilated the wording to the parallel Markan version (Matt 24:23/Mark 13:21; see table 8.14). The remaining differences in wording probably arose through redaction by one Evangelist or the other.

CONCLUSION

The passages examined in this chapter illustrate three reasons for the fact that Matthew and Luke often differ in wording in their parallel material: (1) Matthew often followed an M parallel to Luke's Q material; (2) Matthew often inserted Q material into an M context and assimilated the wording of Q to this new context; and (3) one Evangelist or the other sometimes redacted the same Q version. Here we are primarily interested in the first two of these.

The M material included not only material unique to Matthew, but also material that paralleled some of the material in Q. These M parallels to Q included the beatitudes (Matt 5:3–10), "Against divorce" (Matt 5:31–32), "Against resistance" (Matt 5:38–42), "Against hate" (Matt 5:43–48), the Lord's prayer (Matt 6:9–13), the golden rule (Matt 7:12), "Two paths" (Matt 7:13b–14), "Tree and fruit" (Matt 7:15, 17, 20), "Lord, Lord" (Matt 7:21), "Correct a brother" (Matt 18:15–17), and "Against Pharisees" (Matt 23:23–36). They may also have included "Two houses" (Matt 7:24–27), "Jesus ends words" (Matt 7:28a; 8:5a), and "Forgive 7 times" (Matt 18:21–22). When Matthew knew both an M version and a Q version of the same material, he tended to favor the M version. In some cases he used the M version exclusively. In other cases he conflated the two versions but generally favored M.

Matthew also frequently inserted Q material into an M context. Such Q material includes one of the Q beatitudes (Matt 5:11–12), the sayings on salt and light (Matt 5:13b; 5:15), "Law to remain" (Matt 5:18), "Agree on way" (Matt 5:25–26), "Lost sheep" (Matt 18:12–13), and "Last first" (Matt 20:16). In these cases, Matthew usually reworded the Q material, assimilating it to the language of the M context in which he placed it. This procedure accounts for much of the difference in wording between Matthew and Luke in such material.

Matthew's procedure in combining Q with M resembles his procedure in combining Q with Mark, which we examined in chapter 8. In both cases, the other source takes priority over Q, both with respect to the order of the material and its wording. Mark and M provide the framework into which Matthew inserts the Q material. The order of the Q material is dictated by the order of Mark and M, not by the order of the Q source. Likewise the wording of the Q material is dictated by the wording and context of Mark and M. Matthew assimilates the wording of Q to that of Mark and M and adapts the wording of Q to the Markan or M context in which he places it.

Matthew usually proceeds differently when he is not inserting Q into a Markan or M context. For example, in the Sermon on the Mount, Matthew has assembled a series of four Q pericopes on possessions (Matt 6:19–21, 22–23, 24, 25–33). Though M material precedes this section (Matt 6:16–18), it is set apart from M at the end by other Q material from the Q sermon (Matt 7:1–5/Luke 6:37–42). In this section, Matthew's Q material agrees fairly closely with the parallels in Luke, and most of the differences can be attributed to Luke (Luke 12:33–34; 11:34–36; 16:13; 12:22–31). Here, where Matthew has not integrated Q into an M context, he has not assimilated the wording of Q to M to any great degree.

The same is true for another passage in the Sermon on the Mount: the pericopes "Ask seek, knock" and "Good gifts" (Matt 7:7–8, 9–11). Though M material precedes this section (Matt 7:6) and a conflation of M and Q follows it (Matt 7:12), Matthew has not integrated it with either what precedes or what follows. Hence Matthew's wording agrees closely with that of Luke. Matthew has not assimilated the wording of Q to M. It is when Matthew integrates the Q material with M that he takes greater liberties with the wording of Q.

These results are consistent with the view that Matthew functioned primarily as a compiler and editor rather than as a composer. Matthew had various sources at his disposal, and in combining these sources, he sought to bring a measure of stylistic unity out of their diversity. In this effort, the language of Mark and M took precedence over the wording of Q.

10

COMBINATION OF Q WITH L

We now examine a third cause of differences in wording between Matthew and Luke in Q parallels: Luke often combined Q with L.

Luke's special material, or L, extends from the birth narratives through the resurrection. Critics generally agree that much of it came to Luke from a source or sources.[1] Since it is extensive, constituting about a third of Luke, it would not be surprising to find that it sometimes included the same story or saying as Q. That is in fact what we do find. In some cases Q and L overlapped so that Luke had access to more than one version of the same story or saying. When Matthew and Luke both follow the Q version, they agree in wording. But when Matthew follows Q and Luke follows L, they have hardly any wording in common. We will examine these overlaps in the order in which they occur in Luke.

THREE TEMPTATIONS

After the introduction to the temptation narrative, Matthew and Luke continue with three temptations (Matt 4:2–11a/Luke 4:2b–13). Two of the temptations have a common structure: in both, the devil prefaces his temptation with the phrase "if you are the son of God" (Matt 4:3, 6/Luke 4:3, 9). The third temptation, in which the devil tempts Jesus to worship him, lacks this phrase. While Matthew places the two son of God temptations together before the other, Luke places the distinctive temptation between the two son of God temptations. Critics disagree on whether Matthew or Luke preserves the original order of Q. Luke may have moved the second son of God temptation to the end to serve as the climax because it reflects his interest in Jerusalem or the Temple.[2]

---

1. Fitzmyer, *Luke*, 1:82–85; Paffenroth, *Story of Jesus*, seeks to distinguish between L and Lukan redaction.

2. Fitzmyer, *Luke*, 1:507–8; Allison in Davies and Allison, *Matthew*, 1:364.

Matthew and Luke agree closely in wording when quoting the passages from Deuteronomy in this story since both essentially follow the Septuagint (Matt 4:4, 6, 7, 10/Luke 4:4, 10–11, 12, 8). Elsewhere in the story, they exhibit a mixture of agreement and disagreement. Table 10.1 shows both the agreements and the differences, omitting the passages from the Septuagint. The left-hand column of the table shows Matthew's version of the pericope. The center column shows Luke's verbatim agreements with Matthew, while the right-hand column shows Luke's differences from Matthew.

TABLE 10.1. THREE TEMPTATIONS

Matthew 4:2–11a	Luke 4:2b–13	Luke 4:2b–13
4:2 And	4:2b And	
having fasted forty days and forty nights, afterward		he did not eat anything in those days, and when they were finished,
he hungered.	he hungered.	
3 And approaching,		
the tempter		3 The devil
said to him,	said to him,	
"If you are the son of God, speak	"If you are the son of God, speak	
so that these stones may become loaves."		to this stone so that it may become a loaf of bread."
4 He in reply said …		4 And Jesus replied to him …
5 Then the devil takes him along to the holy city		9 And he brought him to Jerusalem
and stood him on the pinnacle of the temple.	and stood him on the pinnacle of the temple.	
6 And he says to him, "If you are the son of God, throw yourself down …	And he said to him, "If you are the son of God, throw yourself down	
		from here …
		12 And in reply
7 Jesus said to him,	Jesus said to him	
"Again it is written …		that it has been said …

8 Again the devil takes him along to a very high mountain,		5 And bringing him up,
and he shows him all the kingdoms	he showed him all the kingdoms	
of the world		of the inhabited land
and their glory.		
		in a moment of time.
9 And he		6 And the devil
said to him,	said to him,	
		"To you I will give all this authority
cf. 8c	and their glory,	
		because it has been given to me, and I give it to whomever I wish.
		7 You then,
"All these things I will give to you		
if you	if you	
fall down and		
worship	worship	
me."		before me,
		all will be yours."
10 Then		8 And in reply
Jesus says to him,	Jesus said to him,	
"Leave, Satan, for		
it is written …	"It is written …	
11a Then the devil leaves him.		13 And having finished every temptation, the devil withdrew from him until a certain time.

The International Q Project has reconstructed the presumed original form of
Q here, on the assumption that Matthew and Luke both used Q.[3] However, we

---

3. Carruth and Robinson, *Q 4:1–13, 16*, 1–389; Robinson, et al., *Critical Edition of Q*, 22–41; idem, *Sayings Gospel Q*, 78–81.

previously saw a similar mixture of agreement and disagreement in wording in the Beelzebul debate where Matthew conflated Q with the Markan source (table 7.6). Here too, then, it is possible that one Evangelist or the other conflated Q with a parallel from another source.

That Luke did so is suggested by one awkward feature of Luke's narrative. Both Matthew and Luke include the phrase "and their glory" (καὶ τὴν δόξαν αὐτῶν). The phrase makes good grammatical sense in Matthew in the construction "all the kingdoms of the world and their glory" (Matt 4:8). In Luke, however, it does not fit well into its context:[4] "I will give you all this authority {and their glory} because it has been given to me" (Luke 4:6). The possessive pronoun "their" before "glory" requires a plural antecedent, which the preceding term "authority" does not provide. Its antecedent must be the plural "kingdoms" in the preceding sentence (Luke 4:5). When we remove the troublesome phrase, the connection between Luke 4:6ab and 4:6d becomes grammatically correct: the singular noun "authority" is followed correctly by the singular verb "it has been given."[5] It appears therefore that Matthew preserves the more original position of the phrase and that Luke has inserted it into a sentence where it did not originally belong.

One might explain this awkwardness by assuming that Luke moved the phrase "and their glory" from the preceding sentence in Q (Luke 4:5) to place it in Luke 4:6, which he composed.[6] However, it is difficult to see why Luke would move this phrase from a sentence where it fit to one where it does not.

The alternative is to suppose that Luke was combining two distinct sources, Q and L. In this case, Luke did not compose Luke 4:6 but put it together out of two pre-existing components. Table 10.2 shows this conflation of Q and L.

---

4. Beare, *Matthew*, 112; Fitzmyer, *Luke*, 1:516.

5. Matthew 2:19–20 also shows an alternation between singular and plural: while 2:19 refers to the death of Herod (singular), the angel speaking in 2:20 says that "those seeking the life of the child have died" (plural). This alternation, however, is not analogous to that in Luke 4:6. Whereas the alternation in Matthew 2:19–20 corresponds to an alternation between two different speakers (the narrator and the angel), and the sentence spoken by each is grammatical in itself, Luke 4:6 alternates ungrammatically from singular to plural and back to singular within the scope of a single sentence by a single speaker.

6. So Fitzmyer, *Luke*, 1:516.

TABLE 10.2. CONFLATION OF Q AND L IN LUKE 4:5–6

Matthew 4:8bc Q	Luke 4:6c Q	Luke 4:5b–6abd L
4:8b and he shows him all the kingdoms of the world	—	4:5b he showed him all the kingdoms of the inhabited land
		5c in a moment of time.
		6ab And the devil said to him, "To you I will give all this authority,
8c and their glory	6c and their glory	
		6d because it has been given to me and I give it to whomever I wish."

In this alternative, Luke knew an earlier form of 4:6 that consisted of 4:6abd, and into this he inserted 4:6c. Since Luke 4:6c agrees in wording with Matthew, it probably came from Q. Since the passage into which Luke inserted it (Luke 4:5b–6b, 6d) does not agree in wording with Matthew, it probably came not from Q, but from Luke's special material L. In combining Q with L, Luke took the phrase "and their glory" from Q and inserted it into L, where it did not originally belong. Matthew followed Q, which apparently had no parallel to Luke 4:6abd.

If this explanation is correct, then Luke knew two versions of the temptation narrative, one from Q and one from L. Luke's differences from Matthew in wording occur primarily when Luke uses L rather than Q. This conclusion does not rule out the possibility that some of the differences between Matthew and Luke arose from redaction by one Evangelist or the other.

DO NOT JUDGE

In the pericope "Do not judge" in the Q sermon (Matt 7:1–2/Luke 6:37–38), Luke conflated two versions, one from Q (Luke 6:37a, 38c) and one from L (Luke 6:37b–38b). Since we discussed this pericope in chapter 7 (table 7.10), we will not repeat that discussion here.

CENTURION'S BOY

The story of the centurion's boy (Matt 8:5–13/Luke 7:1b–10) provides another example of an overlap between Q and L. This story, in which Jesus heals a centurion's boy at a distance, follows the Q sermon in the sequence of Q. While both Evangelists knew the Q version, it appears that Luke also knew another version from L.

Matthew's version includes a saying on Gentiles coming from east and west that Luke's version lacks (Matt 8:11–12). We can eliminate this from the story as material imported from another context in Q (Luke 13:28–29). Luke in turn has material that Matthew lacks, specifically two delegations from the centurion to Jesus (Luke 7:3–5; 6b, 10). These cannot be dismissed as extrinsic to the story.

The inconsistent features in Luke's account have long been recognized. First, the two delegations to Jesus stand in tension with each other: the centurion sends a delegation of Jewish elders to ask Jesus to come to his house but then sends a delegation of friends to tell him that he does not need to come. Second, the words spoken by the second delegation are in the first person singular as if spoken by the centurion himself. These words seem natural in Matthew, where they are in fact spoken by the centurion, but less natural in Luke, where they are spoken by his friends. Third, Jesus' statement that he had not found such faith in Israel stands in tension with the faith of the Jewish elders who come to Jesus on the centurion's behalf. Fourth, the worthiness attributed to the centurion by the Jewish elders (Luke 7:4) stands in tension with the unworthiness that the centurion attributes to himself (Luke 7:7a). Fifth and finally, Luke uses one set of terms in the material that he shares with Matthew and another set of terms in the material unique to his account. While Matthew refers to the sick person as a "boy" (παῖς) throughout, Luke refers to him as a boy in material that he shares with Matthew (Matt 8:8/Luke 7:7; cf. Matt 8:6, 13), but as a "slave" (δοῦλος) in the rest of the material (Luke 7:2, 3, 10).[7] And while Matthew uses the term "sufficient" (ἱκανός), Luke uses that term in the material that he shares with Matthew (Matt 8:8/Luke 7:6), but the term "worthy" (ἄξιος) elsewhere (Luke 7:4; cf. Luke 7:7a, ἀξιόω).

Various explanations have been proposed to account for these peculiarities in Luke. Fortunately, the International Q Project has published its database for this story, giving easy access to "two centuries of gospel research excerpted, sorted, and evaluated."[8] This database records the following explanations for the fact that Luke includes the two delegations that Matthew

---

7. The term "slave" does occur once in the material common to Matthew and Luke (Matt 8:9/Luke 7:8), but apparently not specifically in reference to the sick person.

8. Steven R. Johnson, ed., *Q 7:1–10: The Centurion's Faith in Jesus' Word* (Documenta Q; Leuven: Peeters, 2002).

lacks.[9] Some scholars think that Luke preserves the more original version of the Q story, which included either the first delegation[10] or the second[11] or both,[12] and that Matthew has simplified it. This explanation would account for Matthew's simplified version, but it would not explain the complexities and inconsistencies in Luke's account. Most scholars therefore think that Matthew preserves the more original version of the Q story, without these delegations, and that Luke has expanded it. But they disagree on the source of that expansion, some attributing it to a revised form of Q known to Luke,[13] others to Luke's special material,[14] and still others to Lukan redaction.[15]

In this discussion, a form-critical argument has played an important role. The story of healing at a distance has been recognized as one particular type of miracle story, and its form has been used as a basis of comparison for the Q story. Two other instances of this type of story also occur in the New Testament. The first, in the Gospel of John (John 4:46–54), is similar to the story of the centurion's boy. In John's version, an official (βασιλικός) goes to Jesus asking him to come heal his son. After some persuasion, Jesus says, "Go, your son lives." The official goes and finds that his son recovered at that exact moment. The second instance, found in Matthew and Mark (Matt 15:21–28/Mark 7:24–30), is the story of a Gentile woman. She comes to Jesus asking him to cast a demon out of her daughter. After some persuasion, Jesus grants her request, she returns home (not mentioned in Matthew), and finds her daughter delivered. In both of these stories, the supplicant goes to the healer personally rather than sending a delegation. In this respect, both are closer in form to Matthew's version of the centurion's son than to Luke's. The effect of this form-critical comparison, therefore, has

---

9. Ibid., 87–131, 240–59.

10. E.g., Allison in Davies and Allison, *Matthew*, 2:19, 22.

11. E.g., Eduard Schweizer, *The Good News according to Luke* (Atlanta: John Knox, 1984), 131.

12. E.g., Robert H. Gundry, *Matthew: A Commentary on His Literary and Theological Art* (Grand Rapids: Eerdmans, 1982), 141.

13. E.g., Sato, *Q und Prophetie*, 55.

14. E.g., Uwe Wegner, *Der Hauptmann von Kafernaum (Mt 7,28a; 8,5–10, 13 par Lk 7,1–10): Ein Beitrag zur Q-Forschung* (WUNT 2/14; Tübingen: Mohr Siebeck, 1985), 247–55.

15. E.g., Robert A. J. Gagnon, "Statistical Analysis and the Case of the Double Delegation in Luke 7:3–7a," *CBQ* 55 (1993): 709–31; idem, "Luke's Motives for Redaction in the Account of the Double Delegation in Luke 7:1–10," *NovT* 36 (1994): 122–45; idem, "The Shape of Matthew's Q Text of the Centurion at Capernaum: Did It Mention Delegations?" *NTS* 40 (1994): 133–42.

been to support the view that Matthew preserves a more original form of the story than Luke.

The problem with this conclusion is that it does not take into consideration all of the evidence. It overlooks another story of healing at a distance, one that is related not in the New Testament, but in the Talmud. The Babylonian Talmud includes several stories about Hanina ben Dosa, a Jewish rabbi in Palestine in the first century CE who had a reputation for total righteousness. In the story that is relevant for our purpose here, Rabbi Gamaliel's son becomes sick. He sends two scholars to ask Rabbi Hanina ben Dosa to pray for him. Ben Dosa prays, then says to them, "Go, the fever has left him." When they return to Rabbi Gamaliel they find that the fever left his son at that very moment (b. Berakoth 34b). Significantly, in this version of the story the supplicant sends a delegation to the healer instead of going personally. In this respect, it resembles the beginning of Luke's version of the centurion's boy.

We need not assume that Luke's version is genetically related to the ben Dosa story. The ben Dosa version does show, however, that the story of healing at a distance could occur in at least two different forms: one in which the supplicant goes personally to the healer and another in which the supplicant sends a delegation on his behalf. Neither is more original than the other; these are simply two different ways of telling the same type of story.

This observation suggests a new way of understanding Luke's account of the centurion's son. Luke has apparently combined two distinct versions of the story: one like that in Matthew, in which the supplicant goes to the healer personally, and one like that in the Talmud, in which the supplicant sends a delegation to the healer. The story shared with Matthew came from Q. Since the second story occurs only in Luke, by definition it belongs to his special material L. While Matthew included only the Q version, Luke combined the Q version with the L version. Thus Luke's similarities to Matthew came from Q, which they both used, and the additional material in Luke came primarily from L, but also from Lukan redaction.

Once we recognize this solution, it is not difficult to identify the material in Luke that belongs to either version. I have set this out in parallel columns in table 10.3. The first column of the table shows Q in Matthew. The second shows Q in Luke along with Luke's redaction, which is enclosed in braces. The third column shows L in Luke.

TABLE 10.3. TWO VERSIONS OF THE CENTURION'S BOY

Matthew 8:5–13 Q	Luke 7:6–9 Q, {R}	Luke 7:1b–5, 10 L
8:5 When he entered Capernaum,		7:1b …he entered Capernaum.
a centurion approached him, entreating him 6 and saying, "Lord, my boy (παῖς) has fallen paralyzed in the house, suffering terribly."	—	2 The slave (δοῦλος) of a certain centurion, who was dear to him, was ill and about to die.
		3 Hearing about Jesus, he sent to him elders of the Jews, asking him to come and heal his slave (δοῦλος). 4 Coming to Jesus, they entreated him earnestly, saying, "The one to whom you would provide this is worthy (ἄξιος), 5 for he loves our nation and himself built the synagogue for us."
7 He said to him, "I will come and heal him."	6 {Jesus went with them.	
	When he was already not far from the house, the centurion sent friends,	
8 In reply the centurion said,	saying to him,}	
"Lord, I am not sufficient (ἱκανός) for you to come under my roof.	"Lord, do not bother, for I am not sufficient (ἱκανός) for you to come under my roof.	
	7 {Therefore neither did I consider myself worthy (ἠξίωσα) to come to you.}	

But only say the word, and my boy (παῖς) will be healed. 9 For I too am a man under authority, having soldiers under myself. And I say to this one go, and he goes; and to another come, and he comes; and to my slave do this, and he does." 10 When Jesus heard, he was amazed and said to those following, "Amen I tell you, with no one in Israel have I found such faith."	But say the word and let my boy (παῖς) be healed. 8 For I too am a man placed under authority, having soldiers under myself. And I say to this one go, and he goes; and to another come, and he comes; and to my slave do this, and he does." 9 When Jesus heard this, he was amazed at him and, turning to the crowd following him, said, "I tell you, not even in Israel have I found such faith."	
13 And Jesus said to the centurion, "Go. As you have believed let it be to you."	—	[Jesus said to them, "Go, the slave is well."]
And his boy (παῖς) was healed in that hour.	—	10 And returning to the house, those who had been sent found the slave (δοῦλος) healthy.

Matthew included the Q version of the story in its entirety, while Luke included only the middle part. In this middle part, where Matthew and Luke both followed Q, they have almost identical wording. Elsewhere, where Luke drew the story from L, Matthew and Luke have hardly any wording in common.

In the Q version, the centurion himself comes to Jesus, and the sick person throughout the story is his "boy" (παῖς). When Jesus offers to come to his house, the centurion states that he is not "sufficient" (ἱκανός) but that Jesus could accomplish the healing without coming. Jesus expresses amazement at his faith, sends him back, and the boy is healed at that moment.

In the L version, the sick person throughout the story is the centurion's "slave" (δοῦλος). The centurion himself does not go to Jesus, but sends a delegation of Jewish elders to ask Jesus to come to his house. When they testify that he is "worthy" (ἄξιος), Jesus himself has the idea of healing at a distance. He sends the Jewish elders back, where they find the slave healed. This version of the story follows the same basic pattern as the story of Hanina ben Dosa in the Talmud.

Luke preserves all of the L version except for Jesus' declaration that the healing is accomplished. I have conjecturally restored this in square brackets in the L column of table 10.3. We can infer that Luke's source included such a declaration, because every version of the story except Luke's has it. In John's version, Jesus says, "Go, your son lives" (John 4:50). In the story of the Gentile woman, Jesus says, "Go, the demon has come out of your daughter" (Mark 7:29).[16] In the Talmud's version, Hanina ben Dosa says, "Go, the fever has left him" (b. Berakoth 34b). And in Q in Matthew, Jesus says, "Go, as you have believed let it be to you" (Matt 8:13). Luke's sources must therefore have included such a declaration, but Luke does not include it from either Q or L. It is not clear why he omitted it. I have restored the declaration in L as "Go, the slave is well," following the pattern provided by the other versions of the story.

Now that we have identified the material from Q and L, respectively, we can see how Luke combined the two. After the end of the Q sermon in Luke 7:1, Luke continues with the L version of the story. It introduces the centurion, his sick slave, and the delegation of Jewish elders, who go to Jesus and ask him to come to the centurion's home (Luke 7:2–5). Luke chose to use this introduction rather than the one from Q, perhaps because it gives such a fine testimonial to the centurion, as one who was worthy because of his philanthropy toward the Jewish community.

After this introduction from L, Luke included the centurion's speech to Jesus from Q. Luke chose to include this, probably because it illustrated the centurion's faith. However, combining this speech with the introduction from L created a problem. In L, the centurion remained at home and therefore did not speak to Jesus personally. How then was Luke to incorporate the centurion's speech to Jesus from Q? Luke could not very well have the centurion himself deliver this message to Jesus, since that would render the Jewish elders unnecessary. Nor could the elders deliver it, since it stated that Jesus did not need to come to the centurion's home, while in L the elders went specifically to invite Jesus to the centurion's home. Luke could have changed the elders' message, but he solved the problem in a different way: he invented a second delegation of "friends" to deliver the message as Jesus is on his way with the elders. This is shown in the middle column of table 10.3, where I have placed Luke 7:6a in braces. Also part of this redaction is Luke 7:7a, where the centurion explains through his friends why he did not come personally. By inventing this second delegation, Luke could keep the centurion at home, as in L, and still have him speak to Jesus, as in Q. But

---

16. Otherwise in Matthew 15:28: "Let it be for you as you wish."

this solution produced a strangely vacillating centurion, one who first sent a delegation to ask Jesus to come and then sent a second delegation to ask him not to come.[17]

For the conclusion of the story, Luke returned to L, as the term "slave" in Luke 7:10 indicates. Here the phrase "those who had been sent" originally referred exclusively to the Jewish elders in L. However, in Luke's conflated and redacted account, it would include the delegation of friends as well.

From these considerations, it seems clear that Luke did not simply revise the Q version of the story of the centurion's son. If that were the case, we would not expect to find two distinct forms of the story represented in Luke, both of which are attested elsewhere. Instead, it appears that Luke combined two distinct forms of the story, adding redaction as necessary to fit them together.

This procedure that I have just attributed to Luke explains all of the peculiar features of Luke's account. First, it explains the tension between the two delegations, one of which asks Jesus to come and the other of which asks him not to come. There was no such tension in Q, which knew neither delegation, nor in L, which knew only the first. The tension arose when Luke created the second delegation as a way of allowing the centurion to speak to Jesus, as in Q, even while staying at home, as in L. Second, it also explains why the words spoken by the second delegation are in the first person singular as if spoken by the centurion himself. Originally, they were in fact spoken by the centurion himself in Q. Third, it explains the tension between Jesus' statement that he had not found such faith in Israel and the fact that the Jewish elders do show faith. Originally these two elements of Luke's account stood in different versions of the story. Q, in which the Jewish elders do not appear, emphasizes the superiority of the centurion's faith to that in Israel. L, however, makes no distinction between the faith of the centurion and the faith of the Jewish elders who represent him. Fourth, it explains the tension between the worthiness attributed to the centurion by the elders (Luke 7:4–5) and the unworthiness that he attributes to himself (Luke 7:7a). The former constituted the perspective of L, while the latter was introduced by Luke's redaction. Fifth and finally, it explains the variation in verbal agreement between Matthew and Luke. Where both follow Q, they agree closely in wording. Where Luke follows L or adds redaction, they have almost no wording in common. So, for

---

17. In two other stories, the supplicant is met by messengers as he returns home. In the Proto-Mark B version of the story of Jairus's daughter, the messengers tell Jairus that his daughter has died (Mark 5:35; Luke 8:49); and in John's story of the official's son, they tell the official that his son has recovered (John 4:51). In neither case, however, do the messengers constitute a delegation from the supplicant himself.

example, where Luke follows Q like Matthew, he uses the term "boy" (Matt 8:8/Luke 7:7; cf. Matt 8:6, 13) and the adjective "sufficient" (Matt 8:8/Luke 7:6); but where he follows L, he uses the term "slave" (Luke 7:2, 3, 10) and the adjective "worthy" (Luke 7:4). In his own redaction he uses neither adjective, but the verb "to regard as worthy" (Luke 7:7a).

In this story, Q and L, while differing in several respects, have one significant feature in common: both identify the supplicant as a centurion, that is, a Gentile.[18] In this respect, they stand closer to the story of the Gentile woman than to the Hanina ben Dosa version or the version in John. The supplicant in the ben Dosa version is certainly not a Gentile, and nothing suggests that the official of John's version is either. Thus the interaction between Jesus and a Gentile constitutes a significant aspect of both Q and L.

While both Q and L present the Gentile in a positive light, Q does so in a unique manner. In all other versions of the story, the idea of healing at a distance comes from the healer. Such is the case in L, John's version, the story of the Gentile woman, and the ben Dosa version. Q, by contrast, is distinctive in attributing the idea of healing at a distance to the supplicant. This feature emphasizes the faith of the centurion, such that Jesus responds with amazement. And since the centurion is a Gentile, the distinctive character of his faith enables the storyteller to laud it as superior to that in "Israel."

It appears then that Luke conflated two distinct versions of the story, one from Q and one from L. When Matthew and Luke both follow Q, they agree in wording; but when Luke follows L, they differ in wording.

ON MISSION

The instructions on mission stood in more sources than perhaps any other tradition in the Synoptic Gospels. Matthew knew various versions of these, all of which he combined in Matthew 10. Luke knew several versions as well, which he combined in two locations, Luke 9:1–6 and Luke 10:1–20. Here we are interested in those instructions that can be attributed to Q, M, or L. These would be found in Luke 10:1–20 and its parallel, as shown in table 10.4.

---

18. Catchpole argues that in Q the centurion was not a Gentile ("Faith," in Catchpole, *Quest for Q*, 280–308). However, he can only maintain this view by attributing the delegation of Jewish elders to Lukan redaction, a view that we have seen reason to doubt. In L, as we have reconstructed it, the centurion was clearly a Gentile, and we have no reason to doubt that the same was true for Q.

TABLE 10.4. ON MISSION

	Matthew M	Matthew Q	Luke Q	Luke L
70 sent				10:1
Pray for workers		9:37–38	10:2	
Sheep of Israel	10:5c–6			
Kingdom come	10:7–8			
No gold/purse	10:9a	—	—	10:4a
No knapsack	10:10a	—	—	10:4b
No sandals	10:10d	—	—	10:4c
Greet no one				10:4d
Worthy of food	10:10f			
Seek one worthy	10:11ab			
Greet the house	10:12–13			10:5–6
Stay in house				10:7
If received		—	10:8–9	
If not received		—	10:10–11	
Better for Sodom		10:15	10:12	
Cities of Israel	10:23			
Woes on cities		11:20–24	10:13–15	
70 return				10:17–20

The middle columns of the table show the Q material in Matthew and Luke, respectively. In three of these passages, Matthew and Luke agree so closely in wording that they must have drawn them with little change from Q: "Pray for workers" (Matt 9:37–38/Luke 10:2), "Better for Sodom" (Matt 10:15/Luke 10:12), and "Woes on cities" (Matt 11:20–24/Luke 10:13–15). The last two of these are linked by the shared sentence, "It will be more tolerable on the day of judgment for X than for Y" (Matt 10:15/Luke 10:12; Matt 11:22/ Luke 10:14; Matt 11:24).

If Luke 10:12 (Matt 10:15) is from Q, then Luke 10:8–12 must be as well, since these verses exhibit a thematic unity. Verses 8–9 tell the messengers what to do in a city that receives them, verses 10–11 tell what to do in a city that does not receive them, and verse 12 gives the consequences for the latter sort of city. That these verses came from Q is confirmed by two stylistic links to other high-agreement Q passages: the sentence "The kingdom of God has drawn near to you" links Luke 10:9 and 11b to the Q Beelzebul debate (Matt 12:28/Luke 11:20), and the phrase "But know this: that" links Luke 10:11b to the Q saying "Unexpected thief" (Matt 24:43/Luke 12:39). Matthew omitted the parallel to Luke 10:8–11 from Q, probably because he had a parallel to verses 8–9 in Matthew 10:7–8 (from M) and a parallel to verses 10–11 in Matthew 10:14 (from the same source as Mark 6:11).

Matthew and Luke have parallel versions of the instructions about what not to take and about greeting a household (table 10.5).

TABLE 10.5. MISSION CHARGE

Matthew 10:9–13 M	Luke 10:4–7 L
10:9a Do not acquire gold	10:4 Do not carry a purse
10a or a knapsack	or a knapsack
10d or sandals.	or sandals,
10f For the worker is worthy of his food.	
	and greet no one along the way.
11ab In whatever city or village you enter, inquire as to who in it is worthy.	
12 As you enter the house,	5 In whatever house you enter,
greet it.	first say, "Peace to this house."
13 And if the house is worthy,	6 And if a son of peace is there,
let your peace come upon it;	let your peace rest on him;
but if it is not worthy,	but if not,
let your peace return to you.	it shall come back upon you.
	7 In that house remain, eating and drinking what they provide. For the worker is worthy of his reward. Do not move from house to house.

In this material, Matthew and Luke have very similar mission charges. Both give similar instructions on what not to take and on staying at someone's house. Their wording, however, differs substantially. Matthew's version is unified by the occurrence of the term "worthy" four times (Matt 10:10f, 11b, 13a, 13c), which Luke includes only once (Luke 10:7), and each version includes material that the other lacks (Matt 10:11ab; Luke 10:4d, 7). Just a few verses before, Matthew and Luke had almost identical wording (Matt 9:37–38/Luke 10:2). What is different about the mission charge that they should now disagree so? It is most likely that Matthew and Luke followed different versions of the mission instructions here.

Manson ascribed most of Matthew's version to M and limited the Q mission charge to Luke 10:8–12 and parallel.[19] If Matthew's version did come from M, we might expect to see some stylistic features of M in the material. One feature fits the requirement. The term "gold" (Matt 10:9a) occurs elsewhere in the Gospels only in M (Matt 23:16, 17, 17) and Matthew (Matt 2:11). It is likely, then, that Matthew 10:9–13 did come from M. The Evangelist Matthew would have found it combined with the M material in Matthew 10:5c–6, 7–8, and 23.

It is also likely that Luke's version came from L, for two reasons.[20] First, in Luke 22:35, a passage unique to Luke, Jesus asks his apostles if they lacked anything when he sent them out "without purse and knapsack and sandals." This question refers back to the instructions in Luke 10:4 not to carry "a purse or a knapsack or sandals." Presumably Luke 22:35 came from L.[21] If so, then so did the mission charge in Luke 10:4–7, to which it refers.[22] Second, Luke 10:8 in Q repeats the instruction in Luke 10:7 about what to eat. These parallel instructions would be redundant in the same source, but explicable if they came from two different sources. Thus if Luke 10:8–12 came from Q, then Luke 10:4–7 must have come from L.[23]

If Luke 10:4–7 came from L and Matt 10:9–13 came from M, it would be a coincidence that both Matthew and Luke placed their respective sources in the same position with respect to the Q material (Luke 10:8–12 par.), unless something in Q guided them both. It is likely, therefore, that Q included at least a partial parallel to the M and L instructions, perhaps a parallel to the instructions on what not to take (Matt 10:9a, 10a, 10d; Luke 10:4abc).

This leaves only Luke 10:1 and 10:17–20 concerning the sending and return of the 70. Since these have no parallel in Matthew, they probably came from L. The L mission charge probably did conclude with the return of the emissaries to Jesus, like the parallel charge in the Markan material (Matt 14:12b; Mark 6:30; Luke 9:10a). However, originally the L mission charge probably referred to the 12 rather than to the 70, since the reference to this charge in Luke 22:35 assumes that it was addressed to the 12. Luke may have revised the L mission charge to address it to the 70 since he had already included a mission charge addressed to the 12 (Luke 9:1–6). Later he

---

19. Manson, *Sayings*, 180–82.

20. *Contra* Fitzmyer, *Luke*, 2:842–43, who assigns this material to Q. Paffenroth (*Story of Jesus*, 46) follows Fitzmyer.

21. So Fitzmyer, *Luke*, 2:1429.

22. Manson, *Sayings*, 74.

23. Ibid., 74.

included Luke 22:35 from L without noticing that it now conflicted with his revised mission charge.

To summarize: Matthew drew part of the mission discourse from Q (Matt 9:37–38; 10:15; 11:20–24) and part from M (Matt 10:5c–8, 23, and probably 10:9–13). Luke drew part of the discourse from Q (Luke 10:2, 8–12, 13–15) and part from L (Luke 10:1, 4–7, 17–20), changing the latter to address the 70 rather than the 12. Where both Evangelists drew from Q ("Pray for workers," "Better for Sodom," "Woes on cities"), they have much the same wording. Their main differences in wording occur where Matthew used M and Luke used L.

Good Gifts

For the Q pericope "Good gifts" (Matt 7:9–11/Luke 11:11–13), Luke may have known a parallel from L. At the end of the pericope, Matthew and Luke agree closely in wording except for two redactional changes, one in Matthew ("your Father who is in the heavens") and one in Luke ("Holy Spirit"). At least this part of the pericope came from Q. At the beginning of the pericope, however, the two Gospels differ not only in wording, but also in content and order (table 10.6).

TABLE 10.6. GOOD GIFTS

Matthew 7:9–10 Q	Luke 11:11–12 L?
9 Or what person is there among you whose son will ask for bread and he will give him a stone?	
Or will ask for fish and he will give him a serpent?	11 What father among you will his son ask for fish, and instead of a fish he will give him a serpent?
	12 Or will ask for an egg and he will give him a scorpion?

Matthew preserves Q here.[24] In Luke, the Q version has been modified to pair "serpent" with "scorpion" as in the L mission discourse: "Behold I have given you the authority to trample upon *serpents* and *scorpions*" (Luke 10:19a). The questions have been reversed in Luke in order to have "scor-

---

24. Catchpole, "Q and 'The Friend at Midnight,'" 414.

pion" follow "serpent." The question is whether Luke himself mimicked this
L motif or whether he found it in L in a parallel version of this pericope. One
consideration favors the latter alternative. To pair "serpent" with "scorpion,"
Luke could have simply changed "stone" to "scorpion"; he had no need to also
change "bread" to "egg." Furthermore, since this pericope is introduced by the
phrase "What person among you," which occurs in L as well as Q (B.34), this
is the sort of pericope that might stand in L. While not certain, it is at least
plausible that Luke has conflated Q with L here.

LAMP OF BODY

The saying "Lamp of body" contains another overlap of Q and L (table
10.7).

TABLE 10.7. LAMP OF BODY

Matthew 6:22–23 Q	Luke 11:34–35 Q	Luke 11:36 L, {R}
6:22 The lamp of the body is the eye.	11:34 The lamp of the body is your eye.	
So if your eye is single,	When your eye is single,	36 If then your {whole body is illuminated},
		not having any part darkened,
your whole body will be illuminated.	your whole body is also illuminated.	the whole {...} will be illuminated
		as when the lamp with its ray illuminates you.
23 But if your eye is evil, your whole body will be darkened.	But when it is evil, your body is also darkened.	
If then the light that is in you is darkness, how great the darkness.	11:35 So watch out that the light that is in you is not darkness.	

The first two columns show the part of the saying that Matthew and Luke
share. Here they agree fairly closely in wording. Both therefore took this material from their common source Q. The third column shows the material unique
to Luke (Luke 11:36), with suspected Lukan redaction in braces. As it stands,
this verse is tautologous, saying that if the body is illuminated it will be illuminated; it therefore makes little sense.[25] I suggest that Luke caused the problem

by adapting an L parallel to the Q saying. Originally the L version would have read, "If then your [eye is single], not having any part darkened, the whole [body] will be illuminated as when the lamp with its ray illuminates you." Like the parallel in Q, it compared the eye to a lamp that illuminated the whole body. But since Luke placed the L version after its Q parallel, which already mentioned the whole body being illuminated, he changed the first part of L (Luke 11:36a) to reflect that state and thus rendered the saying meaningless.

On Possessions

Luke includes a section on possessions that consists of six pericopes: "Not a divider" (12:13–14), "Against greed" (12:15), "Rich fool" (12:16–21), "Do not worry" (12:22–31), "Little flock" (12:32), and "On treasure" (12:33–34). In chapter 5, I argued that "Against greed" and "Rich fool" probably came from Q even though only Luke includes them. The two pericopes "Do not worry" and "On treasure" also stood in Q, since Matthew also includes them (Matt 6:25–33; 6:19–21). An examination of these two pericopes suggests that Luke also knew them in an L version, which he conflated with the Q version.

Do not Worry (Matt 6:25–33/Luke 12:22–31)

In the pericope "Do not worry," Matthew and Luke show a mixture of agreement and disagreement in wording, similar to what we have seen when one Evangelist conflates two sources (e.g., table 7.6). The agreements indicate that both Evangelists used Q. Some of the differences can, no doubt, be ascribed to redaction, such as Matthew's substitution of "your heavenly Father" for "God" (Matt 6:26, 32) and the same Evangelist's addition of the phrase "and his righteousness" (Matt 6:33). Other variations, however, may reflect the differences between two different versions of the material. Table 10.8 shows the most significant variations.

---

25. "The sense of the verse is quite contested" (Fitzmyer, *Luke*, 2:941). Allison supports Torrey's theory that the saying reflects a mistranslation of an Aramaic original (*Jesus Tradition in Q*, 162–63).

TABLE 10.8. DIFFERENCES IN WORDING IN "DO NOT WORRY"

Matthew 6:25–33 Q	Luke 12:22–31 L
6:26a ἐμβλέψατε εἰς τὰ πετεινὰ τοῦ οὐρανοῦ	12:24a κατανοήσατε τοὺς κόρακας
26c οὐδὲ συνάγουσιν εἰς ἀποθήκας	24c οἷς οὐκ ἔστιν ταμεῖον οὐδὲ ἀποθήκη
26e οὐχ ὑμεῖς μᾶλλον διαφέρετε αὐτῶν;	24e πόσῳ μᾶλλον ὑμεῖς διαφέρετε τῶν πετεινῶν.
28a καὶ περὶ ἐνδύματος τί μεριμνᾶτε;	26 εἰ οὖν οὐδὲ ἐλάχιστον δύνασθε, τί περὶ τῶν λοιπῶν μεριμνᾶτε;
31 μὴ οὖν μεριμνήσητε λέγοντες· τί φάγωμεν; ἤ· τί πίωμεν; ἤ· τί περιβαλώμεθα;	29 καὶ ὑμεῖς μὴ ζητεῖτε τί φάγητε καὶ τί πίητε καὶ μὴ μετεωρίζεσθε

Did these differences arise through redaction of the same version by one Evangelist or the other, or do they represent two different versions of the material? One feature of Luke's wording suggests the latter alternative. In Matthew 6:26c, Matthew mentions gathering into granaries (ἀποθήκας), a recurring motif in Q (B.12). In the parallel (Luke 12:24c), Luke mentions two different types of storage places, ταμεῖον and ἀποθήκη. This is the type of doubling that might occur if Luke were conflating two different versions of the material, each using a different term for "storage place." Luke therefore may have known an L version of this pericope as well as a Q version.

The pericope probably ended originally with the admonition "seek first the kingdom of God and all these things will be added to you" (Matt 6:33/ Luke 12:31). Following this ending, Matthew includes an admonition not to worry about tomorrow (Matt 6:34), while Luke has a completely different admonition not to be afraid (Luke 12:32). These probably came from M and L, respectively.

ON TREASURE (MATT 6:19–21/LUKE 12:33–34)

Table 10.9 shows another Q/L overlap in the pericope "On treasure."

TABLE 10.9. ON TREASURE

Matthew 6:19–21 Q	Luke 12:34 Q	Luke 12:33 L
		12:33a Sell your belongings and give charity. Make for yourselves purses that do not grow old,
6:19 Do not treasure up for yourselves treasures on the earth, where moth and rust corrupt and where thieves break in and steal. 20 But treasure up for yourselves	—	
treasures in heaven, where neither moth nor rust corrupts and where thieves do not break in or steal.	33b an inexhaustible treasure in the heavens, where thief does not come near and moth does not ruin.	33b an inexhaustible treasure in the heavens, where thief does not come near and moth does not ruin.
21 For where your (s.) treasure is, there will be your (s.) heart also.	34 For where your (pl.) treasure is, there your (pl.) heart also will be.	

In this saying, the three parts of Luke exhibit three different degrees of agreement with Matthew: Luke 12:33a has no agreement, 12:33b shows a mixture of agreement and disagreement, and 12:34 agrees closely. Streeter and Manson explained this variation by theorizing that while Luke followed Q, Matthew combined Q with M.[26] Manson specified that Matthew 6:19–20 came from M, while 6:21 came from Q. However, features of style and theme indicate that Matthew's version came from Q. The combination of "thief" (κλέπτης; B.43) and "break in" (διορύσσω; B.44) occurs in the New Testament only here and in the Q saying "Unexpected thief" (Matt 24:43/Luke 12:39).

If Matthew used Q,[27] then the differences in Luke 12:33a came either from

---

26. Streeter, Four Gospels, 284; Manson, Sayings, 172, cf. 114.

27. The International Q Project adopts Matthew's version almost in toto as Q: Steven R. Johnson, Q 12:33–34: Storing up Treasures in Heaven (Documenta Q; Leuven: Peeters, 2007); Robinson et al., Critical Edition of Q, 328–33; idem, Sayings Gospel Q, 120–21.

Lukan redaction of Q or from L. The former view, held by some critics,[28] is based on the assumption that the saying contains two stylistic features of Lukan redaction. However, both features more probably came from L. The expression "give charity," δότε ἐλεημοσύνην occurs here and in Luke 11:41, which probably came from L (see table 9.18 and the discussion there). The term "purse," βαλλάντιον, occurs here as well as in Luke 10:4 and 22:35–36, both of which passages probably came from L (see above at tables 10.4–5). It seems likely therefore that Luke 12:33a also came from L.[29]

Luke 12:34 has much the same wording as Matthew 6:21, an indication that both verses came from Q. The main question is whether Luke 12:33b came from Q or L. The term "inexhaustible" (ἀνέκλειπτος) may have come from Luke's hand, since it occurs only here in the New Testament. However, the related verb ἐκλείπω is L vocabulary, occurring three times in L (Luke 16:9; 22:32; 23:45 v.l.) but nowhere else in the Gospels. This term suggests that Luke 12:33b continued 12:33a in L. However, other wording in Luke 12:33b matches that of Q in Matthew. Thus neither Q nor L can be ruled out as the source for Luke 12:33b. It may be that Luke conflated them here.

If these conclusions are correct, Luke conflated Q with L in the two pericopes "Do not worry" and "On treasure." Matthew and Luke agree in wording when both follow Q but differ when Luke follows L.

Faithful or Not

In the Q pericope "Faithful or not," Matthew and Luke have the same wording for the most part. They also exhibit several differences (table 10.10).

TABLE 10.10. DIFFERENCES IN WORDING IN "FAITHFUL OR NOT"

Matthew 24:45–51 Q	Luke 12:42–46, 47–48a Q, {L}
slave	manager
appointed	will appoint
household	staff
food	grain allowance
amen	truly

---

28. Fitzmyer, *Luke*, 2:981; Allison in Davies and Allison, *Matthew*, 1:630–31; Paffenroth, *Story of Jesus*, 42.

29. It is doubtful that Mark 10:21 (Luke 18:22) influenced Luke 12:33a since the only word in common is "sell."

his fellow slaves	the boys and girls
with the drunks	and get drunk
hypocrites	unbelievers
51b There, there will be weeping and gnashing of teeth.	{47 That slave who knew the will of his Lord, but did not prepare for or do his will, will be beaten with many blows. 48a But the one who did not know, but did things worthy of blows, will be beaten with few blows.}

For the first part of this pericope, the differences are probably not exten-sive enough to indicate that one Evangelist used a source that overlapped with Q. More likely, they can be explained as redaction of Q by one Evangelist or the other. The International Q Project credits Matthew with better preserving the Q version, except for the term "hypocrites."[30]

The ending is a different matter. The Q pericope probably concluded with the sentence "There, there will be weeping and gnashing of teeth," as in Matthew 24:51b. Since this description of eschatological punishment occurs several times in Matthew, it is often assigned to Matthean redaction; but since it also occurs once in Luke (Luke 13:28), it is probably a sentence from Q that Luke tended to omit. In the present instance, he did not simply omit it, but replaced it with an alternative vision of eschatological punishment in Luke 12:47–48a. This came from L.[31] While the description in Q did not dis-tinguish between degrees of punishment, Luke replaced it with a description that did.

SIGNS OF TIMES

We discussed the pericope "Signs of times" (Matt 16:2–3/Luke 12:54–56) in chapter 8. Matthew's version probably came from Q, and Matthew inserted it into a Markan context. Luke's version probably came from L, since the plural "hypocrites" (Luke 12:56) occurs elsewhere in Luke only in the L story of the crippled woman (Luke 13:15). Thus the two versions of the saying probably represent an overlap of Q and L. Matthew and Luke differ in wording here primarily because they used different versions of the saying.

---

30. Robinson et al., *Critical Edition of Q*, 366–75; idem, *Sayings Gospel Q*, 124–27.

31. Fitzmyer, *Luke*, 2:991.

FEW SAVED

Luke's section "Few saved" (Luke 13:23–30) consists of a series of sayings which threaten that most people will be excluded from the kingdom (table 10.11).

TABLE 10.11. FEW SAVED

	Matthew M	Matthew Q	Luke Q	Luke L
Are few saved				13:23
Narrow gate		7:13a	—	13:24
Don't know you	25:10–12	7:22–23	13:26–27	13:25
Sons excluded		8:11–12	(13:28–29)	(13:28–29)
Last first		20:16	—	13:30

As the table shows, these sayings stand adjacent to one another in Luke 13:23–30, while in Matthew the Q sayings are separated, though still in the same order. Luke probably preserved the original unity of these sayings.[32]

Luke knew two versions of this section, one shared with Matthew (Q) and one unique to Luke (L). The presence of L is clearest in Luke 13:25/13:26–27, where Luke includes both the Q version and the L version, and in Luke 13:28–29, where Luke conflates the two versions. Luke 13:24 and 13:30 might come from either Q or L.

Matthew has a parallel for all of this material except Luke 13:23, in which someone asks Jesus if the saved are few. Either Luke found this verse in L or composed it himself as an introduction to the section. We will examine the remaining sayings individually.

NARROW GATE (MATT 7:13A/LUKE 13:24)

The first item in the series is the pericope "Narrow gate." As we saw previously (table 9.11), Matthew affixed the first part of the saying (Matt 7:13a) to a saying from M on two ways (Matt 7:13b–14). Luke may have followed L for the term "door" in contrast to "gate" in Matthew, which probably came from Q.

---

32. So Kloppenborg, *Formation of Q*, 225; Fitzmyer is uncertain that Luke 13:24–29 formed a unit in Q (*Luke*, 2:1022).

Don't Know You (Matt 7:22–23/Luke 13:25)

The next item in the series is the pericope "Don't know you." Both Matthew and Luke include two versions of this (table 10.12).

TABLE 10.12. DON'T KNOW YOU

Matthew 25:10–12 M	Matthew 7:22–23 Q	Luke 13:26–27 Q	Luke 13:25 L
25:10 and the door was closed.			13:25 From the time the householder rises and closes the door,
11 Later the rest of the virgins come, saying, "Lord, Lord, open to us."	7:22 Many will say to me on that day, "Lord, Lord, did we not prophesy in your name, and in your name cast out demons, and in your name perform many miracles?"	13:26 Then you will begin to say, "We ate and drank before you, and you taught in our streets."	and you begin to knock on the door saying, "Lord, open to us,"
12 But in reply he said, "Amen I tell you, I do not know you."	23 And then I will confess to them, "I never knew you.	27 And he will say to you, "I do not know [you], where you are from.	and in reply he will say to you, "I do not know you, where you are from."
	Depart from me, you who work lawlessness."	Stay away from me, all you workers of unrighteousness."	

The middle columns of table 10.12 show the Q pericope in Matthew and Luke respectively. The two versions differ considerably in wording. Jesus speaks in the first person in Matthew, but Luke speaks about him in the third person. Conversely, Luke addresses the unrighteous in second person, while Matthew speaks about them in third person. In Matthew, the evildoers prophesied, cast out demons, and performed miracles, while in Luke, they simply ate, drank, and heard Jesus teach.

Matthew has inserted this Q pericope into the conclusion of the Q sermon (Matt 7:21–27). Since in the sermon Jesus is the speaker, Matthew changed the saying's speech about Jesus to speech by Jesus when he incorporated it into the sermon. Matthew also made other redactional changes to the saying, such as turning the evildoers into Christian prophets, exorcists, and miracle workers.[33] By turning those working "lawlessness" into other Christians, Matthew adapted the saying to the concerns of his own community. Matthew apparently agreed with the view expressed elsewhere in Matthew that the Law should be kept (Matt 5:17–20), but he knew of other Christians, such as those in Paul's camp, who taught that one no longer needed to follow the Law. Matthew condemns such Christians as lawless, even if they exhibit miraculous powers.[34]

Luke's version of the Q saying may better reflect its original wording. In at least one instance, however, Luke too has redacted it, changing "lawlessness," in the quotation from the Septuagint (Ps 6:8 [9]), to "unrighteousness."[35] The differences between Matthew and Luke in the Q saying thus stem from redaction of both parallels.

The outer columns of table 10.12 show two other versions of the saying "Don't know you." In Matthew this serves as the conclusion to the M parable of ten virgins (Matt 25:10–12), an indication that Matthew found it in that source. Luke has a similar version in Luke 13:25, which must have come from L. Luke apparently knew two versions of the section "Few saved," one from Q and one from L. He included the saying "Don't know you" from both versions, thus creating a doublet.

SONS EXCLUDED (MATT 8:11–12/LUKE 13:28–29)

In the third item in the series, the pericope "Sons excluded," Luke again drew from both the Q and L versions, this time conflating them (table 10.13).

TABLE 10.13. SONS EXCLUDED

Matthew 8:11–12 Q	Luke 13:28a, 29 Q	Luke 13:28bcde L
8:11a But I tell you that many from east and west will come	13:29a And they will come from east and west	—
	29b and from north and south	

---

33. So Allison in Davies and Allison, *Matthew*, 1:714.

34. *Contra* ibid., 1:718–19.

35. Ibid., 1:718.

11b and recline	29c and recline	—
11c with Abraham and Isaac and Jacob	—	13:28b when you see Abraham and Isaac and Jacob
		28c and all the prophets
11d in the kingdom of the heavens.	29d in the kingdom of God.	28d in the kingdom of God,
12a But the sons of the kingdom will be cast out into the outer darkness.	—	28e but yourselves cast out.
12b There, there will be weeping and gnashing of teeth.	→ 28a There, there will be weeping and gnashing of teeth.	

As the pericope stands, the elements within it have a different order in Matthew than in Luke. Kloppenborg attributes the differences primarily to Lukan redaction.[36] Allison attributes the differences to Matthean redaction: Matthew altered the pericope to fit it into its new context when he moved it from its original position in Q into the story of the centurion's boy.[37] Fitzmyer doubts that one can know whether to ascribe the differences to Matthean redaction, Lukan redaction, or to Luke's use of L.[38]

Three features of the material suggest that the differences arose because Luke combined two different versions of the pericope.

First, when we list the elements of this pericope in Matthew's order, as in the first column of table 10.13, the corresponding material in Luke falls into two distinct sequences, shown in the last two columns of the table. These two sequences when combined do not produce a single sequence that has the same order in Luke as in Matthew. However, when viewed separately, each sequence in Luke has the same order as the corresponding material in Matthew. These two distinct sequences in Luke provide the first clue that Luke knew two distinct versions of the pericope, which he has combined.

Second, Luke's version includes doublets: where Matthew has only one instance of the expression "in the kingdom of God," Luke has two. Since one of these occurs in the first Lukan sequence (Luke 13:29d) and the other in the second (Luke 13:28d), they provide confirmation that each Lukan sequence represents a parallel version of the pericope.

36. Kloppenborg, *Formation of Q*, 225–27.
37. Allison in Davies and Allison, *Matthew*, 2:26.
38. Fitzmyer, *Luke*, 2:1021–22.

Third, as further confirmation, the two versions differ stylistically. The material in Luke's first sequence agrees with Matthew's version in using third-person discourse, while the material in Luke's second sequence differs by using second-person direct address.

These three features of the material point to the same conclusion: Luke has combined two different versions of the pericope, one using third-person discourse like that in Matthew (Q) and one using second-person discourse (L). In combining these two different versions, Luke created a doublet by using the same phrase ("in the kingdom of God") from both versions. With the exception of Luke 13:28a, Luke kept the elements of each version in their original order. Thus when each version is viewed separately, it has the same order as Matthew's version. However, when Luke combined the two versions, he placed L before the corresponding material in Q. Hence in Luke's conflated version of the pericope, the elements do not have the same order as the corresponding elements in Matthew.

Once we place Luke's two versions in different columns, the only item in Luke out of sequence with Matthew is the sentence "There, there will be weeping and gnashing of teeth" (Luke 13:28a). This sentence usually serves as a conclusion, as it does here in Matthew 8:12b (cf. Matt 13:42; 13:50; 22:13; 24:51; 25:30). Only in Luke 13:28a does it serve as an introduction. It is likely, therefore, that Matthew here preserves it in its original position at the end of the Q pericope, while Luke moved it from there to serve as the introduction to his conflated version of the saying.

Luke's conflation of Q and L accounts for most of the differences in wording between Matthew and Luke in this pericope. Redaction by one Evangelist or the other would account for the rest.

LAST FIRST (MATT 20:16/LUKE 13:30)

The final item in this section is the saying "Last first." As we saw previously (table 9.17), Matthew attached the Q version of the saying to the end of the parable of the hired workers from M (Matt 20:1–15). Luke knew an L version of this saying, and, since he seems to favor L in this section, his version may have come from that source.

AT A MEAL

Luke includes a section set in the house of a Pharisee during a Sabbath meal (Luke 14:1–24). This consists of a series of three pericopes: "Man with dropsy" (14:1–6), "Banquet teachings" (14:7–14), and "Great supper" (14:15–24). The second has no parallel in Matthew and therefore probably came from L.[39] The other two have a parallel or a partial parallel in Matthew, so that one might infer that Luke's version of these came from Q. Our examination will indicate, however, that these pericopes in Luke came from L, just as the second one did.

MAN WITH DROPSY (MATT 12:10C, 11/LUKE 14:1–6)

The first item in this section of Luke is the pericope "Man with dropsy" (Luke 14:1–6). Since only Luke includes this in its entirety, some scholars attribute it to L.[40] Others assign it to Q.[41] The fact that it mentions "lawyers" (Luke 14:3), a term limited to L among the Gospel sources (Luke 7:30; 10:25; 11:45, 46, 52), suggests that it came from L. So does the combination "donkey or ox," which occurs elsewhere only in the L pericope "Crippled woman" (Luke 13:15).[42]

A parallel to Luke 14:5 in this story also appears in Matthew (Matt 12:10c, 11), inserted into a similar story that Matthew shared with Mark (Matt 12:9–14/Mark 3:1–6). Neirynck, following Bultmann and others, regards this insertion as an isolated saying.[43] However, Kloppenborg is probably right that such a saying by itself would have no point unless it were connected to something more.[44] Since Matthew knew a parallel to Luke 14:5, he probably knew a parallel to the story in which it occurs, Luke 14:1–6.

The parallels in Matthew and Luke both include the rhetorical question "What person among you," which occurs elsewhere in both Q and L (B.34). Matthew's version must therefore have come from Q. Where we can compare the two, the Q version in Matthew and the L version in Luke have hardly any wording in common. For "sheep" in Q (Matt 12:11), L has "donkey or ox" (Luke 14:5). For "fall into a pit" (εἰς βόθυνον ἐμπεσεῖν) in Q (Matt 12:11), L has "fall into a well" (εἰς φρέαρ πεσεῖν, Luke 14:5). For the rhetorical question "What person among you" (τίς ἔσται ἐξ ὑμῶν ἄνθρωπος) in Q (Matt 12:11), L has "Which of you" (τίνος ὑμῶν, Luke 14:5).

---

39. Manson, *Sayings*, 27; Fitzmyer, *Luke*, 2:1044; Paffenroth, *Story of Jesus*, 59.

40. Fitzmyer, *Luke*, 2:1038–39; Paffenroth, *Story of Jesus*, 58–59.

41. Examples are given by Neirynck, "Luke 14,1–6," 243–46.

42. At Luke 14:5, some manuscripts read υιος ("son") instead of ονος ("donkey"). The latter reading is to be preferred (Manson, *Sayings*, 277). *Contra* Neirynck, "Luke 14,1–6," 254–55.

43. Ibid., 247, 259.

44. John S. Kloppenborg, *Q Parallels: Synopsis, Critical Notes, and Concordance* (Foundation and Facets: New Testament; Sonoma, Calif.: Polebridge, 1988), 160.

We conclude therefore that the L story in Luke 14:1–6 had a parallel in Q that Luke omitted in favor of the L version. Matthew took the main point from the Q version of this story and inserted it into a similar story from his Markan source. Matthew and Luke differ in wording in the one verse that they share because while Matthew used Q, Luke used L.

GREAT SUPPER (MATT 22:1–10/LUKE 14:15–24)

The last pericope in this section is the parable of the great supper (Matt 22:1–10/Luke 14:15–24). In this, Matthew and Luke have almost completely different wording. Table 10.14 shows the beginning of the parable.

TABLE 10.14. GREAT SUPPER, BEGINNING

Matthew 22:2	Luke 14:16b
2 The kingdom of heaven is like a king man who held a wedding for his son.	16b A certain man gave a great dinner and invited many.

Here the only word in common is "man," and this lack of agreement in wording extends through the rest of the story as well. The only other words shared by Matthew and Luke are "and he sent his slave(s)," "to the guests," "ready," and "to the roads." Furthermore, Matthew includes the addendum "No garment" (Matt 22:11–14) that Luke lacks. If Matthew and Luke both used Q,[45] then one or both must have revised heavily. However, we previously saw the same high degree of disagreement in wording in the Beelzebul debate, where Matthew followed the Markan source while Luke used Q (table 7.5). Here too, therefore, it is possible that Matthew and Luke knew different versions of the story.

Allison conjectures that Matthew's version came from M, understood as oral tradition adopted by Matthew.[46] If this were the case, we would expect the addendum in Matthew 22:11–14 to come from M. Instead, it contains features of style that are typical of Q: the term "cast out" (ἐκβάλλειν; Matt 22:13; B.49; B.51; B.52) and the sentence, "There, there will be weeping and gnashing of teeth" (Matt 22:13; B.47). This sentence is often considered Matthean redaction, because it occurs more frequently in Matthew than in Luke. However, since we concluded in chapter 1 that Luke did not use Matthew, the presence

---

45. So Fitzmyer, *Luke*, 2:1052; Paffenroth, *Story of Jesus*, 44.
46. Allison in Davies and Allison, *Matthew*, 3:194.

of this sentence in Luke 13:28 indicates that it came from Q. It appears then that Matthew's version of the story came from Q.

Two considerations indicate that Luke's version may come from L. First, it is the third in a series of pericopes (Luke 14:1–6, 7–14, 15–24) with the same setting (Luke 14:1). Since the first two of these pericopes came from L, it is reasonable to think that the third did as well. Second, a stylistic and thematic link between the second and third pericopes supports this conclusion. The second pericope exhorts hosts to invite "the poor, the crippled, the lame, the blind" (Luke 14:13). Likewise, in Luke's version of the great supper, the host has his slave bring in "the poor and the crippled and the blind and the lame" (Luke 14:21). While this phrase could be Lukan redaction, it could just as plausibly represent a stylistic feature of L.

On balance, it seems reasonable to conclude that Matthew and Luke differ in wording in this parable because their respective stories came from different sources: Matthew's from Q and Luke's from L.

Lost Sheep

In the parable of the lost sheep (Matt 18:12–13/Luke 15:3–7), Matthew and Luke have only minimal wording in common, such as "a hundred sheep" and "the ninety-nine." We saw in chapter 9 that Matthew's version is a Q saying inserted into an M context. While Luke's version may also have come from Q,[47] it is more likely that it came from L.[48] It begins with the rhetorical question "What person among you," which could come from either Q or L (B.34). More decisively, it stands as the first in a series of three parables on the lost (Luke 15:3–7, 8–10, 11–32), which have the same introduction (Luke 15:1–2). Since the introduction and the other two parables are unique to Luke and probably came from L, it is likely that the first parable in this series also came from L.

A stylistic and thematic link between the first two parables, the lost sheep and the lost coin, confirms that they came from the same source. In both parables, an individual who has lost an item finds it and calls on friends and neighbors to celebrate the fact. Both comment on how much joy there is in heaven over one repentant sinner. If one assumes that the parable of the lost sheep came from Q, then these affinities would suggest that the parable of the lost coin also came from Q.[49] However, if one does not make that assumption,

47. So Fitzmyer, *Luke*, 2:1073

48. So Manson, *Sayings*, 283; Paffenroth, *Story of Jesus*, 49–50.

49. Kloppenborg Verbin, *Excavating Q*, 96–98.

then the absence of the parable of the lost coin from Matthew suggests that it came from L, and its affinities with the parable of the lost sheep suggest that the latter came from L as well.

The differences in wording between Matthew and Luke thus have two causes: they used different sources for the parable, Q and L respectively, and the wording of Matthew's version diverged further when Matthew adapted it to an M context.

ON RECOMPENSE

The last two items of Q in Luke's order are the parable of the pounds and the saying "Twelve thrones." Both deal with eschatological recompense or reward of Jesus' followers. Both show an overlap of Q with L.

PARABLE OF POUNDS (MATT 25:14–30/LUKE 19:12–27)

Matthew and Luke have distinctly different versions of the parable of pounds, with hardly any wording in common (Matt 25:14–30/Luke 19:12–27). Some critics ascribe the parable to Q, assuming that one or both Evangelists redacted it heavily.[50] Allison represents another common response to this difference: "the disagreements are so many and so significant that many—we include ourselves—hesitate to suppose that Matthew and Luke both used Q."[51] Manson, for example, assigned Matthew's version to M and Luke's to L.[52] Streeter thought Matthew's version was a conflation of Q with M. However, he based this view on Eusebius's description of this parable in the Gospel according to the Hebrews, which could simply be an expansion of Matthew.[53]

Features of style and theme indicate that Matthew's version came from Q. The theme of being "faithful" (Matt 25:21, 23/Luke 19:17) comes from Q (B.45) as does the motif of "casting out" (Matt 25:30a; B.49, B.51). Likewise Q accounts for the last sentence: "There, there will be weeping and gnashing of teeth" (Matt 25:30b). We have identified this sentence as a feature of Q, even though Luke tends to omit it (B.47).

---

50. Fitzmyer (*Luke*, 2:1230–31) and Paffenroth (*Story of Jesus*, 52–53) suppose that Luke has heavily redacted the Q parable. The International Q Project also reconstructs a presumed original Q version: Robinson et al., *Critical Edition of Q*, 524–57; idem, *Sayings Gospel Q*, 148–51.

51. Allison in Davies and Allison, *Matthew*, 3:376.

52. Manson, *Sayings*, 245.

53. Streeter, *Four Gospels*, 282–83.

The Q version in Matthew tells a consistent story. A man has three slaves, to each of whom he gives a different number of talents to work with while he is gone. When he returns, the slaves with five talents and two talents, respectively, have doubled their money, while the slave with one talent has made nothing. The parable concludes with the master's command to cast out the useless slave (Matt 25:30).

Luke's version, apart from its wording, has two significant differences. First, it includes a series of passages about a well-born man who goes to a distant country to receive a kingdom. This description corresponds closely to the events surrounding the accession of Archelaus after the death of his father, Herod the Great, in 4 B.C.E. Archelaus went to Rome to ask to be appointed king over Judea, Samaria, and Idumea (Luke 19:12); the Jews sent an embassy to Rome protesting his appointment (Luke 19:14); and when Archelaus returned (Luke 19:15a), he slew many (Luke 19:27).[54] Removing these passages makes Luke's version of the parable correspond more closely to that of Matthew.

Second, Luke's version is troubled by an inconsistency in the narrative. The story begins with a different premise than Matthew's: the man has ten slaves instead of three, to each of whom he gives an equal amount of money, a mina apiece. Yet when he settles accounts with them, we hear of only three slaves, as in Matthew: the first, the second, and "the other" (Luke 19:16, 18, 20).[55] Furthermore the objection in Luke 19:25, "Lord, he has ten (minas)," would fit better in Matthew's account, where the first slave has ten (talents) than in Luke's account, where the first slave has eleven minas as well as ten cities. The continuation of the story thus does not correspond well with the beginning.

The difficulties in Luke's account can best be explained if Luke knew two versions of the story, a three-slave version like that in Matthew from Q, and a ten-slave version from L.[56] Luke used the L version for the most part, which explains the ten slaves and the lack of agreement in wording with Matthew. However, Luke also drew a few elements from the three-slave Q version, which accounts for the inconsistencies in the narrative.

---

54. Josephus, *Ant.* 17.196–341; *Bell.* 2.80–100; see Allison in Davies and Allison, *Matthew*, 3:402–3.

55. The narrative would be less inconsistent if we adopted the variant reading "another" of A and other manuscripts.

56. Allison mentions this idea: "We have also wondered whether Mt 25.14–30 is not close to Q, Lk 19.11–27 a conflation of Q and some other source" (Davies and Allison, *Matthew*, 3:376).

Stylistic features tend to bear out this conclusion. Four features of style in Luke's story are stylistic traits of the Evangelist: ἄνθρωπός τις (19:12), ὑποστρέφω (19:12), καὶ ἐγένετο ἐν τῷ (19:15), and παραγίνομαι (19:16). These occur not only in L but in all strands of the material in Luke. However, eight other stylistic traits occur only in material unique to Luke: εἰς χώραν μακράν,[57] δέκα,[58] πολίτης,[59] πρεσβεία,[60] ἐν τῷ + ἐπανέρχομαι,[61] φωνέω = "summon,"[62] ἐξουσία over political entities,[63] and πράσσω = "exact payment."[64] The most significant of these is the number "ten," which is the number of drachmas owned by the woman who lost one of them (Luke 15:8) and the number of lepers whom Jesus healed (Luke 17:12, 17). Since both of these stories occur in L, they make it plausible to think that L also included a story about ten slaves.

Three, possibly four, of the stylistic traits that occur only in material unique to Luke are found in the passages that correspond to the story of Archelaus. It is likely therefore that these passages were part of the L story.

Twelve Thrones (Matt 19:28b/Luke 22:28–30)

The final item of Q in Luke's order is the saying "Twelve thrones," which we discussed in chapter 8 (table 8.15). Matthew and Luke have little wording in common for several reasons. Matthew adapted the saying to the Markan context in which he placed it and added a temporal phrase and a temporal clause to clarify when the disciples would receive their reward. Luke conflated the saying with a saying from L (Luke 22:29–30a), which resembles another L saying (Luke 12:32). Thus L affected the wording of the saying in Luke.

Conclusion

In this chapter, we have surveyed a third cause for the differences in wording between Matthew and Luke in Q parallels. Not infrequently, Luke knew both a Q version and an L version of the same pericope. At times he used one or the other, but at other times, he combined the two. When Matthew used Q

---

57. Luke 19:12; cf. 15:13.
58. Luke 19:13, 13, 16, 17, 24, 25; cf. 13:16; 14:31; 15:8; 17:12, 17.
59. Luke 19:14; cf. 15:15.
60. Luke 19:14; cf. 14:32.
61. Luke 19:15; cf. 10:35.
62. Luke 19:15; cf. 16:2.
63. Luke 19:17, 19; cf. 4:6.
64. Luke 19:23; cf. 3:13.

and Luke used L, their wording has little in common. When Matthew used Q and Luke conflated Q with L, their wording exhibits a mixture of agreement and disagreement. Luke's procedure is consistent with the view that the Evangelists functioned primarily as compilers and editors rather than as composers.

11

OTHER CAUSES OF DIFFERENCES IN WORDING

Most of the differences between Matthew and Luke in the wording of the double tradition can be traced to one of the three causes that we have discussed in previous chapters: the Evangelists combined Q with Mark, Matthew combined Q with M, and Luke combined Q with L. Two other causes account for the remaining differences: insertion of one Q passage into another, and editorial revision per se.

ONE Q PASSAGE IN ANOTHER

Matthew three times and Luke once inserted one Q passage into another. Matthew inserted the Q pericope "Don't know you" into the end of the Q sermon (Matt 7:22–23), the Q pericope "Sons excluded" into the Q story of the centurion's boy (Matt 8:11–12), and the Q pericope "Law until John" into the Q discourse of Jesus on John (Matt 11:12–13). Luke inserted two sentences from the Q pericope "On words" (Matt 12:33–37) into the Q pericope "Tree and fruit" in the Q sermon (Luke 6:45).

We have discussed all of these except "Law until John," which we will examine here. Table 11.1 shows this pericope.

TABLE 11.1. LAW UNTIL JOHN

Matthew 11:12–13 Q	Luke 16:16 Q
	16:16 The Law and the prophets were until John.
11:12 From the days of John the Baptist until now, the kingdom of the heavens	From that time, the kingdom of God
	has been proclaimed, and everyone in it
has been treated violently,	has been treated violently.

and violent men have ravaged it.	
13 For all the prophets and the Law prophesied until John.	

As Kloppenborg states, "This pericope is a notorious *crux interpretum* and virtually every detail is disputed."[1] Allison refers to it as "without a doubt, one of the NT's great conundrums,"[2] and his review of its various interpretations confirms this judgment. Any attempt to solve the puzzle must begin by reconstructing the original form of the saying.

In Luke, this saying probably came from Q rather than L, since it is one of three sayings (Luke 16:16–18) that interrupt the L material, separating the parable of the rich man and Lazarus (Luke 16:19–31) from its introduction (Luke 16:14–15). Matthew has inserted this Q saying into a different context in Q, following Jesus' testimony to John (Matt 11:7–11/Luke 7:24–28). Since Matthew tends to abhor an isolated saying, he has joined this one to other material on the same theme, the role of John the Baptist.[3]

Matthew's version shares only a few words of verbatim agreement with Luke's (ὁ νόμος, οἱ προφῆται, ἀπὸ Ἰωάννου, ἡ βασιλεία, and βιάζεται) and has the two sentences reversed. Some of the differences from Luke can be traced to Matthew's efforts to fit the Q saying into its new context. Luke probably preserves the original order of the saying, with the statement about the old order preceding the statement about the new.[4] Matthew reversed this order, probably so that "the kingdom of the heavens" in the (originally) second sentence would follow on from the same expression at the end of Jesus' testimony (Matt 11:11/Luke 7:28). In the original order, "until John" preceded "From that time," but Matthew's transposition shifted the phrase "From that time" to the beginning of the saying, where it no longer had an antecedent, so Matthew had to expand it to "From the days of John the Baptist" (Matt 11:12).

Another difference arose as Matthew sought to clarify the first cryptic sentence in Q, which literally reads, "The Law and the prophets up to John." Matthew apparently interpreted this to mean that the scriptures prophesied about or toward John, so he added the verb "prophesied" to make this clear. And since it was primarily the prophets who prophesied, he changed the order of the compound subject to put "prophets" first.

---

1. Kloppenborg, *Formation of Q*, 112–15, esp. 113.

2. Allison in Davies and Allison, *Matthew*, 2:254.

3. Ibid., 2:253; Fitzmyer, *Luke*, 2:1114.

4. Allison in Davies and Allison, *Matthew*, 2:253.

Another difference may have arisen as an oversight on the part of Matthew or an earlier scribe. Matthew omitted the words "has been proclaimed, and everyone in it" so that the verb "has been treated violently" (βιάζεται) came to have "the kingdom of the heavens" as its subject rather than the original "everyone in it." Alternatively, some critics take the words that are absent from Matthew as Lukan redaction, since Luke favors the verb εὐαγγελίζομαι.[5] However, this verb occurs once elsewhere in Q as well (Matt 11:5/7:22) and therefore need not be Lukan redaction here.

Matthew's "and violent men have ravaged it" looks to be a restatement in the active voice of the passive "and everyone in it has been treated violently." This repetition suggests that the original saying was structured in parallel strophes, a parallelism that Luke has spoiled by omitting the second strophe as redundant.

If this analysis is accurate, then the original saying ran as follows:

The Law and the prophets (were) until John;
from that time the kingdom of God has been proclaimed.
And everyone in it has been treated violently;
and violent men have ravaged it.

The saying looks back on the deaths of John and Jesus from the perspective of the early Christian community. John began the proclamation of the kingdom of God, followed by Jesus. Both were treated violently by violent men. The violence has extended to "everyone" in the kingdom, which would include the followers of Jesus as well, who have also proclaimed the kingdom.

The evolution of this saying is instructive. Luke has preserved it better than Matthew except for omitting the final strophe. The changes in Matthew's version were due to three different causes: adaptation of the saying to a new context in Q, clarification (and hence interpretation) of the meaning of the saying, and omission, possibly by scribal oversight.

Editorial Revision

All of the changes to the wording of Q that we have discussed so far occur in passages that have a parallel in another source or that have been inserted into the context of another source, whether the Markan source, M, L, or Q itself. In such passages, the wording of Q was frequently influenced by the other

---

5. Ibid. The International Q Project follows Matthew in omitting these words (Robinson et al., *Critical Edition of Q*, 464–67; idem, *Sayings Gospel Q*, 140–41).

source. Yet we have also seen changes that adaptation to the other source did not necessitate. Such redaction or editorial revision per se also occurs in passages that have no overlaps or other such interference from other sources. In most cases, such passages have close to the same wording in Matthew and Luke. We previously listed these in table 7.1. In other cases, parallels of this kind show more significant differences in wording that can be attributed to redaction. We will examine one of these here.

In the section on Jesus and John (Matt 11:2–19/Luke 7:18–35), each Gospel has some material that the other lacks. Matthew has a saying on John and the Law that the Evangelist inserted here from elsewhere in Q (Matt 11:12–13/Luke 16:16). Matthew also includes a saying identifying John as Elijah (Matt 11:14–15). Beare leaves open the possibility that this stood in Q and was omitted by Luke because he rejected the identification of John as Elijah.[6] It is more likely that this saying is Matthean redaction since Matthew makes a similar redactional identification in material shared with Mark (Matt 17:13; cf. Mark 9:11–13).[7]

Luke probably inserted 7:29–30 as an explanation for 7:35. The International Q Project includes this passage in their reconstruction of Q as Luke's parallel to Matthew 21:32, though with a degree of uncertainty of "C" in a descending scale from "A" to "D." While Kloppenborg Verbin considers it probable that this passage stood in Q,[8] Fitzmyer regards Matthew 21:32 as too remote a parallel to establish this.[9] The presence of the term "lawyers" in the Lukan passage suggests that it came from L, since this term occurs elsewhere in the Gospels only in that source (Luke 10:25; 11:45, 46, 52; 14:3).

The Q material for this section, then, consists of the three pericopes, "John's question" (Matt 11:2–6/Luke 7:18–23), "Jesus on John" (Matt 11:7–11/ Luke 7:24–28), and "Children in market" (Matt 11:16–19/Luke 7:31–35).

In all three pericopes, Matthew and Luke agree closely in wording. Some variation, though, occurs in the pericope "John's question." Luke includes a list of miracles that Jesus performed at that time (Luke 7:21). Most scholars agree that Luke added this to provide instances of the cures claimed in Luke 7:22.[10] Some differences in wording also occur in the introduction to the story (table 11.2).

---

6. Beare, *Matthew*, 259.

7. Manson, *Sayings*, 185; Kloppenborg, *Formation of Q*, 110; Allison in Davies and Allison, *Matthew*, 2:246, 258.

8. Kloppenborg Verbin, *Excavating Q*, 100.

9. Fitzmyer, *Luke*, 1:671.

10. Manson, *Sayings*, 66; Fitzmyer, *Luke*, 1:663, 667; Allison in Davies and Allison, *Matthew*, 2:241–42.

TABLE 11.2. ARE YOU THE ONE

Matthew 11:2–3 Q	Luke 7:18–20 Q
11:2 John having heard	7:18 And his disciples reported to John
in the prison	
of the deeds of the Christ,	about all these things.
	And summoning a certain two of his disciples,
sending	John 19 sent
through his disciples,	
	to the Lord,
3 he said to him,	saying,
"Are you the one coming or do we wait for a different one?"	"Are you the one coming or do we wait for another?
	20 When they came to him, the men said, "John the Baptist sent us to you, saying, 'Are you the one coming or do we wait for another?'"

Here redaction by one or both of the Evangelists probably accounts for the differences in wording. The International Q Project attributes most of the redaction to Luke, favoring Matthew's version for all except the phrases "in the prison" and "of the deeds of the Christ."[11] However, since Matthew tended to omit redundant detail, Luke's longer, repetitive version may stand closer to the original.[12]

---

11. Robinson et al, *Critical Edition of Q*, 118–21; idem, *Sayings Gospel Q*, 92–93.
12. Manson, *Sayings*, 66.

12
Summary and Conclusions

Our conclusions can be summarized under three headings: the existence of Q, the unity of Q, and the plurality of Q.

The Existence of Q

I set out to answer two disputed questions in the study of Q. First, is Q really necessary? I have concluded that any plausible theory of Synoptic relations requires the Q hypothesis. Attempts by Goodacre and others to discredit Streeter's arguments for Q have not succeeded, and other arguments for Q have confirmed the hypothesis.

The Unity of Q

Most of this study has been devoted to the second question: did the Q material come from a single source or more than one? The double tradition seems to exhibit unity with respect to order and features of style and theme, but plurality with respect to wording in the parallels. Previous scholarship has not adequately established either its unity or its plurality. With respect to the unity of Q, the evidence that I have presented suggests the following conclusions.

1. The double tradition includes a series of pericopes unified by a common order in Matthew and Luke, recurring features of style and theme, and a tendency to organize sayings into larger complexes (table 3.2). This series constitutes the minimal assured contents or core of a unified Q source. It shows that Q existed as a written source with a unified stylistic and thematic character.

2. The double tradition passages outside the core exhibit a stylistic and thematic coherence or unity with the core. Apart from a few short sayings, these passages are linked to the core and to each other by a web of stylistic and thematic connections. These are listed in appendix B. Such unity indi-

cates that this material came from the same milieu; and such unity is at least consistent with the view that these passages came from the same source as the core, that is, from Q.

3. The one exception is the discourse "On confession" (Matt 10:24–39 par). This discourse shows very little stylistic or thematic affinity with the core or other double tradition material. It probably did not come from the same source (Q) as the rest of the double tradition material.

4. A number of passages unique to Matthew or Luke share distinctive features of style and theme with the Q material. The chances are good therefore that these also came from Q. These are identified in chapter 5.

5. Luke probably better preserves the original order of Q than Matthew. However, Luke too probably relocated material in a few instances. Table 6.1 provides a preliminary list of the Q material in its presumed original order.

The Plurality of Q

The primary argument for the plurality of Q is the wording in Q parallels. A large part of the Q material falls into one of two extremes: either Matthew and Luke agree almost completely in wording or they disagree almost completely. Such extremes of verbal agreement might suggest that the double tradition material came from more than one source or more than one version of the same source.

With respect to this apparent plurality, our study indicates that Q per se existed as a single unified written source with much the same wording in the copies known to Matthew and Luke. However, the Evangelists also knew parallels to Q from various overlapping sources or traditions, such as the Markan source, M, and L. These parallels affected the wording of Q passages in various ways. The tables in appendices C and D summarize our conclusions concerning which double tradition passages came from Q and which came from M or L.

The evidence that I have presented suggests that differences between Matthew and Luke in the wording of the double tradition arose for the following reasons.

1. The large amount of verbatim agreement between Matthew and Luke in Q passages suggests that the Evangelists functioned primarily as compilers and editors rather than as composers. These Evangelists had inherited a variety of sources and traditions that they wished to combine into some sort of a unified whole, and this task required a measure of creativity and adaptation of their sources. Much of their disagreement in wording arose as they combined overlapping sources or incorporated material from one source into the context of another.

2. Where the Markan source overlapped with Q, or the Evangelists placed Q material in a Markan context, the Markan source often influenced the wording of Q in either Matthew or Luke. Such influence took several forms. One Evangelist or the other might conflate Q with the Markan version, replace the Q version with the Markan version, adapt the wording of Q to that of the Markan version, or adapt the wording of Q to the Markan context.

3. Matthew often knew an M version of a pericope in Q in addition to the Q version. He generally gave priority to M, though sometimes he conflated Q with M. Matthew also sometimes inserted Q material into an M context and in such cases consistently reworded Q. Matthew gave priority to M, adapting the wording of Q to the language, perspective, and context of M.

4. Luke often knew an L version of a pericope in addition to the Q version. At times he used one or the other, but at other times he combined the two. Matthew and Luke agree in wording when both follow Q, but differ when Luke follows L.

5. Changes to the wording of Q also occurred occasionally when an Evangelist inserted one Q passage into another and adapted the passage to its new context.

6. The Evangelists sometimes made changes to the wording of Q that were not necessitated by the influence of some other source or context. In some cases, they omitted redundant language or improved the grammar and style of Q. In other cases they clarified the meaning of Q, in the process becoming interpreters as well as editors. In yet other cases, they adapted Q to make it relevant to the situations of their own communities.

IMPLICATIONS FOR THE STUDY OF Q

Hopefully, this study has clarified both the unity and the plurality of Q to some degree. We have tried to determine the original contents and order of Q, the stylistic and thematic features of Q, and the reasons for variations in verbal agreement in Q parallels. We have identified various passages from other sources that overlapped with Q and identified a discourse in the double tradition that may have circulated independently of Q.

The results of this study also have broader implications for the study of Q. It confirms that Q existed as a unified written source that was known in much the same wording to Matthew and Luke. It therefore legitimates the quest to reconstruct the original wording of Q and to understand the social and religious context out of which this source emerged. At the same time, it makes clear that future study of Q must go hand in hand with further study of parallel material from M and L, not only to avoid confusing Q with such parallels, but also to better understand the relationship between Q and these other strands of the Gospel tradition.

Appendix A

"Editorial Fatigue" as an Argument against Q

One of Mark Goodacre's arguments against Q is based on "editorial fatigue," a term coined by Michael Goulder.[1] According to this view, certain inconsistencies in narration are best explained as the result of inconsistent editing: an editor makes changes at the beginning of his source but fails to sustain the changes throughout the account. The editor becomes "fatigued" and lapses into "docile reproduction" of the source. Without using the term "editorial fatigue," G. M. Styler earlier gave examples of the same phenomenon along with other editorial blunders in Matthew.[2] Goodacre gives examples of the phenomenon in the triple tradition in both Matthew and Luke. He also finds examples in the double tradition in Luke but not Matthew. With respect to the instances in the double tradition, he makes the argument that Luke became fatigued in copying Matthew, not Q, because

> if the Two Source Theory is correct, one will expect to see not only Luke but also Matthew showing signs of fatigue in double tradition material.... On the Q theory it does strain plausibility that Luke should often show fatigue in double tradition material and that Matthew should never do so, especially given Matthew's clearly observable tendency to become fatigued in his editing of Mark.[3]

There are several problems with this argument. The first is Goodacre's assumption that we should expect Matthew to show editorial fatigue when editing Q since he shows such fatigue when editing Mark. We do not know enough about the circumstances of Matthew's editing to make such an assumption. Perhaps Matthew simply paid more careful attention to Q than to Mark.

---

1. Goodacre, "Fatigue in the Synoptics," 45–58; idem, *Synoptic Problem*, 71–76, 154–56.
2. Styler, "Priority of Mark," 293–98.
3. Goodacre, "Fatigue in the Synoptics," 57–58.

The second is Goodacre's assumption that we should expect Matthew to show editorial fatigue when editing Q because Luke does. We have no reason to think that Matthew's style of editing Q would necessarily be the same as Luke's. Matthew may simply have been more careful than Luke in editing Q.

Third, Foster argues that Matthew does show editorial fatigue at least once in the double tradition. Matthew tends to replace the phrase "the kingdom of God" with "the kingdom of the heavens," but in one instance (Matt 12:28/Luke 11:20) he lapses back into using the phrase "the kingdom of God" from his source.[4]

Fourth, Goodacre cites only six inconsistencies in Luke, and not all of these arose from editorial fatigue. Four of them probably arose because Luke conflated two somewhat inconsistent sources, neither of which was Matthew. And in the remaining instances, we can just as easily suppose that Luke used Q as that he used Matthew.

1. In the mission instructions in Matthew 10, Matthew mentions both entering a city and leaving it (Matt 10:11a, 14b), while the parallel in Luke speaks only of leaving it (Luke 9:5b). Goodacre takes this as an instance in which Luke lapsed into editorial fatigue while editing Matthew: Luke edited out of Matthew the instruction about entering a city but then forgot and retained the instruction about leaving it.[5] However, table A.1 shows another possible explanation for Luke's inconsistency.

TABLE A.1. LUKE 9:4A, 9:5B

Matthew	Luke	Mark
10:11a In whatever city or village you enter	9:4a And in whatever house you enter	6:10 Wherever you enter a house
10:14b as you come out of that house or city	9:5b as you come out of that city	6:11b as you go out from there

In this passage, Mark speaks of entering and leaving a house, while Matthew speaks of entering and leaving a city. Luke shares the first part (Luke 9:4a) with Mark and the second (Luke 9:5b) with Matthew, thus creating an inconsistent reference to entering a house but leaving a city. Apparently Luke conflated two different sources, one that he shared with Mark and one that he shared with Matthew. Luke's inconsistency, therefore, arose from combining two different sources, not from experiencing fatigue as he edited a single

---

4. Foster, "Is It Possible," 330–32.
5. Goodacre, "Fatigue in the Synoptics," 54–55.

source. And the source that he shared with Matthew need not have been the Gospel of Matthew.

2. In the story of the centurion's boy, Matthew refers to the child as a "boy" (παῖς) throughout (Matt 8:6, 8, 13), while Luke alternates between "slave" (δοῦλος, Luke 7:2, 3, 10) and "boy" (παῖς, Luke 7:7). Goodacre assumes again that Luke became fatigued while editing Matthew: he changed Matthew's "boy" to "slave" but forgot to do so in Luke 7:7. However, another explanation is more likely. In chapter 10, I showed that Luke knew two distinct versions of this story, one from Q that used παῖς and one from L that used δοῦλος (see table 10.3 and the discussion there). Matthew used only the Q version with παῖς, while Luke combined the two. Here, as in the preceding instance, Luke created an inconsistency not by becoming fatigued as he edited Matthew, but by combining two inconsistent versions of the material.

In these two instances, Luke conflated two distinct sources. An editor who combines inconsistent sources is more likely to create inconsistencies than one who follows a single source. Therefore Matthew, who followed a single source in these instances, was less likely than Luke to create inconsistencies in them. The same explanation is at least possible for the next two instances as well.

3. In the parable of the pounds, Matthew tells a consistent story with three slaves (Matt 25:14–30). Luke, on the other hand, begins with ten slaves but finishes with only three (Luke 19:12–27). Goodacre takes this as another example of Luke initially revising Matthew and then lapsing back into docile reproduction of Matthew. However, this is again not the only explanation for Luke's inconsistency. It is more likely that Luke combined two distinct versions of the parable, one with three slaves from Q and one with ten from L (see ch. 10). While Matthew maintained consistency by preserving only the version with three slaves from Q, Luke created an inconsistency not by becoming fatigued as he edited a single source, but by combining two inconsistent versions of the parable.

4. The same explanation accounts for another inconsistency that Goodacre points out in this same parable. In Luke's version, the first servant receives ten cities as his reward (Luke 19:17), yet a later statement presupposes that he received money as in Matthew (Matt 25:28; Luke 19:24). Here, too, Luke's inconsistency probably arose because he conflated Q with L. We need not assume that Luke used Matthew.

5. A fifth instance cited by Goodacre may or may not be a case of editorial fatigue. Matthew 13:16–17 refers to eyes and ears, then symmetrically to seeing and hearing. The parallel in Luke 10:23–24, however, lacks this symmetry, since Luke has no reference to ears. Goodacre assumes that Luke created this asymmetry: he forgot that he omitted the reference to ears found

in Matthew, then unthinkingly reproduced the following reference to hearing. If so, this would constitute a case of editorial fatigue. However, it is also possible that Luke preserves the more original form of the saying and that Matthew added a reference to ears in order to correct a perceived lack of symmetry in the original. Matthew would have had adequate motivation to make such a change, since he inserts this saying into a context which mentions both eyes and ears (Matt 13:13–15). This instance is therefore not a clear-cut case of editorial fatigue unless one assumes what must be demonstrated, i.e., that Matthew preserves the more original version of the saying.

6. The sixth and final instance cited by Goodacre probably is a case of editorial fatigue. In Luke 17:2, Luke speaks of "these little ones" but has not previously mentioned any little ones. Presumably he omitted such a reference that would have stood prior to 17:2. Matthew and Mark also refer to "one of these little ones" (Matt 18:6; Mark 9:42) but have a preceding referent for the expression (Matt 18:2; Mark 9:36). However, while Luke has apparently omitted part of his source, we have no reason to identify that source as Matthew.

Goodacre's argument from Luke's editorial fatigue in the double tradition thus appears less impressive than he assumed. In four of six instances, it is more likely that Luke created inconsistencies not by becoming fatigued in editing a single source, but by conflating two somewhat inconsistent sources, neither of which was Matthew. Goodacre's fifth example may or may not be a case of editorial fatigue, though his sixth probably is. The actual editorial fatigue in Luke's double tradition thus dwindles to one probable instance and one other possible instance. And these are just as easily explained by supposing that Luke used Q as by supposing that he used Matthew. Since Luke apparently created only a few such inconsistencies in the Q material, we should not take it as significant if Matthew created one or even none. Goodacre's argument therefore does not pose a problem for the Q hypothesis or make it more likely that Luke used Matthew rather than Q.

APPENDIX B
FEATURES OF STYLE AND THEME IN Q

This appendix lists features of style and theme in Q material in the order of their first appearance in Q in Luke's order, and it shows the passages in Q where each feature appears.

B.1. Reference to John the Baptist
   John appears (Matt 3:5b/Luke 3:2b–3a)
   Coming wrath (Matt 3:7a/Luke 3:7a)
   John's question (Matt 11:2, 4/Luke 7:18, 20, 22)
   Jesus on John (Matt 11:7–11/Luke 7:24–28)
   Children at market (Matt 11:18/Luke 7:33)
   Lord's prayer (Luke 11:1)
   Law until John (Matt 11:12–13/Luke 16:16)
   Elsewhere than Q: Mark, etc.

B.2. Implicit or explicit identification of John as a prophet
   John appears (Matt 3:5b/Luke 3:2b–3a)
   Jesus on John (Matt 11:9/Luke 7:26)
   Elsewhere than Q: Mark 1:6 par; 11:32 parr

B.3. Expression "brood of vipers": γεννήματα ἐχιδνῶν
   Coming wrath (Matt 3:7b/Luke 3:7b)
   On words (Matt 12:34)
   On Pharisees (Matt 23:33)

B.4. Theme of fleeing from judgment
   Coming wrath (Matt 3:7b/Luke 3:7b)
   On Pharisees (Matt 23:33)

B.5. Theme of bearing good or bad fruit
   Coming wrath (Matt 3:8, 10/Luke 3:8, 9)

Tree and fruit (Matt 7:18, 16/Luke 6:43–44)
Bad tree burned (Matt 7:19)
On words (Matt 12:33)
Elsewhere than Q: Matt 7:17 (M)

B.6. Theme of repentance: μετάνοια, μετανοέω
Coming wrath (Matt 3:8/Luke 3:8)
Greater one (Matt 3:11, not Luke 3:16)
Woes on cities (Matt 11:20; Matt 11:21/Luke 10:13)
Something more (Matt 12:41/Luke 11:32)
Correct a brother (Luke 17:3, not Matt 18:15)
Forgive 7 times (Luke 17:4, not Matt 18:21–22)
Elsewhere in L: Luke 13:3, 5; 15:7, 10; 16:30
Elsewhere: Matt 3:2; Matt 4:17/Mark 1:15; Mark 1:4/Luke 3:3; Mark 6:12;
    Luke 5:32; 24:47

B.7. Theme of cutting down a fruitless tree
Coming wrath (Matt 3:10/Luke 3:9)
Bad tree burned (Matt 7:19)
Elsewhere in L: Luke 13:6–9

B.8. Destroying something worthless by fire as analogy for judgment
Coming wrath (Matt 3:10/Luke 3:9)
Wheat and chaff (Matt 3:12/Luke 3:17)
Bad tree burned (Matt 7:19)
Weeds in wheat (Matt 13:30)
Weeds explained (Matt 13:40)
Elsewhere than Q: John 15:6

B.9. Reference to Jesus as "the one coming": ὁ ἐρχόμενος
Greater one (Matt 3:11, not Luke 3:16)
John's question (Matt 11:3/Luke 7:19, 20)
Deserted house (Matt 23:39/Luke 13:35)

B.10. Reference to the Spirit
Greater one (Matt 3:11/Luke 3:16)
Jesus' baptism (Matt 3:16/Luke 3:22)
Jesus tested (Matt 4:1/Luke 4:1b)
Jewish exorcists (Matt 12:28, not Luke 11:20)
Unforgivable sin (Matt 12:32/Luke 12:10)

Elsewhere than Q: Matt 10:20; 12:18; 22:43; 28:19; Luke 4:1a, 14, 18; 10:21; 11:13; 12:12

B.11. Analogies for separating righteous from wicked
Wheat and chaff (Matt 3:12/Luke 3:17)
Weeds in wheat (Matt 13:24–30)
Weeds explained (Matt 13:36b–43)
Parable of net (Matt 13:47–50)
Elsewhere than Q: Matt 25:32 (M)

B.12. Theme of gathering wheat into granary: συνάγειν εἰς ἀποθήκην
Wheat and chaff (Matt 3:12/Luke 3:17)
Do not worry (Matt 6:26; cf. Luke 12:24)
Weeds in wheat (Matt 13:30)
Rich fool (Luke 12:18)

B.13. Identification of Jesus as God's son
Jesus' baptism (Matt 3:17; cf. Luke 3:22)
Three temptations (Matt 4:3/Luke 4:3; Matt 4:5/Luke 4:9)
Father and son (Matt 11:27/Luke 10:22)

B.14. Theme of the kingdom of Satan
Three temptations (Matt 4:8–9/Luke 4:5–6)
Satan divided (Matt 12:26/Luke 11:18)

B.15. Form of a blessing: μακάριος
Beatitudes (Luke 6:20b, 21a, 21b)
You persecuted (Matt 5:11/Luke 6:22)
John's question (Matt 11:6/Luke 7:23)
Blessed eyes (Matt 13:16/Luke 10:23)
Hear and do (Luke 11:27, 28)
Waiting for Lord (Luke 12:37, 38)
Faithful or not (Matt 24:46/Luke 12:43)
Elsewhere in M: Matt 5:3, 4, 5, 6, 7, 8, 9, 10; 16:17
Elsewhere in L: Luke 14:14, 15; 23:29

B.16. Theme of the kingdom of God
You poor (Luke 6:20b; cf. M Matt 5:3)
Lord, Lord (Matt 7:21, not Luke 6:46)
Jesus on John (Matt 11:11/Luke 7:28)
Lord's prayer (Matt 6:10/Luke 11:2)

Do not worry (Matt 6:33/Luke 12:31)
Sons excluded (Matt 8:11/Luke 13:29; Luke 13:28)
Great supper (Matt 22:2; cf. Luke 14:15)
Law until John (Matt 11:12/Luke 16:16)
Weeds in wheat (Matt 13:24)
Weeds explained (Matt 13:38, 41, 43)
Treasure and pearl (Matt 13:44, 45)
Parable of net (Matt 13:47)
New and old (Matt 13:52)
Elsewhere in L: Parable of pounds (Luke 19:11, 12, 15)
Elsewhere: Mark (*passim*), etc.

B.17. Theme of rejected or persecuted prophets or messengers
You persecuted (Matt 5:11–12/Luke 6:22–23)
Children in market (Matt 11:16–17/Luke 7:31–35)
Seeking signs (Matt 12:38–42/Luke 11:16, 29–32)
On Pharisees (Matt 23:29–36/Luke 11:47–51)
Prophet's fate (Luke 13:33)
Deserted house (Matt 23:37/Luke 13:34)
Great supper (Matt 22:3–6/cf. L Luke 14:17–20)
Rejection first (Luke 17:25)
Elsewhere in L: Luke 4:24–27
Elsewhere: Mark 6:4/Matt 13:57; John 4:44

B.18. Expression "Son of Man"
You persecuted (Luke 6:22, not Matt 5:11)
Children in market (Matt 11:19/Luke 7:34)
On following (Matt 8:20/Luke 9:58)
Sign of Jonah (Matt 12:40/Luke 11:30)
Unforgivable sin (Matt 12:32/Luke 12:10)
Unexpected thief (Matt 24:44/Luke 12:40)
Eschatology (Matt 24:27, 37, 39/Luke 17:22, 24, 25, 26, 30)
Weeds explained (Matt 13:37, 41)
Elsewhere: Mark (*passim*), etc.

B.19. Term "reward": μισθός
You persecuted (Matt 5:12/Luke 6:23): ὁ μισθὸς ὑμῶν πολύς
Love enemies (Luke 6:35c): ὁ μισθὸς ὑμῶν πολύς
Love enemies (Matt 5:46)
Elsewhere in M: Matt 6:1, 2, 5, 16; 20:8
Elsewhere in L: Luke 10:7, not Matt 10:10

Elsewhere: Mark 9:41/Matt 10:42; Matt 10:41

B.20. Form of a woe: οὐαί
Woes on rich (Luke 6:24, 25, 26)
Woes on cities (Matt 11:21/Luke 10:13)
Inside and out (Matt 23:25, not L Luke 11:39)
On tithing (Matt 23:23/Luke 11:42)
Tombs/graves (Matt 23:27/Luke 11:44)
Tombs of prophets (Matt 23:29/Luke 11:47)
Offender's fate (Matt 18:7/Luke 17:1)
Elsewhere in M: Matt 23:15, 16
Elsewhere in M/L: Luke 11:46, not Matt 23:4; Matt 23:13/Luke 11:52
Elsewhere: Mark 13:17; 14:21; Matt 23:14; Luke 11:43

B.21. Reference to God as father
Lord's prayer (Matt 6:9; Luke 11:2)
Good gifts (Matt 7:11/Luke 11:13)
Do not worry (Matt 6:32/Luke 12:30)
Elsewhere than Q: M Matt 5:45, 48/L Luke 6:35e, 36; M Matt 7:21, not Q
    Luke 6:46

B.22. Term "condemn": καταδικάζω
On words (Matt 12:37)
Elsewhere: Matt 12:7; L Luke 6:37b; James 5:6

B.23. Theme of falling into hole
Blind lead blind (Matt 15:14b/Luke 6:39): βόθυνος
Man with dropsy (Q Matt 12:11 βόθυνος/L Luke 14:5 φρέαρ)

B.24. Term "hypocrite(s)": ὑποκριταί
Mote and beam (Matt 7:5/Luke 6:42)
On Pharisees (Matt 23:23, 25, 27, 29, not Luke 11:42, 39, 44, 47)
Faithful or not (Matt 24:51, not Luke 12:46)
Elsewhere in M: Matt 6:2, 5, 16; 23:13, 14, 15
Elsewhere in L: Luke 12:56, not Q Matt 16:3; Luke 13:15
Elsewhere: Matt 15:7/Mark 7:6; Matt 22:18

B.25. Reference to John's disciples
John's question (Matt 11:2/Luke 7:18)
Lord's prayer (Luke 11:1)
Elsewhere than Q: Mark 2:18 parr; 6:29 par; John 1:35, 37; 3:25

B.26. Theme of hearing and doing the word
    Lord, Lord (Matt 7:21/Luke 6:46)
    Two houses (Matt 7:24, 26/Luke 6:47, 49)
    Hear and do (Luke 11:28)
    Elsewhere than Q: Hear and do (Matt 12:50; Mark 3:35; Luke 8:21)

B.27. Imperative "Go tell": πορευθέντες ἀπαγγείλατε or εἴπατε
    John's question (Matt 11:4/Luke 7:22)
    Prophet's fate (Luke 13:32)
    Elsewhere than Q: Matt 28:7

B.28. Expression "this generation"
    Children in market (Matt 11:16/Luke 7:31)
    Sign of Jonah (Matt 12:39/Luke 11:29, 30
    Something more (Matt 12:42, 41/Luke 11:31, 32)
    Return of spirit (Matt 12:45b, not Luke 11:26)
    On Pharisees (Matt 23:36/Luke 11:50, 51)
    Rejection first (Luke 17:25)
    Elsewhere than Q: Mark 8:12; 8:38; 13:30 parr

B.29. Theme of "wisdom": σοφία, σοφοί
    A.   as characteristic of those inside the community
        Children in market (Matt 11:19/Luke 7:35)
        Something more (Matt 12:42/Luke 11:31)
        On Pharisees (Matt 23:34/Luke 11:49)
    B.   as characteristic of those outside the community
        Father and son (Matt 11:25/Luke 10:21)
    Elsewhere than Q: Mark 6:2/Matt 13:54; Luke 2:40, 52; 21:15

B.30. Sentence "the kingdom of God has drawn near (or come) [to you]":
ἤγγικεν or ἔφθασεν [ἐφ' ὑμᾶς] ἡ βασιλεία τοῦ θεοῦ
    Mission charge (Matt 10:7/Luke 10:9)
    Mission charge (Luke 10:11b)
    Jewish exorcists (Matt 12:28/Luke 11:20)
    Elsewhere than Q: Matt 3:2; Matt 4:17/Mark 1:15

B.31. Phrase "But know this: that…": τοῦτο δὲ γινώσκετε ὅτι
    Mission charge (Luke 10:11b)
    Unexpected thief (Matt 24:43/Luke 12:39)
    Elsewhere than Q: 2 Tim 3:1

B.32. Theme of the day of judgment
Mission charge (Matt 10:15/Luke 10:12)
Woes on cities (Matt 11:22, 24/Luke 10:14)
Something more (Matt 12:42, 41/Luke 11:31, 32)
On words (Matt 12:36)
Elsewhere than Q: Matt 5:21, 22; 1 John 4:17 etc.

B.33. Theme of Sodom and Lot
Mission charge (Matt 10:15/Luke 10:12)
Woes on cities (Matt 11:23, 24)
Eschatology (Luke 17:28–29, 32)

B.34. Phrase "Who (What man/woman) among you"
Friend at night (Luke 11:5)
Good gifts (Matt 7:9/L Luke 11:11)
Do not worry (Matt 6:27/Luke 12:25)
Man with dropsy (Matt 12:11/L Luke 14:5)
Elsewhere only in L: Luke 14:28; 15:4, not Q Matt 18:12; Luke 15:8; 17:7

B.35. Term χρῄζω
Friend at night (Luke 11:8)
Do not worry (Matt 6:32/Luke 12:30)
Elsewhere than Q: Rom 16:2; 2 Cor 3:1

B.36. Expression "(you) being evil": πονηροὶ ὄντες or ὑπάρχοντες
Good gifts (Matt 7:11/Luke 11:13)
On words (Matt 12:34a)

B.37. Eschatological correlative
Sign of Jonah (Matt 12:40/Luke 11:30)
Return of spirit (Matt 12:45b, not Luke 11:26)
Weeds explained (Matt 13:40)
Parable of net (Matt 13:48–49)
Eschatology (Matt 24:27, 37, 38–39/Luke 17:24, 26, 30)

B.38. Theme of something greater
Something more (Matt 12:42, 41/Luke 11:31, 32)
Elsewhere than Q: Matt 12:5–7; cf. 9:13a

B.39. Theme that life is more than possessions
Do not worry (Matt 6:25b/Luke 12:23)

Elsewhere than Q: Against greed (L Luke 12:15)

B.40. Expression "today and tomorrow": σήμερον καὶ αὔριον
Do not worry (Matt 6:30/Luke 12:28)
Prophet's fate (Luke 13:32, 33)
Elsewhere than Q: James 4:13

B.41. Term "store up": θησαυρίζω
On treasure (Matt 6:19, 20, not Luke 12:33a)
Rich fool (Luke 12:21)

B.42. Term "treasure": θησαυρός
On treasure (Matt 6:19, 20, 21/Luke 12:33b, 34
On words (Matt 12:35/Luke 6:45a)
Hidden treasure (Matt 13:44)
New and old (Matt 13:52)
Elsewhere than Q: Mark 10:21 parr; Matt 2:11

B.43. Term "thief": κλέπτης
On treasure (Matt 6:19, 20/Luke 12:33b)
Unexpected thief (Matt 24:43/Luke 12:39)

B.44. Term "break in": διορύσσω
On treasure (Matt 6:19, 20, not Luke 12:33b)
Unexpected thief (Matt 24:43/Luke 12:39)

B.45. Theme of being "faithful": πιστός
Faithful or not (Matt 24:45/Luke 12:42)
Faithful in little (Luke 16:10–12)
Parable of pounds (Matt 25:21, 23/Luke 19:17)

B.46. Theme of prudent (φρόνιμος) manager or slave
Faithful or not (Matt 24:45/Luke 12:42)
Fired manager (Luke 16:8)

B.47. Sentence "There, there will be weeping and gnashing of teeth": ἐκεῖ ἔσται
ὁ κλαυθμὸς καὶ ὁ βρυγμὸς τῶν ὀδόντων
Faithful or not (Matt 24:51, not Luke 12:46)
Sons excluded (Matt 8:12/Luke 13:28)
No garment (Matt 22:13)
Parable of pounds (Matt 25:30, not L Luke 19:27)

Weeds explained (Matt 13:42)
Parable of net (Matt 13:50)

B.48. Animals in argument from lesser to greater to justify Sabbath healing
Man with dropsy (Q Matt 12:11/ L Luke 14:5)
Elsewhere in L: Crippled woman (Luke 13:15)

B.49. Expression "cast out": ἐκβάλλειν ἔξω
Sons excluded (Luke 13:28; cf. Matt 8:12)
Spoiled salt (Matt 5:13b/Luke 14:35)
Parable of net (Matt 13:48)
Elsewhere than Q: Mark 12:8 parr; Luke 4:29

B.50. Expression "the sons of the kingdom": οἱ υἱοὶ τῆς βασιλείας[1]
Sons excluded (Matt 8:12, not L Luke 13:28)
Weeds explained (Matt 13:38)

B.51. Phrase "cast out into the outer darkness": ἐκβάλλειν εἰς τὸ σκότος τὸ ἐξώτερον[2]
Sons excluded (Matt 8:12, cf. L Luke 13:28e)
No garment (Matt 22:13)
Parable of pounds (Matt 25:30, not L Luke 19:27)

B.52. Phrase "cast them into the furnace of fire": βαλοῦσιν αὐτοὺς εἰς τὴν κάμινον τοῦ πυρός[3]
Weeds explained (Matt 13:42)
Parable of net (Matt 13:50)

B.53. Term "mammon": μαμωνᾶς
Fired manager (Luke 16:9)
Faithful in little (Luke 16:11)

---

1. Since this expression occurs only in Matthew, it could be Matthean redaction. However, since both instances occur in a Q context, the expression probably came from Q.

2. Since this phrase occurs only in Matthew, it may be Matthean redaction. However, since it occurs nowhere except before the Q sentence, "There, there will be weeping and gnashing of teeth," it probably represents Matthean revision of the Q expression "cast out" (ἐκβάλλειν ἔξω).

3. Since this phrase occurs only in Matthew, it could be Matthean redaction. However, since both instances occur in what is probably a Q context, it probably represents Matthean revision of the Q expression "cast out" (ἐκβάλλειν ἔξω).

Two masters (Matt 6:24/Luke 16:13)

B.54. Expression "useless slave(s)": δοῦλοι ἀχρεῖοι
     Parable of pounds" (Q Matt 25:30, not L Luke 19:27)
     Elsewhere in L: Useless slaves (Luke 17:10)

APPENDIX C
Q IN MATTHEW'S ORDER

The table below lists the Q material in Matthew's order with related material from M and L.

- The first column names the passage.
- The second column shows relevant M material in Matthew.
- The third and fourth columns show Q material in Matthew and Luke respectively.
- The last column shows relevant L material in Luke.
- A line (—) indicates a place where one Evangelist or the other has probably omitted material.
- An arrow preceding a reference in smaller font (e.g., → 4:6b) indicates a place to which one Evangelist or the other probably moved the material so indicated. While the reference appears where the material originally stood in its source, the arrow points to the place to which the Evangelist moved it.

	Matthew M	Matthew Q	Luke Q	Luke L
John and Jesus				
John appears		—	3:2b	
Region of Jordan		3:5b	3:3a	
Coming wrath		3:7–10	3:7–9	
Greater one		3:11	3:16	
Wheat and chaff		3:12	3:17	
To fulfill all	3:14–15			
Jesus' baptism		3:16–17	3:21–22	
Jesus tested		4:1	4:1b–2a	
Bread alone		4:2–4	4:2b–4	
Angel hands		4:6–7	4:9–12	

All kingdoms		4:8–11a	→ 4:6c	4:5–8, 13
A sermon				
The poor	5:3	—	6:20b	
The grieving	5:4			
The meek	5:5			
The hungry	5:6	—	6:21a	
The weeping		—	6:21b	
The merciful	5:7			
The pure	5:8			
The peacemakers	5:9			
The persecuted	5:10	5:11–12	6:22–23	
Woes on rich		—	6:24–26	
Salt of earth	5:13a			
Spoiled salt		5:13b	14:34–35b	
Light of world	5:14			
Lamp on stand		5:15	11:33	
Let light shine	5:16			
Not abolished	5:17			
Law to remain		5:18	16:17	
Least command	5:19			
More righteous	5:20			
Against anger	5:21–22			
Be reconciled	5:23–24			
Agree on way	5:25	5:26	12:57–59	
Against lust	5:27–28			
Cut off member	5:29–30			
Against divorce	5:31–32	5:32	16:18	
Against oaths	5:33–37			
Against resistance	5:38–39a			
Turn the cheek	5:39b	—	→ 6:29a	
Tunic, cloak	5:40	—	→ 6:29b	
Second mile	5:41			
Give if asked	5:42	—	→ 6:30	
Against hate	5:43			
Love enemies	5:44ab		6:27	
Bless, pray	5:44c		6:28	

Sons of Father	5:45			
If you love	5:46–47	—	6:32–33	
If you lend				6:34
Love enemies		—	6:35abd	6:35c
Sons of Father			6:35ef	
Be like Father	5:48		6:36	
Secret devotions	6:1–8			
Lord's prayer	6:9–13	—	11:1–4	
Secret fasting	6:16–18			
Sell belongings				12:33a
On treasure		6:19–20	12:33b	12:33b
Where heart is		6:21	12:34	
Lamp of body		6:22–23	11:34–35	11:36
Two masters		6:24	16:13	
Do not worry		6:25–33	12:22–31	12:22–31
Today's trouble	6:34			
Do not judge		7:1	6:37a	6:37b
Same judgment		7:2a	—	6:37c
Same measure		7:2b	6:38c	6:38ab
Mote and beam		7:3–5	6:41–42	
Dogs, swine	7:6			
Ask, seek, knock		7:7–8	11:9–10	
Good gifts		7:9–11	11:13	11:11–12
Golden rule	7:12	7:12	→ 6:31	
Are few saved				13:23
Narrow gate		7:13a	—	13:24
Two paths	7:13b–14			
False prophets	7:15			
Tree and fruit	7:17	7:18	6:43	
Known by fruits	7:20	7:16a	6:44a	
Figs, grapes		7:16b	6:44b	
Tree cut down		7:19		
Lord, Lord	7:21	—	6:46	
Don't know you		7:22–23	—	13:26–27
Two houses	7:24–27	—	6:47–49	
Jesus ends words	7:28a	—	7:1a	

To Capernaum		→ 8:5a	7:1b	
Miscellaneous				
Centurion's plea		8:5b–6	—	7:2
Jewish elders				7:3–5
Centurion's faith		8:7–10	7:6–9	
Sons excluded		8:11–12	13:29, 28a	13:28bcde
Boy healed		8:13	—	7:10
Two followers		8:19–22	9:57–60	
Another follower		—	9:61–62	
On mission				
70 sent				10:1
Pray for workers		9:37–38	10:2	
Sheep of Israel	10:5c–6			
Kingdom come	10:7–8			
No purse/gold	10:9a	—	—	10:4a
No knapsack	10:10a	—	—	10:4b
No sandals	10:10d	—	—	10:4c
Greet no one				10:4d
Worthy of food	10:10f			
One worthy	10:11ab			
Greet the house	10:12–13			10:5–6
Stay in house				10:7
If received		—	10:8–9	
If not received		—	10:10–11	
Better for Sodom		10:15	10:12	
Cities of Israel	10:23			
70 return				10:17–20
Miscellaneous				
John's question		11:2–6	7:18–23	
Jesus on John		11:7–11	7:24–28	
Law until John		11:12–13	16:16	
Children in market		11:16–19	7:31–35	
Woes on cities		11:20–24	10:13–15	
Father and son		11:25–27	10:21–22	
Come unto me	11:28–30			
Man with dropsy		12:10c, 11	—	14:1–6

Friend at night		—	11:5–8	
Mute demoniac	12:22–23	12:22–23	11:14	
By Beelzebul	12:24	12:24	11:15	
Satan divided		12:25–26	11:17–18	
Jewish exorcists		12:27–28	11:19–20	
Strong man		—	11:21–22	
With or against		12:30	11:23	
Hear and do		—	11:27–28	
Unforgivable sin	12:31	12:32	12:10	
On words		12:33–37	→ 6:45	
Request for sign		12:38	—	
Sign of Jonah		12:39–40	11:29–30	
Something more		12:42, 41	11:31–32	
Return of spirit		12:43–45	→ 11:24-26	
Parables				
Blessed eyes		13:16–17	10:23–24	
Weeds in wheat		13:24–30		
Weeds explained		13:36b–43		
Treasure and pearl		13:44–46		
Parable of net		13:47–50		
New and old		13:51–52		
Miscellaneous				
Peter on water	14:28–31			
Blind lead blind		15:14b	6:39	
Signs of times		16:2–3	—	12:54–56
Peter the rock	16:16–19			
Effective faith		17:20b	17:5–6	
Temple tax	17:24–27			
On community				
Who is greatest	18:1			
Humble like child	18:4			
Offender's fate		18:7	17:1–2	
Angels see God	18:10			
Lost sheep		18:12–13	—	15:3–7
Father's will	18:14			
Correct a brother	18:15	18:15	17:3	

Tell church	18:16–17		
Bind, agree	18:18–20		
Forgive 7 times	18:21–22	—	17:4	
Unforgiving slave	18:23–35		
Miscellaneous			
On eunuchs	19:10–12		
12 thrones		19:28b	22:28, 30b	22:29–30a
Workers' pay	20:1–15		
Last first		20:16	—	13:30
Mouth of babes	21:14–16		
Two sons	21:28–32		
Great supper		22:1–10	—	14:15–24
No garment		22:11–14	—	
On Pharisees			
Pharisee's dinner				11:37–38
Inside and out				11:39–41
Lawyer objects				11:45
Moses' seat	23:1–3		
Heavy burdens	23:4			11:46
To be seen	23:5		
Called rabbi	23:7b–12		
Kingdom locked	23:13			11:52
Proselytes, oaths	23:15–22		
On tithing	23:23	—	11:42	
Gnat and camel	23:24		
Inside and out	23:25–26	—	—	
Tombs/graves	23:27–28	—	11:44	
Prophets' tombs	23:29–32	—	11:47–48	
Brood of vipers		23:33	—	
Blood avenged	23:34–36	—	11:49–51	
Foes plot				11:53–54
Against greed		—	12:15	
Rich fool		—	12:16–21	
Little flock				12:32
On Jerusalem			
Prophet's fate		—	13:31–33	

Deserted house		23:37–39	13:34–35	
Fired manager		—	16:1–9	
Faithful in little		—	16:10–12	
Eschatology				
Days will come		—	17:22	
Apostasy, hate	24:10–12			
Here or there		24:26	17:23	
Like lightning		24:27	17:24	
Rejection first		—	17:25	
Where body is		24:28		
Sign, tribes	24:30ab			
Great trumpet	24:31b			
Days of Noah		24:37–39a	17:26–27	
Days of Lot		—	17:28–29	
So it will be		24:39b	17:30	
No turning back		—	17:31	
Lot's wife		—	17:32	
Taken or left		24:40–41	17:34–35	
Where body is			17:37	
Keep watch		24:42	—	
Loins and lamps		—	12:35	
Unexpected thief		24:43–44	12:39–40	
Faithful or not		24:45–51a	12:42–46	
Gnashing teeth		24:51b	—	12:47–48a
Much required				12:48b
Ten virgins	25:1–9			
Don't know you	25:10–12			13:25
Banquet lesson				14:7–14
Parable of pounds		25:14–30	19:12–27	19:12–27
Nations judged	25:31–46			

APPENDIX D
Q IN LUKE'S ORDER

The table below lists the Q material primarily in Luke's order with related material from M and L.

- The first column names the passage.
- The second column shows relevant M material in Matthew.
- The third and fourth columns show Q material in Matthew and Luke respectively.
- The last column shows relevant L material in Luke.
- A line (—) indicates a place where one Evangelist or the other has probably omitted material.
- An arrow preceding a reference in smaller font (e.g., → 4:6b) indicates a place to which one Evangelist or the other probably moved the material so indicated. While the reference appears where the material originally stood in its source, the arrow points to the place to which the Evangelist moved it.

	Matthew M	Matthew Q	Luke Q	Luke L
John and Jesus				
John appears		—	3:2b	
Region of Jordan		3:5b	3:3a	
Coming wrath		3:7–10	3:7–9	
Greater one		3:11	3:16	
Wheat and chaff		3:12	3:17	
Jesus' baptism		3:16–17	3:21–22	
Jesus tested		4:1	4:1b–2a	
Bread alone		4:2–4	4:2b–4	
All kingdoms		4:8–10	→ 4:6c	4:5–8
Angel hands		4:6–7	4:9–12	
Devil leaves		4:11a	—	4:13

A sermon				
The poor	5:3	—	6:20b	
The grieving	5:4			
The meek	5:5			
The hungry	5:6	—	6:21a	
The weeping		—	6:21b	
The merciful	5:7			
The pure	5:8			
The peacemakers	5:9			
The persecuted	5:10	5:11–12	6:22–23	
Woes on rich		—	6:24–26	
Against resistance	5:38–39a			
Turn the cheek	5:39b	—	→ 6:29a	
Tunic, cloak	5:40	—	→ 6:29b	
Second mile	5:41			
Give if asked	5:42	—	→ 6:30	
Golden rule		→ 7:12	→ 6:31	
Against hate	5:43			
But I say	5:44a	—	6:27a	
Love enemies	5:44b	—	6:27bc	
Bless, pray	5:44c	—	6:28	
Sons of Father	5:45			
If you love	5:46	—	6:32	
If you do good	5:47	—	6:33	
If you lend				6:34
Love enemies		—	6:35abd	6:35c
Sons of Father		—	6:35ef	
Be like Father	5:48	—	6:36	
Do not judge		7:1	6:37a	6:37b
Same judgment		7:2a	—	6:37c
Same measure		7:2b	6:38c	6:38ab
Blind lead blind		15:14b	6:39	
Mote and beam		7:3–5	6:41–42	
Golden rule	7:12			
False prophets	7:15			
Tree and fruit	7:17	7:18	6:43	
Known by fruits	7:20	7:16a	6:44a	

Figs, grapes		7:16b	6:44b	
Tree cut down		7:19		
Lord, Lord	7:21	—	6:46	
Two houses	7:24–27	—	6:47–49	
Jesus ends words	7:28a	—	7:1a	
To Capernaum		8:5a	7:1b	
Miscellaneous				
Centurion's plea		8:5b–6	—	7:2
Jewish elders				7:3–5
Centurion's faith		8:7–10	7:6–9	
Boy healed		8:13	—	7:10
John's question		11:2–6	7:18–23	
Jesus on John		11:7–11	7:24–28	
Children in market		11:16–19	7:31–35	
Two followers		8:19–22	9:57–60	
Another follower		—	9:61–62	
On mission				
70 sent				10:1
Pray for workers		9:37–38	10:2	
Sheep of Israel	10:5c–6			
Kingdom come	10:7–8			
No purse/gold	10:9a	—	—	10:4a
No knapsack	10:10a	—	—	10:4b
No sandals	10:10d	—	—	10:4c
Greet no one				10:4d
Worthy of food	10:10f			
One worthy	10:11ab			
Greet the house	10:12–13			10:5–6
Stay in house				10:7
If received		—	10:8–9	
If not received		—	10:10–11	
Better for Sodom		10:15	10:12	
Cities of Israel	10:23			
Woes on cities		11:20–24	10:13–15	
70 return				10:17–20
Father and son		11:25–27	10:21–22	
Blessed eyes		13:16–17	10:23–24	

Miscellaneous				
Lord's prayer	6:9–13	—	11:1–4	
Friend at night		—	11:5–8	
Ask, seek, knock		7:7–8	11:9–10	
Good gifts		7:9–11	11:13	11:11–12
Mute demoniac	12:22–23	12:22–23	11:14	
By Beelzebul	12:24	12:24	11:15	
Satan divided		12:25–26	11:17–18	
Jewish exorcists		12:27–28	11:19–20	
Strong man		—	11:21–22	
With or against		12:30	11:23	
Hear and do		—	11:27–28	
On words		12:33–37	→ 6:45	
Request for sign		12:38	—	
Sign of Jonah		12:39–40	11:29–30	
Something more		12:42, 41	11:31–32	
Return of spirit		12:43–45	→ 11:24–26	
Lamp on stand		5:15	11:33	
Lamp of body		6:22–23	11:34–35	11:36
Weeds in wheat		13:24–30		
Weeds explained		13:36b–43		
Treasure and pearl		13:44–46		
Parable of net		13:47–50		
New and old		13:51–52		
On Pharisees				
Pharisee's dinner				11:37–38
Inside and out				11:39–41
Lawyer objects				11:45
Moses' seat	23:1–3			
Heavy burdens	23:4			11:46
To be seen	23:5			
Called rabbi	23:7b–12			
Kingdom locked	23:13			11:52
Proselytes, oaths	23:15–22			
On tithing	23:23	—	11:42	
Gnat and camel	23:24			
Inside and out	23:25–26	—	—	

Tombs/graves	23:27–28	—	11:44	
Prophets' tombs	23:29–32	—	11:47–48	
Brood of vipers		23:33		
Blood avenged	23:34–36	—	11:49–51	
Foes plot				11:53–54
Miscellaneous				
Unforgivable sin		12:32	12:10	
Against greed		—	12:15	
Rich fool		—	12:16–21	
Do not worry		6:25–33	12:22–31	12:22–31
Little flock				12:32
Sell belongings				12:33a
On treasure		6:19–20	12:33b	12:33b
Where heart is		6:21	12:34	
Keep watch		24:42	—	
Loins and lamps		—	12:35	
Unexpected thief		24:43–44	12:39–40	
Faithful or not		24:45–51a	12:42–46	
Gnashing teeth		24:51b	—	12:47–48a
Signs of times		16:2–3	—	12:54–56
Agree on way	5:25	5:26	12:57–59	
Are few saved				13:23
Narrow gate		7:13a	—	13:24
Don't know you	25:10–12	7:22–23	13:26–27	13:25
East and west		8:11a	13:29a	
North and south			13:29b	
And recline		8:11b	13:29c	
With patriarchs		8:11c	—	13:28b
And prophets				13:28c
In the kingdom		8:11d	13:29d	13:28d
Sons cast out		8:12a	—	13:28e
Gnashing teeth		8:12b	→ 13:28a	
Last first		20:16	—	13:30
Prophet's fate		—	13:31–33	
Deserted house		23:37–39	13:34–35	
Man with dropsy		12:10c, 11	—	14:1–6
Banquet lesson				14:7–14

Great supper		22:1–10	—	14:15–24
No garment		22:11–14	—	
Spoiled salt		5:13b	14:34–35b	
Lost sheep		18:12–13	—	15:3–7
Fired manager		—	16:1–9	
Faithful in little		—	16:10–12	
Two masters		6:24	16:13	
Law until John		11:12–13	16:16	
Law to remain		5:18	16:17	
On divorce	5:31–32	5:32	16:18	
Offender's fate		18:7	17:1–2	
Angels see God	18:10			
Father's will	18:14			
Correct a brother	18:15	18:15	17:3	
Tell church	18:16–17			
Bind, agree	18:18–20			
Forgive 7 times	18:21–22	—	17:4	
Unforgiving slave	18:23–35			
Effective faith		17:20b	17:5–6	
Eschatology				
Days will come		—	17:22	
Apostasy, hate	24:10–12			
Here or there		24:26	17:23	
Like lightning		24:27	17:24	
Where body is		24:28		
Rejection first		—	17:25	
Sign, tribes	24:30ab			
Great trumpet	24:31b			
Days of Noah		24:37–39a	17:26–27	
Days of Lot		—	17:28–29	
So it will be		24:39b	17:30	
No turning back		—	17:31	
Lot's wife		—	17:32	
Taken or left		24:40–41	17:34–35	
Where body is			17:37	
Parable of pounds		25:14–30	19:12–27	19:12–27
12 thrones		19:28b	22:28, 30b	22:29–30a

APPENDIX E
DID THE EVANGELIST COMPOSE
MATTHEW 13:36–43 AND 13:49–50?

In chapter 5, I argued that the parable discourse unique to Matthew (Matt 13:24–30, 36b–52) may have come from Q. In contrast, Joachim Jeremias argued that Matthew composed at least some of this material, specifically, the interpretation of the parable of the weeds (Matt 13:36–43) and the interpretation of the parable of the net (Matt 13:49–50).[1] In arguing for Matthew's composition of the former, he cited 37 examples in this pericope of what he claimed were linguistic characteristics of the Evangelist Matthew. On closer examination, however, most of his examples are not particularly impressive.

For Matthew 13:36, Jeremias cites ἀφείς as Matthean redaction, noting that "The use of an introductory participial construction to link up with the preceding sentence is a typical Matthaean usage."[2] This may be so, but use of an introductory participial construction is a typical usage of most other authors as well (e.g., Mark 1:10, 16, 18, 19, 20, 26; Luke 1:22, 28, 39, 60, 63). This construction tells us nothing about the author of the passage.

For the same verse, Jeremias finds a further Matthean characteristic in the plural "crowds." While the plural occurs 30 times in Matthew, it also occurs once in Mark and 22 times in Luke-Acts, as Jeremias himself observes.[3] It is therefore hardly a definitive indicator of Matthean composition.

Jeremias further attributes ἦλθεν to Matthew on the grounds that the aorist indicative following an aorist participle to describe an action following a preceding one is "a Matthaean stylistic peculiarity."[4] Once again, it may be true that Matthew uses this construction, but other authors use it frequently as well (e.g., Mark 1:18, 19, 20, 26, 29, 31, 35, 41, 43, 45, etc.).

---

1. Jeremias, *Parables*, 81–85.
2. Ibid., 82 n. 53.
3. Ibid., 82 n. 54.
4. Ibid., 82 n. 55.

According to Jeremias, the phrase εἰς τὴν οἰκίαν in the sense "into the house" occurs in the New Testament only in Matthew.[5] That claim is simply mistaken. It occurs not infrequently in Mark and Luke-Acts as well (Mark 1:29; 3:27; cf. 10:10; Luke 4:38; 7:44; 8:51; 22:10; 22:54; Acts 9:17).

Similarly Jeremias claims that the sequence of words αὐτῷ οἱ μαθηταὶ αὐτοῦ is a peculiarity of Matthew.[6] Yet it occurs not infrequently elsewhere as well (Mark 5:31; 6:1; 6:35; 8:4; 14:12; Luke 7:11; cf. Luke 9:18; 22:39; John 11:8).

Perhaps most astonishingly, Jeremias cites the participle λέγων as a stylistic peculiarity of Matthew,[7] though it occurs regularly in all the Gospels.

Moving on to Matthew 13:37, Jeremias finds a Matthean characteristic in the expression ὁ δὲ ἀποκριθεὶς εἶπεν.[8] While this occurs 17 or 18 times in Matthew, it also occurs twice in Mark and three times in Luke, as Jeremias recognized. Once it occurs in the triple tradition (Matt 12:48; Luke 8:21; cf. Mark 3:33) and once in a source common to Matthew and Mark (Matt 19:4; Mark 10:3). Thus while Matthew favors it, it does not definitively indicate Matthean composition.

In Matthew 13:38, Jeremias points to the term ὁ κόσμος as a favorite word of Matthew.[9] While Matthew uses it nine times, Mark has it two or three times, Luke-Acts four times, and the Fourth Gospel about seventy-seven times. It occurs twice in the triple tradition (Matt 16:26; Mark 8:36; Luke 9:25; also Matt 26:13; Mark 14:9) and probably in Q (Luke 11:50; cf. M Matt 23:35). Thus while Matthew uses it more frequently than Mark or Luke, it need not be Matthean composition.

For the same verse, Jeremias also lists "οὗτοι (casus pendens)" as a Matthean characteristic. He is apparently referring to the superfluous use of οὗτος as a resumptive pronoun following another subject. While Matthew has ten or eleven instances of this (Matt 5:19; 7:21 v.l.; 10:22; 13:20, 22, 23; 13:38; 18:4; 21:42; 24:13; 26:23), Mark has four (Mark 3:35; 6:16; 12:10; 13:13), and Luke has six (Luke 8:14, 15; 9:24; 9:48; 20:17; 23:52). It occurs at least three times in the triple tradition (Matt 13:22, 23; Luke 8:14, 15; cf. Mark 4:18, 20; also Matt 21:42; Mark 12:10; Luke 20:17; also Matt 10:22; 24:13; Mark 13:13) and also in M (Matt 5:19; 18:4). Again, while Matthew uses this construction more frequently than Mark or Luke, one cannot for this reason assume that it is Matthean composition in Matthew 13:38.

---

5. Ibid., 82 n. 56.
6. Ibid., 82 n. 58.
7. Ibid., 83 n. 59.
8. Ibid., 83 n. 64.
9. Ibid., 83 n. 65.

Jeremias lists the expression οἱ υἱοὶ τῆς βασιλείας as a Matthean expression because it occurs only here and in Matthew 8:11.[10] However, the expression in Matthew 8:11 could be from Q instead of Matthew (see table 10.13). From the same expression he also lists ἡ βασιλεία separately because the term "the kingdom" without further qualification occurs six times (elsewhere) in Matthew and only in Luke 12:32 elsewhere in the New Testament.[11] Actually, "the kingdom" without qualification occurs twice in Luke-Acts (Luke 12:32; Acts 20:25) and once in Revelation (Rev 1:9).

Jeremias takes ὁ πονηρός in the sense "the Devil" as another Matthean characteristic.[12] It occurs five times in Matthew and eight times in the New Testament outside the Gospels. In Matthew it occurs three times in M (Matt 5:37; 5:39; 6:13). In the parable of the sower (Matt 13:19), it may reflect Matthean redaction, but not necessarily so if one does not subscribe to Markan priority. It therefore does not clearly indicate Matthean composition.

Furthermore, Jeremias includes the expression οἱ υἱοὶ τοῦ πονηροῦ in his list of Matthean characteristics because it occurs only here in the New Testament and probably came from the same hand as οἱ υἱοὶ τῆς βασιλείας.[13] However, as I mentioned above, the latter expression may have come from Q.

In Matthew 13:40, Jeremias lists both ὥσπερ and οὕτως ἔσται as favorite expressions of Matthew.[14] He fails to consider that here they form an eschatological correlative, a typical feature not of Matthew but of Q (see table 5.2).

From the same verse, Jeremias identifies οὖν in connection with another particle (here ὥσπερ) as a Matthean characteristic because it occurs eleven times in Matthew but only five times in Luke.[15] However, it occurs in Q (Matt 7:11/Luke 11:13; Matt 6:22b/Luke 11:34b [cf. 11:36]; Matt 6:23b/Luke 11:35; Matt 6:28/Luke 12:26; Luke 16:11) and therefore in Matthew 13:40 it could have come from Q rather than Matthew.

In Matthew 13:41, Jeremias also lists τὸ σκάνδαλον as a characteristic Matthean expression because it occurs five times in Matthew and only once in Luke.[16] The term in Matthew 16:23 is probably Matthean redaction. However, it also occurs in Q (Matt 18:7/Luke 17:1), and therefore in Matthew 13:41 it could have come from Q rather than Matthew.

---

10. Ibid., 83 n. 68.
11. Ibid., 83 n. 67.
12. Ibid., 83 n. 69.
13. Ibid., 83 n. 70.
14. Ibid., 83 n. 72, 74.
15. Ibid., 84 n. 73.
16. Ibid., 84 n. 78.

Jeremias also ascribes ἡ ἀνομία to Matthew because it occurs four times in Matthew (7:23; 13:41; 23:28; 24:12) and nowhere else in the Gospels.[17] He overlooks the fact that Matthew 7:23 is a Q passage where Matthew's ἀνομία preserves the more original reading of Q, a quotation of Psalm 6:8. Furthermore Matthew 23:28 and 24:12 probably came from M rather than Matthew (see ch. 9 notes 57 and 61). Thus the term in Matthew 13:41 could have come from either Q or M.

Moving on to Matthew 13:42, Jeremias attributes the expression ἡ κάμινος τοῦ πυρός to Matthew because it occurs only here and Matthew 13:50.[18] However, this argument is somewhat circular. Both passages belong to the parable material unique to Matthew in Matthew 13 and probably came from the same hand. The question is whether this hand was Matthew, Q, or M. To simply attribute this expression to Matthew is to presuppose what must be proved.

From the same verse, Jeremias also lists the sentence "There, there will be weeping and gnashing of teeth" as a characteristic expression in Matthew because it occurs six times in Matthew and only once in Luke.[19] Again Jeremias overlooks the fact that this sentence comes from Q. Luke includes it once from Q (Matt 8:12/Luke 13:28) but otherwise avoids it (see the discussion of Matthew's parable discourse in ch. 5). Thus the sentence in Matthew 13:42 could have come from Q.

In Matthew 13:43, Jeremias takes οἱ δίκαιοι as a Matthaen expression because this term in relation to the last judgment and with an allusion to Daniel 12:2–3 occurs only in Matthew (13:43, echoed in 13:49; 25:46).[20] But since only Matthew 13:43 alludes to Daniel 12:2–3, such an allusion does not indicate whether this verse came from Matthew or M or Q. And the term "the righteous" in relation to the last judgment is not unique to Matthew, but also occurs in Luke 14:14.

Jeremias further claims the term ἐκλάμπειν as Matthean because it is a *hapax legomenon* in the New Testament, found only in Matthew.[21] But if a word occurs only once, it is impossible to determine its source on the basis of that fact. It could have occurred once in either Q or M.

In the phrase ἐν τῇ βασιλείᾳ τοῦ πατρὸς αὐτῶν, Jeremias considers ἡ βασιλεία τοῦ πατρός as a Matthean expression because a reference to the kingdom of the Father occurs in the New Testament only here and in Mat-

---

17. Ibid., 84 n. 79.
18. Ibid., 84 n. 80.
19. Ibid., 84 n. 81.
20. Ibid., 84 n. 83.
21. Ibid., 84 n. 84.

thew 26:29, though it occurs seven times in the Gospel of Thomas.[22] However, the fact that the expression came from Matthew one time in Matthew 26:29 does not necessarily mean that it came from Matthew in 13:43. The Lord's prayer, which addresses God as "Father" and refers to "your kingdom" would provide M or Q with the material from which to draw the expression "kingdom of the Father."

In the same phrase, Jeremias also considers the possessive construction ὁ πατὴρ αὐτῶν as Matthean because "Father" with a possessive pronoun (σου, ἡμῶν, ὑμῶν, αὐτῶν) "is a characteristic Matthaean circumlocution for the divine name," and he notes that this expression occurs with the third personal pronoun only here in the New Testament.[23] Actually, the construction occurs with the third singular ("his Father") in the triple tradition (Matt 16:27; Mark 8:38; cf. Luke 9:26). The expression does occur in Matthean redaction (Matt 6:26; 7:11; 10:20, 29, 32, 33; 12:50; 15:13; 20:23; 26:29, 39, 42). However, in the great majority of instances, the construction in Matthew comes from M (Matt 5:16, 45, 48; 6:1, 4, 6, 6, 8, 9, 18, 18; 7:21; 16:17; 18:10, 14, 19, 35; 23:9; 25:34, 41; 26:53). It also occurs in Q (Luke 6:36/M Matt 5:45; Matt 6:32/Luke 12:30; Matt 11:27/Luke 10:22), in a source common to Matthew and Mark (Mark 11:25, [26]; Matt 6:14, 15), and in L (Luke 1:49; 12:32; 22:29; 24:49). It therefore provides no evidence for Matthean composition.

Jeremias also regards the sentence ὁ ἔχων ὦτα ἀκουέτω as a characteristic of Matthew because the form without the infinitive ἀκούειν after ὦτα and with the plural ὦτα is found only in Matthew.[24] This call to hear occurs seven or eight times in the Gospels: once in the triple tradition (Matt 13:9; Mark 4:9; Luke 8:8), once or twice more in Mark (Mark 4:23; 7:16 v.l.), twice in Matthew (Matt 11:15; 13:43), and once in Luke (Luke 14:35). All seven or eight of these sentences in the Gospels use the plural ὦτα. In all three instances in Matthew, some manuscripts include the infinitive ἀκούειν and others do not: i.e. ὁ ἔχων ὦτα [ἀκούειν] ἀκουέτω. Since the text is uncertain, we cannot certainly identify the form in Matthew 13:43 as Matthean.

Once we have weeded out the questionable examples from Jeremias's list, there remain the following legitimate indications of the Evangelist Matthew's hand: τότε (13:36, 43); προσῆλθον (13:36); διασάφησον ἡμῖν τὴν παραβολὴν (13:36); τὴν παραβολὴν τῶν ζιζανίων τοῦ ἀγροῦ (13:36); τοῦ ἀγροῦ (13:36); συντέλεια αἰῶνος (13:39, 40); αὐτοῦ in the expression "his angels" (13:41); αὐτοῦ in the expression "his kingdom" (13:41); and ὡς ὁ ἥλιος (13:43).

---

22. Ibid., 84 n. 86.
23. Ibid., 84 n. 87.
24. Ibid., 84 n. 88.

This much more modest list of Matthean characteristics provides less reason to think that Matthew composed this pericope. Most of the characteristics occur in the introductory sentence (Matt 13:36) and not in the interpretation itself. This distribution is compatible with the view that the Evangelist revised a pre-existing pericope, especially the introduction. However, even part of the introduction is pre-Matthean. The initial phrase (τότε ἀφεὶς τοὺς ὄχλους) corresponds to Mark 4:36a (καὶ ἀφέντες τὸν ὄχλον) at the conclusion of the parable material shared by Mark and Matthew. Matthew's redaction is apparent in the initial τότε, but otherwise either Matthew or Mark could preserve the more original reading.

Jeremias also attributes to Matthew the interpretive conclusion of the parable of the net (Matt 13:49–50 in 13:47–50) because of the Matthean characteristics that he finds there.[25] I have already shown that most of these do not support Matthean composition: οὕτως ἔσται, οἱ δίκαιοι, ἡ κάμινος τοῦ πυρός, and the sentence "There, there will be weeping and gnashing of teeth." Jeremias also regards the verb ἀφορίζειν as a Matthean characteristic because it occurs with reference to the last judgment only here and in Matthew 25:32 (twice).[26] However, the occurrences in Matthew 25:32 may be from M rather than Matthean redaction. Of the characteristics cited by Jeremias, only the expression ἡ συντέλεια τοῦ αἰῶνος is clearly Matthean.

Thus we have no reason to think that Matthew composed either the interpretation of the parable of the weeds or the interpretation of the parable of the net. This conclusion is consistent with our thesis that the Evangelists functioned primarily as compilers rather than as composers.

25. Ibid., 85.
26. Ibid., 85 n. 90.

WORKS CITED

Allison, Dale C. *The Jesus Tradition in Q*. Harrisburg, Pa.: Trinity Press International, 1997.

Bailey, Kenneth E. "Informal Controlled Oral Tradition and the Synoptic Gospels." *Asia Journal of Theology* 5 (1991): 34–54. Repr. in *Themelios* 20.2 (January 1995): 4–11.

———. "Middle Eastern Oral Tradition and the Synoptic Gospels." *ExpT* 106 (1995): 363–67.

Barrett, C. K. "Q: A Re-examination." *ExpT* 54 (1942–43): 320–23. Repr. as pages 259–68 in *The Two-Source Hypothesis: A Critical Appraisal*. Edited by Arthur J. Bellinzoni Jr., Joseph B. Tyson, and William O. Walker Jr. Macon, Ga.: Mercer University Press, 1985.

Beare, Francis W. *The Gospel according to Matthew: Translation, Introduction and Commentary*. Harper & Row, 1981. Repr., Peabody, Mass.: Hendrickson, 1987.

Bellinzoni, Arthur J., Jr., Joseph B. Tyson, and William O. Walker Jr., eds. *The Two-Source Hypothesis: A Critical Appraisal*. Macon, Ga.: Mercer University Press, 1985.

Bergemann, Thomas. *Q auf dem Prüfstand: Die Zuordnung des Mt/Lk-Stoffes zu Q am Beispiel der Bergpredigt*. FRLANT 158. Göttingen: Vandenhoeck & Ruprecht, 1993.

Betz, Hans Dieter. *The Sermon on the Mount: A Commentary on the Sermon on the Mount*. Hermeneia. Minneapolis: Fortress, 1995.

Brooks, Stephenson H. *Matthew's Community: The Evidence of His Special Sayings Material*. JSNTSup 16. Sheffield: Sheffield Academic Press, 1987.

Burkett, Delbert. *Rethinking the Gospel Sources: From Proto-Mark to Mark*. New York: T&T Clark, 2004.

Bussmann, Wilhelm. *Synoptische Studien*. 3 vols. in 2. Halle (Saale): Buchhandlung des Waisenhauses, 1925–31.

Carruth, Shawn, and Albrecht Garsky. *Q 11:2b–4: The Lord's Prayer*. Edited by Stanley D. Anderson. Documenta Q. Leuven: Peeters, 1996.

Carruth, Shawn, and James M. Robinson. *Q 4:1–13, 16: The Temptations of Jesus; Nazara*. Edited by Christoph Heil. Documenta Q. Leuven: Peeters, 1996.

Casey, Maurice. *An Aramaic Approach to Q: Sources for the Gospels of Matthew and Luke*. SNTSMS 122. Cambridge: Cambridge University Press, 2002.

Catchpole, David R. "The Beginning of Q: A Proposal." *NTS* 38 (1992): 205–21.

———. "Did Q Exist?" Pages 1–59 in idem, *The Quest for Q*. Edinburgh: T&T Clark, 1993.

———. "Q and 'The Friend at Midnight' (Luke xi. 5–8/9)." *JTS* NS 34 (1983): 407–24.

———. *The Quest for Q*. Edinburgh: T&T Clark, 1993.

———. "Reproof and Reconciliation in the Q Community: A Study of the Tradition-History of Mt 18,15–17,21–22/Lk 17,3–4." *SNTU* 8 (1983): 79–90.

Davies, W. D., and Dale C. Allison Jr. *A Critical and Exegetical Commentary on the Gospel according to Saint Matthew*. 3 vols. ICC. Edinburgh: T&T Clark, 1988–97.

Delobel, Joël, ed. *Logia: Les paroles de Jésus—The Sayings of Jesus. Mémorial Joseph Coppens*. BETL 59. Leuven: Leuven University Press, 1982.

Denaux, Adelbert. "Criteria for Identifying Q-Passages: A Critical Review of a Recent Work by T. Bergemann." *NovT* 37 (1995): 105–29.

Derrenbacker, Robert A., Jr. *Ancient Compositional Practices and the Synoptic Problem*. BETL 186. Leuven: Peeters, 2005.

———. "Greco-Roman Writing Practices and Luke's Gospel: Revisiting 'The Order of a Crank.'" Pages 61–83 in *The Gospels according to Michael Goulder*. Edited by Christopher A. Rollston. Harrisburg, Pa.: Trinity Press International, 2002.

———. "The Relationship of the Gospels Reconsidered." *TJT* 14 (1998): 83–88.

Dewey, Joanna. "Response to Kelber, Horsley, and Draper." Pages 101–8 in *Oral Performance, Popular Tradition, and Hidden Transcript in Q*. Edited by Richard A. Horsley. SemeiaSt 60. Atlanta: Society of Biblical Literature, 2006.

Downing, F. Gerald. "Compositional Conventions and the Synoptic Problem." *JBL* 107 (1985): 69–85.

———. "Disagreements of Each Evangelist with the Minor Close Agreements of the Other Two." *ETL* 80 (2004): 445–69.

———. "Dissolving the Synoptic Problem through Film?" *JSNT* 84 (2001): 117–19.

———. *Doing Things with Words in the First Christian Century*. JSNTSup 20. Sheffield: Sheffield Academic Press, 2000.

———. "A Paradigm Perplex: Luke, Matthew and Mark." *NTS* 38 (1992): 15–36.

———. "Redaction Criticism: Josephus' *Antiquities* and the Synoptic Gospels." *JSNT* 8 (1980): 46–65; 9 (1980): 29–48.

———. "Towards the Rehabilitation of Q." *NTS* 11 (1964/65): 169–81. Repr. as pages 269–85 in *The Two-Source Hypothesis: A Critical Appraisal*. Edited by Arthur J. Bellinzoni Jr., Joseph B. Tyson, and William O. Walker Jr. Macon, Ga.: Mercer University Press, 1985.

———. "Word Processing in the Ancient World: The Social Production and Performance of Q." *JSNT* 64 (1996): 29–48.

Dunn, James D. G. *Jesus Remembered*. Vol. 1 of *Christianity in the Making*. Grand Rapids: Eerdmans, 2003.

Edwards, Richard Alan. *The Sign of Jonah in the Theology of the Evangelists and Q*. SBT 2/18. London: SCM; Napierville, Ill.: Allenson, 1971.

Farmer, William R. *The Synoptic Problem: A Critical Analysis*. New York: Macmillan, 1964. Repr., Dillsboro, N.C.: Western North Carolina Press, 1976.

Farrer, A. M. "On Dispensing with Q." Pages 55–88 in *Studies in the Gospels: Essays in Memory of R. H. Lightfoot*. Edited by D. E. Nineham. Oxford: Blackwell, 1955. Repr. as pages 321–56 in *The Two-Source Hypothesis: A Critical Appraisal*. Edited by Arthur J. Bellinzoni Jr., Joseph B. Tyson, and William O. Walker Jr. Macon, Ga.: Mercer University Press, 1985.

Fitzmyer, Joseph A. *The Gospel according to Luke: Introduction, Translation, and Notes*. 2 vols. AB 28–28A. Garden City, N.Y.: Doubleday, 1981–85.

———. "The Priority of Mark and the 'Q' Source in Luke." Pages 16–23 in idem, *To Advance the Gospel: New Testament Studies*. New York: Crossroad, 1981.

Fleddermann, Harry T. "The Beginning of Q." Pages 153–59 in *Society of Biblical Literature 1985 Seminar Papers*. Missoula, Mont.: Scholars Press, 1985.

Foster, Paul. "Is It Possible to Dispense with Q?" *NovT* 45 (2003): 313–37.

———. "The M-Source: Its History and Demise in Biblical Scholarship." In *New Studies in the Synoptic Problem*. Edited by Paul Foster, Andrew Gregory, John S. Kloppenborg, and Joseph Verheyden. Leuven: Peeters, forthcoming.

———. Review of Maurice Casey, *An Aramaic Approach to Q: Sources for the Gospels of Matthew and Luke*. *NovT* 46 (2004): 289–91.

Fuller, Reginald H. *The New Testament in Current Study*. New York: Scribner's, 1962.

Gaboury, Antonio. *La structure des évangiles synoptiques*. Leiden: Brill, 1970.

Gagnon, Robert A. J. "Luke's Motives for Redaction in the Account of the Double Delegation in Luke 7:1–10." *NovT* 36 (1994): 122–45.

———. "The Shape of Matthew's Q Text of the Centurion at Capernaum: Did It Mention Delegations?" *NTS* 40 (1994): 133–42.

———. "Statistical Analysis and the Case of the Double Delegation in Luke 7:3–7a." *CBQ* 55 (1993): 709–31.

Garsky, Albrecht, et al. *Q 12:49–59: Children against Parents; Judging the Time; Settling out of Court.* Edited by Shawn Carruth. Documenta Q. Leuven: Peeters, 1997.

Goodacre, Mark. *The Case against Q: Studies in Markan Priority and the Synoptic Problem.* Harrisburg, Pa.: Trinity Press International, 2002.

———. "Fatigue in the Synoptics." *NTS* 44 (1998): 45–58.

———. *Goulder and the Gospels: An Examination of a New Paradigm.* JSNTSup 133. Sheffield: Sheffield Academic Press, 1996.

———. "A Monopoly on Marcan Priority? Fallacies at the Heart of Q." Pages 538–622 in *Society of Biblical Literature 2000 Seminar Papers.* Atlanta: Society of Biblical Literature, 2000.

———. "On Choosing and Using Appropriate Analogies: A Response to F. Gerald Downing." *JSNT* 26 (2003): 237–40.

———. "The Synoptic Jesus and the Celluloid Christ: Solving the Synoptic Problem through Film," *JSNT* 80 (2000): 31–44. Repr. as pages 121–32 in idem, *The Case against Q: Studies in Markan Priority and the Synoptic Problem.* Harrisburg, Pa.: Trinity Press International, 2002.

———. *The Synoptic Problem: A Way through the Maze.* The Biblical Seminar 80. Sheffield: Sheffield Academic Press, 2001.

———. "A World without Q." Pages 174–79 in *Questioning Q: A Multidimensional Critique.* Edited by Mark Goodacre and Nicholas Perrin. Downers Grove, Ill.: InterVarsity Press, 2004.

Goodacre, Mark, and Nicholas Perrin, eds. *Questioning Q: A Multidimensional Critique.* Downers Grove, Ill.: InterVarsity Press, 2004.

Goulder, Michael D. "Is Q a Juggernaut?" *JBL* 115 (1996): 667–81.

———. *Luke: A New Paradigm.* 2 vols. JSNTSup 20. Sheffield: Sheffield Academic Press, 1989.

———. *Midrash and Lection in Matthew.* London: SPCK, 1974.

———. "On Putting Q to the Test." *NTS* 24 (1978): 218–34.

———. "The Order of a Crank." Pages 111–30 in *Synoptic Studies: The Ampleworth Conferences of 1982 and 1983.* Edited by C. M. Tuckett. JSNTSup 7. Sheffield: JSOT Press, 1984.

———. "Self-Contradiction in the IQP." *JBL* 118 (1999): 506–17.

Gundry, Robert H. "Matthean Foreign Bodies in Agreements of Luke with Matthew against Mark: Evidence That Luke Used Matthew." Pages 1466–95 in vol. 2 of *The Four Gospels 1992.* Edited by F. van Segbroeck et al. 3 vols. BETL 100 Leuven: Leuven University Press, 1992.

———. *Matthew: A Commentary on His Literary and Theological Art.* Grand Rapids: Eerdmans, 1982.

———. "A Rejoinder on Matthean Foreign Bodies in Luke 10, 25–28." *ETL* 71 (1995): 139–50.

Harnack, Adolf. *The Sayings of Jesus: The Second Source of St. Matthew and St. Luke.* Translated by J. R. Wilkinson. New York: Putnam's Sons, 1908.

Hengel, Martin. *The Four Gospels and the One Gospel of Jesus Christ: An Investigation of the Collection and Origin of the Canonical Gospels.* Harrisburg, Pa.: Trinity Press International, 2000.

Hickling, C. J. A. "The Plurality of 'Q.'" Pages 425–29 in *Logia: Les paroles de Jésus—The Sayings of Jesus. Mémorial Joseph Coppens.* Edited by Joël Delobel. BETL 59. Leuven: Leuven University Press, 1982.

Hieke, Thomas. *Q 6:20–21: The Beatitudes for the Poor, Hungry, and Mourning.* Documenta Q. Leuven: Peeters, 2001.

Hoffmann, Paul, et al. *Q 12:8–12: Confessing or Denying; Speaking against the Holy Spirit; Hearings before Synagogues.* Edited by Christoph Heil. Documenta Q. Leuven: Peeters, 1997.

———. *Q 22:28, 30: You Will Judge the Twelve Tribes of Israel.* Edited by Christoph Heil. Documenta Q. Leuven: Peeters, 1999.

Horsley, Richard A. "Recent Studies of Oral-Derived Literature and Q." Pages 150–74 in Richard A. Horsley and Jonathan A. Draper, *Whoever Hears You Hears Me: Prophets, Performance, and Tradition in Q.* Harrisburg, Pa.: Trinity Press International, 1999.

———, ed. *Oral Performance, Popular Tradition, and Hidden Transcript in Q.* SemeiaSt 60. Atlanta: Society of Biblical Literature, 2006.

Horsley, Richard A., and Jonathan A. Draper. *Whoever Hears You Hears Me: Prophets, Performance, and Tradition in Q.* Harrisburg, Pa.: Trinity Press International, 1999.

Huggins, Ronald V. "Matthean Posteriority: A Preliminary Proposal." *NovT* 34 (1992): 1–22. Repr. as pages 204–25 in *The Synoptic Problem and Q: Selected Studies from Novum Testamentum.* Edited by David E. Orton. Leiden: Brill, 1999.

Jacobson, Arland D. *The First Gospel: An Introduction to Q.* Sonoma, Calif.: Polebridge, 1992.

———. "The Literary Unity of Q." *JBL* 101 (1982): 365–89. Repr. in part as pages 98–115 in *The Shape of Q: Signal Essays on the Sayings Gospel.* Edited by John S. Kloppenborg. Minneapolis: Fortress, 1994.

———. "The Literary Unity of Q: Lc 10,2–16 and Parallels as a Test Case." Pages 419–23 in *Logia: Les paroles de Jésus—The Sayings of Jesus. Mémorial Joseph Coppens.* Edited by Joël Delobel. BETL 59. Leuven: Leuven University Press, 1982.

Jeremias, Joachim. *The Parables of Jesus.* 2nd ed. New York: Scribner's, 1972.

Johnson, Steven R. *Q 7:1–10: The Centurion's Faith in Jesus' Word.* Documenta Q. Leuven: Peeters, 2002.

———. *Q 12:33–34: Storing up Treasures in Heaven.* Documenta Q. Leuven: Peeters, 2007.

Kelber, Werner H. "The Verbal Art in Q and *Thomas*: A Question of Epistemology." Pages 25–42 in *Oral Performance, Popular Tradition, and the Hidden Transcript in Q*. Edited by Richard A. Horsley. SemeiaSt 60. Atlanta: Society of Biblical Literature, 2006.

Kloppenborg, John S. "Didache 16 6–8 and Special Matthean Tradition." *ZNW* 70 (1979): 54–67.

———. *The Formation of Q: Trajectories in Ancient Wisdom Collections*. Philadelphia: Fortress, 1987.

———. "On Dispensing with Q? Goodacre on the Relation of Luke to Matthew." *NTS* 49 (2003): 210–36.

———. *Q Parallels: Synopsis, Critical Notes, and Concordance*. Foundation and Facets: New Testament. Sonoma, Calif.: Polebridge, 1988.

———. "Variation in the Reproduction of the Double Tradition and an Oral Q?" *ETL* 83 (2007): 53–80.

———, ed. *The Shape of Q: Signal Essays on the Sayings Gospel*. Minneapolis: Fortress, 1994.

Kloppenborg Verbin, John S. *Excavating Q: The History and Setting of the Sayings Gospel*. Minneapolis: Fortress, 2000.

———. "Goulder and the New Paradigm: A Critical Appreciation of Michael Goulder on the Synoptic Problem." Pages 29–60 in *The Gospels according to Michael* Goulder. Edited by Christopher A. Rollston. Harrisburg, Pa.: Trinity Press International, 2002.

Knox, Wilfred L. *St Luke and St Matthew*. Vol. 2 of *The Sources of the Synoptic Gospels*. Cambridge: Cambridge University Press, 1957.

Kosch, Daniel. *Die eschatologische Tora des Menschensohnes: Untersuchungen zur Rezeption der Stellung Jesu zur Tora in Q*. NTOA 12. Fribourg: Universitätsverlag; Göttingen: Vandenhoeck & Ruprecht, 1989.

———. "Q: Rekonstruktion und Interpretation: Eine methodenkritische Hinführung mit einem Exkurs zur Q-Vorlage des Lk." *FZPT* 36 (1989): 409–25.

Kümmel, Werner Georg. *Introduction to the New Testament*. Rev. ed. Nashville: Abingdon, 1975.

Luz, Ulrich. *Matthew 1–7*. Translated by W. Linss. Continental Commentaries. Minneapolis: Augsburg, 1989.

———. *Matthew 1–7: A Commentary*. Translated by James E. Crouch. Hermeneia. Minneapolis: Fortress, 2007.

———. "Sermon on the Mount/Plain: Reconstruction of Q^{Mt} and Q^{Lk}." Pages 473–79 in *Society of Biblical Literature 1983 Seminar Papers*. SBLSP 22. Chico, Calif.: Scholars Press.

Manson, T. W. *The Sayings of Jesus*. London: SCM, 1937. Repr., Grand Rapids: Eerdmans, 1957.

Matson, Mark A. "Luke's Rewriting of the Sermon on the Mount." Pages 43–70 in *Questioning Q: A Multidimensional Critique*. Edited by Mark Goodacre and Nicholas Perrin. Downers Grove, Ill.: InterVarsity Press, 2004.

McNicol, Allan J., ed. *Beyond the Q Impasse: Luke's Use of Matthew. A Demonstration by the Research Team of the International Institute for Gospel Studies*. With David L. Dungan and David B. Peabody. Valley Forge, Pa.: Trinity Press International, 1996.

Meier, John P. *Law and History in Matthew's Gospel: A Redactional Study of Mt. 5:17–48*. AnBib 71. Rome: Biblical Institute Press, 1976.

Meijboom, Hajo Uden. *A History and Critique of the Origin of the Marcan Hypothesis 1835–1866: A Contemporary Report Rediscovered*. Translated and edited by John J. Kiwiet. New Gospel Studies 8. Macon, Ga.: Mercer University Press, 1993.

Mournet, Terence C. *Oral Tradition and Literary Dependency: Variability and Stability in the Synoptic Tradition and Q*. WUNT 2/195. Tübingen: Mohr Siebeck, 2005.

Neirynck, Frans. "The First Synoptic Pericope: The Appearance of John the Baptist in Q?" *ETL* 72 (1996): 41–74.

———. "Goulder and the Minor Agreements," *ETL* 73 (1997): 84–93.

———. "Luke 10:25–28: A Foreign Body in Luke?" Pages 149–65 in *Crossing the Boundaries: Essays in Biblical Interpretation in Honour of Michael D. Goulder*. Edited by Stanley E. Porter et al. Biblical Interpretation Series 8. Leiden: Brill, 1994.

———. "Luke 14,1–6: Lukan Composition and Q Saying." Pages 243–63 in *Der Treue Gottes trauen: Beiträge zum Werk des Lukas: Für Gerhard Schneider*. Edited by Claus Bussmann and Walter Radl. Freiburg: Herder, 1991.

———. "Matthew 4:23–5:2 and the Matthean Composition of 4:23–11:1." Pages 23–46 in *The Interrelations of the Gospels*. Edited by David L. Dungan. BETL 95. Leuven: Leuven University Press, 1990.

———. "Q^{Mt} and Q^{Lk} and the Reconstruction of Q." *ETL* 66 (1990): 385–90.

———. "Recent Developments in the Study of Q." Pages 29–75 in *Logia: Les paroles de Jésus—The Sayings of Jesus. Mémorial Joseph Coppens*. Edited by Joël Delobel. BETL 59. Leuven: Leuven University Press, 1982.

———. "The Sermon on the Mount in the Gospel Synopsis." *ETL* 52 (1976): 350–57. Repr. as pages 729–36 of *Evangelica: Gospel Studies—Études d'évangile: Collected Essays*. Edited by F. van Segbroeck. BETL 60. Leuven: Leuven University Press, 1982.

Neville, David. "The Demise of the Two-Document Hypothesis? Dunn and Burkett on Gospel Sources." *Pacifica* 19 (Feb 2006): 78–92.

Orton, David E., ed. *The Synoptic Problem and Q: Selected Studies from Novum Testamentum*. Leiden: Brill, 1999.

Paffenroth, Kim. *The Story of Jesus according to L.* JSNTSup 147. Sheffield: Sheffield Academic Press, 1997.

Peterson, Jeffrey. "Order in the Double Tradition and the Existence of Q." Pages 28–42 in *Questioning Q: A Multidimensional Critique.* Edited by Mark Goodacre and Nicholas Perrin. Downers Grove, Ill.: InterVarsity Press, 2004.

Piper, Ronald A., ed. *The Gospel behind the Gospels: Current Studies on Q.* NovTSup 75. Leiden: Brill, 1995.

Robinson, James M. "Basic Shifts in German Theology." *Interpretation* 16 (1962): 76–97.

———. "The Incipit of the Sayings Gospel Q." *RHPR* 75 (1995): 9–33.

Robinson, James M., Paul Hoffmann, and John S. Kloppenborg, eds. *The Critical Edition of Q: Synopsis Including the Gospels of Matthew and Luke, Mark and Thomas with English, German, and French Translations of Q and Thomas.* Hermeneia. Minneapolis: Fortress; Leuven: Peeters, 2000.

———. *The Sayings Gospel Q in Greek and English with Parallels from the Gospels of Mark and Thomas.* Leuven: Peeters, 2001.

Rollston, Christopher A., ed. *The Gospels according to Michael Goulder.* Harrisburg, Pa.: Trinity Press International, 2002.

Sanday, W., ed. *Studies in the Synoptic Problem: By Members of the University of Oxford.* Oxford: Clarendon, 1911.

Sanders, E. P. "The Argument from Order and the Relationship Between Matthew and Luke." *NTS* 15 (1968–69): 249–61. Repr. as pages 409–25 in *The Two-Source Hypothesis: A Critical Appraisal.* Edited by Arthur J. Bellinzoni Jr., Joseph B. Tyson, and William O. Walker Jr. Macon, Ga.: Mercer University Press, 1985.

Sanders, E. P., and Margaret Davies. *Studying the Synoptic Gospels.* Philadelphia: Trinity Press International, 1989.

Sandt, Huub van de, and David Flusser. *The Didache: Its Jewish Sources and Its Place in Early Judaism and Christianity.* CRINT 3/5. Assen: Van Gorcum; Minneapolis: Fortress, 2002.

Sato, Migaku. *Q und Prophetie: Studien zur Gattungs- und Traditionsgeschichte der Quelle Q.* WUNT 2/29. Tübingen: Mohr Siebeck, 1988.

Schürmann, Heinz. "Sprachliche Reminiszenen an abgeänderte oder ausgelassene Bestandteile der Sprachsammlung im Lukas- und Matthäusevangelium." *NTS* 6 (1959/60): 193–210. Repr. as pages 111–25 of idem, *Traditionsgeschichtliche Untersuchungen zu den synoptischen Evangelien.* Düsseldorf: Patmos, 1968.

Schweizer, Eduard. *The Good News according to Luke.* Atlanta: John Knox, 1984.

Solages, Paul Marie Bruno de. *La composition des évangiles: De Luc et de Matthieu et leurs sources.* Leiden: Brill, 1973.

Stein, Robert H. *Studying the Synoptic Gospels: Origin and Interpretation.* 2nd ed. Grand Rapids: Baker, 2001.

Streeter, Burnett Hillman. *The Four Gospels: A Study of Origins.* [1924] Rev. ed. London: Macmillan, 1930.

———. "On the Original Order of Q." Pages 140–64 in *Studies in the Synoptic Problem: By Members of the University of Oxford.* Edited by W. Sanday. Oxford: Clarendon, 1911.

Styler, G. M. "The Priority of Mark." Pages 285–316 in C. F. D. Moule, *The Birth of the New Testament.* 3rd ed. San Francisco: Harper & Row, 1982.

Taylor, Vincent. "The Order of Q." *JTS* NS 4 (1953): 27–31. Repr. as pages 90–94 in idem, *New Testament Essays.* London: Epworth, 1970.

———. "The Original Order of Q." Pages 246–69 in *New Testament Essays: Studies in Memory of Thomas Walter Manson, 1893–1958.* Edited by A. J. B. Higgins. Manchester: Manchester University Press, 1959. Repr. as pages 95–118 in idem, *New Testament Essays.* London: Epworth, 1970. Repr. as pages 295–317 in *The Two-Source Hypothesis: A Critical Appraisal.* Edited by Arthur J. Bellinzoni Jr., Joseph B. Tyson, and William O. Walker Jr. Macon, Ga.: Mercer University Press, 1985.

Tuckett, Christopher M. "The Beatitudes: A Source-Critical Study." *NovT* 25 (1983): 193–207. With a reply by M. D. Goulder, 207–16.

———. "The Existence of Q." Pages 19–47 in *The Gospel behind the Gospels: Current Studies in Q.* Edited by Ronald A. Piper. Leiden: Brill, 1995. Rev. and repr. as pages 1–39 in Tuckett, *Q and the History of Early Christianity: Studies on Q.* Edinburgh: T&T Clark; Peabody, Mass.: Hendrickson, 1996.

———. "On the Relation between Matthew and Luke." *NTS* 30 (1984): 130–42.

———. *Q and the History of Early Christianity: Studies on Q.* Edinburgh: T&T Clark; Peabody, Mass.: Hendrickson, 1996.

———. Review of Mark Goodacre, *The Case against Q: Studies in Markan Priority and the Synoptic Problem. NovT* 46 (2004): 401–403.

———. Review of Maurice Casey, *An Aramaic Approach to Q: Sources for the Gospels of Matthew and Luke. JTS* NS 54 (2003): 683–87.

———. Review of R. A. Derrenbacker, *Ancient Compositional Practices and the Synoptic Gospels. JTS* NS 58 (2007): 187–90.

———. "Synoptic Problem." *ABD* 6:263–70.

Vassiliadis, Petros. "The Nature and Extent of the Q Document." *NovT* 20 (1978): 49–73.

Weeden, Theodore J., Sr. "Theories of Tradition: A Critique of Kenneth Bailey." *Forum* (Westar Institute) 7.1 (2004): 45–69.

Wegner, Uwe. *Der Hauptmann von Kafernaum (Mt 7,28a; 8,5–10, 13 par Lk 7,1–10): Ein Beitrag zur Q-Forschung.* WUNT 2/14. Tübingen: Mohr Siebeck, 1985.

Index of Ancient Sources

Index of Modern Authors

Allison, Dale C., Jr. vii, 29, 51, 51 n. 2, 52, 53, 54, 72 n. 10, 73 n. 12, 79, 79 n. 25, 94, 94 n. 2, 95, 106 n. 22, 108, 108 nn. 25–26, 110 n. 28, 120, 120 n. 10, 121 n. 11, 123 nn. 13–14, 125, 125 n. 21, 128 nn. 23–24, 129 n. 26, 133 n. 29, 135, 135 n. 2, 137 nn. 5–6, 140, 140 n. 10, 142, 143 nn. 12–13, 144 nn. 14–16, 145 nn. 17–18, 146 nn. 20–21, 154, 155 n. 34, 156 n. 35, 159, 159 n. 41, 162 nn. 46–47, 165 n. 50, 167 n. 65, 171 n. 2, 177 n. 10, 189 n. 25, 192 n. 28, 197, 197 n. 37, 200 n. 46, 202, 202 n. 51, 203 nn. 54 and 56, 208, 208 nn. 2 and 4, 210 nn. 7 and 10, 251, 252

Anderson, Stanley D. 151 n. 26, 251

Bailey, Kenneth E. 48, 48 nn. 53–54, 251, 259

Barrett, C. K. 41, 41 nn. 24–27, 42, 44, 61, 61 n. 1, 251

Beare, Francis W. 73 n. 12, 174 n. 4, 210, 210 n. 6, 251

Bellinzoni, Arthur J., Jr. 7 n. 24, 15 n. 37, 20 n. 61, 25 n. 76, 34 nn. 4–5, 41 n. 24, 251, 253, 258, 259

Bergemann, Thomas 43, 43 n. 34, 44, 73 n. 11, 99, 251, 252

Betz, Hans Dieter 42, 42 n. 31, 251

Brooks, Stephenson H. 106 n. 22, 108, 108 n. 24, 128 n. 24, 135 n. 2, 140, 140 n. 10, 142, 142 n. 12, 143 n. 13, 145 n. 18, 148 n. 23, 162 n. 46, 164 n. 48, 251

Burkett, Delbert 1 n. 2, 2 n. 6, 4 nn. 14 and 16, 5 n. 21, 9 n. 30, 24 nn. 73–74, 27 n. 83, 44 n. 35, 46 n. 48, 54 n. 6, 113 n. 1, 115 n. 4, 119 n. 6, 135 n. 3, 251, 257

Bussmann, Claus 80 n. 27, 257

Bussmann, Wilhelm 40, 40 nn. 21–23, 41, 42, 251

Carruth, Shawn 119 n. 7, 125 nn. 16–18, 151 nn. 26–27, 173 n. 3, 251, 254

Casey, Maurice 44, 44 n. 37, 45, 45 nn. 39–40, 99, 252, 253, 259

Catchpole, David R. 2 n. 9, 20 n. 62, 80, 80 nn. 28–30, 113 n. 2, 161 n. 44, 183 n. 18, 187 n. 24, 252

Coppens, Joseph 36 n. 13, 252, 255, 257

Crouch, James E. 42 n. 30, 256

Davies, Margaret 17 n. 43, 258

Davies, W. D. 51 n. 2, 72 n. 10, 73 n. 12, 79 n. 25, 94 n. 2, 106 n. 22, 108 nn. 25–26, 110 n. 28, 120 n. 10, 121 n. 11, 123 nn. 13–14, 125 n. 21, 128 nn. 23–24, 129 n. 26, 133 n. 29, 135 n. 2, 137 nn. 5–6, 140 n. 10, 143 nn. 12–13, 144 nn. 14–16, 145 nn. 17–18, 146 nn. 20–21, 147 n. 22, 148 nn. 23 and 25, 153 n. 31, 155 n. 34, 156 n. 35, 159 n. 41, 161 n. 45, 162 nn. 46–47, 165 n. 50, 167 n. 65, 171 n. 2, 177 n. 10, 192 n. 28, 197 n. 37, 200 n. 46, 202 n. 51, 203 nn. 54 and 56, 208 nn. 2–4, 210 nn. 7 and 10, 252

Delobel, Joël 36 n. 13, 70 n. 5, 252, 255, 257

Denaux, Adelbert 43 n. 34, 44 n. 36, 252

-279-

Printed in the United States
219964BV00001B/4/P